WOMAN'S DAY

Book of American Needlework

ROSE WILDER LANE

SIMON AND SCHUSTER · NEW YORK · 1963

Appliquéd and embroidered rug, reminiscent of Paisley designs. [PENNSYLVANIA FARM MUSEUM OF LANDIS VALLEY, LANCASTER, PA.]

THIRD PRINTING

LIBRARY OF CONGRESS CATALOG CARD NUMBER: 63-17731
MANUFACTURED IN THE UNITED STATES OF AMERICA BY WESTERN PRINTING AND LITHOGRAPHING CO., NEW
YORK, N. Y. TYPE COMPOSITION BY YANKEE TYPESETTERS, INC., CONCORD, N. H.

*Grateful acknowledgment is made to the following contributors for their cooperation and for the use of
material from their collections:*

Art Institute of Chicago, Chicago, Ill.
Brooklyn Museum, Brooklyn, N.Y.
Chester County Historical Society, West Chester, Pa.
Colonial Williamsburg, Va.
Cooperstown Museum, Cooperstown, N.Y.
Farmers' Museum, Cooperstown, N.Y.
Fenimore House, Cooperstown, N.Y.
Henry Ford Museum, Dearborn, Mich.
Kenmore, Fredericksburg, Va.
Maryland Historical Society, Baltimore, Md.
Metropolitan Museum of Art, American Wing, New York, N.Y.
Mount Vernon Ladies' Association, Mount Vernon, Va.
Museum of the Daughters of the American Revolution, Washington, D.C.
Museum of Fine Arts, Boston, Mass.
National Gallery of Art, Index of American Design, Washington, D.C.
Newark Museum, Newark, N.J.
New Hampshire Historical Society, Concord, N.H.
New York Historical Society, New York, N.Y.

New York State Historical Association, Cooperstown, N.Y.
Old Deerfield, Mass.
Old Sturbridge Village, Sturbridge, Mass.
Pennsylvania Farm Museum of Landis Valley, Lancaster, Pa.
Rochester Memorial Art Gallery, Rochester, N.Y.
Rochester Museum of Arts and Sciences, Rochester, N.Y.
Abby Aldrich Rockefeller Folk Art Collection, Williamsburg, Va.
Shelburne Museum, Shelburne, Vt.
Sleepy Hollow Restorations, Tarrytown, N.Y.
Smithsonian Institution, Washington, D.C.
Stamford Historical Society, Inc., Stamford, Conn.
Valentine Museum, Richmond, Va.
Wadsworth Atheneum, Hartford, Conn.
Mary Washington House, Fredericksburg, Va.
Wenham Historical Association and Museum, Wenham, Mass.
Laura Ingalls Wilder Home Museum, Mansfield, Mo.
Witte Museum, San Antonio, Tex.

Photographs are by Ben Calvo of the Woman's Day *Studio, except for those on page 43, Samuel Chamberlain; pages 106-107, Raymond M. Sato; pages 147-150, Robert E. Coates.*

Preface

Five years ago the editors of Woman's Day began work on the Story of American Needlework. It was an ambitious project. It would entail months of travel to all the great museums in the country. It would mean countless hours of extracurricular work. Our needlework editors, our photographers, our service editors and many other members of our staff would be burdened with added responsibilities and the time-consuming details of selection, authentication, reproduction and presentation of the most treasured examples of American Needlework. We thought the task a worthy one. From museums all over the country we collected our material, a priceless heritage of our past.

As the great canvas unfolded, we, as editors, took pride anew in the work of past generations of American women who had created the art of American Needlework. The beauty, the patterns, the colors, the whole flavor and feeling of the needlework art were a true expression of American individuality and the American way of life. The canvas was so dramatic and so inspiring and, in these troubled times, so reassuring and so illustrative of our great past and of the strength and meaning of America, that

we invited one of America's most distinguished authors, Rose Wilder Lane, to write the story of the history and development of the needlework arts in America. Mrs. Lane is an expert needlewoman as well as an historian, novelist and essayist. Her words give beauty and meaning to the great needlework canvas.

It was a worthy task. The story of American Needlework and of the generations of American women who created it was recorded for posterity. The appreciation of our readers was overwhelming; their gratitude was heart-warming. As one reader said, "This is American history through the eye of a needle." From thousands of our readers came the request that the series of articles be collected in book form for permanency.

Here is the book. It is, for our editors, another dream come true. We hope that the book will become a treasured collector's item in American homes throughout the country. We hope, also, that it will encourage the creative women of our generation to carry on the great tradition of American Needlework, bringing beauty to their lives and homes and lasting satisfaction to themselves and their families.

THE EDITORS OF *Woman's Day*

Contents

Introduction

EEDLEWORK is the art that tells the truth about the real life of people in their time and place. The great arts, music, sculpture, painting, literature, are the work of a few unique persons whom lesser men emulate, often for generations. Needlework is anonymous; the people create it. Each piece is the work of a woman who is thinking only of making for her child, her friend, her home or herself a bit of beauty that pleases her.

So her needlework expresses what she is, more clearly than her handwriting does. It expresses everything that makes her an individual unlike any other person—her character, her mind and her spirit, her experience in living. It expresses, too, her country's history and culture, the traditions, the philosophy, the way of living that she takes for granted.

The first thing that American needlework tells you is that Americans live in the only classless society. This republic is the only country that has no peasant needlework. Everywhere else, peasant women work their crude, naive, gay patterns, suited to their humble class and frugal lives, while ladies work their rich and formal designs proper to higher birth and breeding.

American needlework is not peasant's work or aristocrat's. It is not crude and it is not formal. It is needlework expressing a new and unique spirit, more American than American sculpture, painting, literature or classical music.

Three hundred years ago the colonies in America were European. Gentlemen and their ladies brought to North America the absolute monarchies of the Continent, the feudal system of England, and the arts and cultures of the Old World. They also brought the lower classes to do the hard work.

The workers who cleared the forests, planted the crops, hunted for the fur traders, and did the brewing, building, spinning and weaving were peasants hardly more free than serfs, bound servants no more free than slaves, poor families imprisoned for poverty who were herded out of debtors' prisons and shipped to America, and poor girls who, having no dowries, were auctioned in American ports to woodsmen and freed servants who could afford to buy wives.

They came from the hungry classes in all the famine-plagued kingdoms of the Old World. They had nothing in common but their poverty, their humanity, and a wild hope. Long before British victory in European wars had seized for the British Empire all the colonies in America except the Spanish Floridas and New France west of the Mississippi, the land that is now these States was the home of all mankind.

The Dutch built the town on Manhattan Island, and the patroons' large estates on Long Island and up the Hudson River valley. German peasants slowly defeated the Pennsylvania wilderness. Scotch-Irish struggled into the Carolina mountains. Swedes settled Delaware. New France ran from Maine to Detroit to St. Louis and up the Mississippi from Mobile and New Orleans to Illinois, Missouri and the Dakota headwaters of the Missouri River. New Spain stretched from Peru and Mexico to San Antonio, Los Angeles, San Francisco. The Russians came down from Alaska to Monterey. Among all these pioneers, only a few at first, were Italians, Danes, Poles, Armenians, Assyrians, Czechs, Slovaks, Finns, Greeks, Norwegians, Hungarians, Africans, Arabs, Egyptians, Levantines. Protestants ruled New England; Catholics governed Maryland; Jews were in all the colonies. All varieties of humankind were here, and all the languages, faiths, cultures.

By painful stages on wagon tracks through forests and by boats sailing along empty coasts, the English, Irish, Scottish, Dutch, French and Spanish gentlemen were meeting on the neutral ground of their lofty social class. Beneath them the lower classes were mingling and intermarrying with each other and with the Indians—the farmers, the peddlers, the sailors, the little merchants, the wilderness fighters; the first Americans.

Struggling for bare life itself, against the forests, the grudging soil, the weather, the sea, they learned that differences between human beings are superficial and that a common human nature and a common need, a common hope, unite all humankind on this hostile earth. In sharing danger and hardship, they learned that every person is self-controlling, responsible for his acts; that each one makes his own life what it is and that all alike must struggle to survive and to make human living better than it is.

This truth was not in the feudal idea that God creates inferior and superior classes of human beings. It was not in the Acts of Parliament and Kings. It was not in the schools that taught gentlemen's sons the duties of their privileged status. It was not in the arts and writings that expressed the Old World's concept of the nature of man, and it was not in the colonies' social order of authority above, obedience below. But it was in the first American needlework.

Needlework is a pretty occupation for a

woman's hands. No governor and no scholar noticed it, and the women who made it did not guess that their needles were prophesying the World Revolution. They believed that they belonged in the class where they were born; they thought that they were loyal subjects of their King. But they did not like the old needlework patterns.

They made new patterns. A hundred years before the time when their grandsons would attack the Old World belief that persons are merely particles of the State, American women rejected that ancient fallacy as it was expressed in European needlework.

In typical Old World needlework, each detail is a particle of the whole; no part of the design can stand alone, whole and complete in itself. The background is solid, the pattern is formal, and a border encloses all.

American women smashed that rigid order to bits. They discarded backgrounds, they discarded borders and frames. They made the details create the whole, and they set each detail in boundless space, alone, independent, complete.

They did in needlework what Americans would later do in the human world of living human beings. As Americans were the first to know and to declare that a person is the unit of human life on earth, that each human being is a self-governing source of the life-energy that creates, controls, and changes societies, institutions, governments, so American women were the first to reverse the old meaning in needlework design. They no longer copied the stiff, formal order imposed upon enclosed patterns; they made each detail free, self-reliant, complete by itself, not quite like any other, and they let these details create their whole effect.

Just as individual freedom suddenly released the terrific human energy that swept the Old World's Great Powers from this hemisphere and wholly transformed North America in a third of the time that those Old World Powers had held it, so this reversal of meaning gives American needlework an almost explosive energy. No other needlework is so alive. There are no stiff forms in it, no monotonous repetitions. Leaves and flowers spring vigorously from living stems; buds burst open, squirrels frisk, deer leap, birds fly. Colors are clear and fresh and vibrant. No other needlework on earth is so strong, so free, so full of energy and movement.

Women in the European colonies began this revolution in needlework more than a hundred years before Americans broke clean away from the Old World and began to create a wholly new world.

English, French, and German women in the white towns and red farmhouses of New England and in the great houses of Maryland and Virginia took old patterns of Persia, India, Portugal, Holland and England and wrought them in crewel work transformed by the new American spirit. They made the feather crest of the Prince of Wales into airy quilting patterns. French women changed the Lilies of France into living flowers. Dutch women on Long Island and German girls in Pennsylvania took the stiff tulip from their painted chests and worked it into their unique patterns of wholly American patchwork.

American women changed the English Rose into the Cherokee Rose, the Prairie Wild Rose, and the Texas Rose that vies with the Lone Star; different patterns all, and all charming.

Then from starving Ireland the Irish women brought the lace that America transformed into the wholly new crocheted lace that is the American "real" lace, the most varied, flexible, and free of the world's fine laces, the only lace that is made "in the air."

Spread Eagle counterpane, made by the Spears family in Shelburne, Vermont early in the nineteenth century, with narrow strips of blanketing stitched together and decorated in wool. Semicircles converge upon a centered circle with eagle and 25 stars. Since Arkansas, our 25th state, was not admitted to the Union until 1836, the stars on the blanket are purely decorative. [SHELBURNE MUSEUM, SHELBURNE, VT.]

The Italians and the Russians brought the cross-stitch; the Spanish brought outline; the Danes brought cutwork, the grandmother of all laces; Madeira sent drawnwork; Scots added the woven plaid, Scandinavians the hooked coverlet that American women transformed into our hooked rug; American Indians gave beadwork; Mexicans gave the Aztec patterns and the desert's blazing colors.

American women, children of all these lands, took all this and more and made it American in spirit. They changed it, combined its symbols, gave it space and freedom and energy; and they created a new folk art: American needlework.

We are still creating it. As colonial women made such designs as the Log Cabin, the Bear's Paw, the Tomahawk, the Pine Tree, the Wild Goose Flight; as nineteenth-century Americans made Martha Washington's Flower Garden, the Oregon Trail, the Lone Star of Texas, the Atlantic Cable, so today American women are making patterns of the skyscraper sky lines, civic centers and parks, airplanes, Hawaii's Island Garden. They are working into needlework murals our legends of Paul Bunyan and Johnny Appleseed and Daniel Boone.

Only one form of American needlework is wholly American, without root or kin in the Old World; that is our pieced patchwork. Oh, patches are nothing new. Ancient Egyptians sewed fabric to fabric, and in medieval Europe women applied cloth to cloth. Patches are as old as poverty. In rags and patches the first workers came to America. Patches belonged to workers, to the poor, low-class subjects of the ruling classes. Patchwork was always a task, not an art.

Poverty came across the ocean with the immigrants. Here on the farthest rim of the known world, it became direst need. The smallest scrap of cloth was precious to a woman who could have no more cloth until the trees were cut and burned, the land spaded and sown to flax or to grass for sheep,

then next year the wool sheared, washed, combed, carded and spun, or the flax pulled and carefully rippled, retted, dried, beetled, scutched, heckled, spun, and at last the loom made, the warp threaded, the shuttles wound and the cloth woven.

In a wilderness thousands of miles from home, depending only upon themselves for their very lives, these poor immigrants learned the inescapable fact that a person is the only source of the only energy that preserves human life on this planet. With their minds and hands they made houses, they produced food, they wove cloth and built towns, and each ceased to think of himself as a bit of a class in a nation. They knew that each one was creating the neighborhood, the town, the colony.

To women who knew this, every precious scrap of cloth had a new meaning; they thought of what the small pieces, together, could make. And they began to make a pattern of them.

From this simple beginning, in the crazy quilt and the Log Cabin pattern. American women developed the whole vast treasure of American patchwork, pieced and appliquéd, that we are still developing.

From scraps and bits they made the English Rose, the French Lily, the Dutch Tulip, the Irish Chain, the Indian Tree of Life, and with patches they recorded American history, all of it, from Bear's Paw and Tomahawk to California Poppy and Hawaiian Pineapple.

They quilted—and quilt—their patchwork in webs of tiny stitches; they added touches of embroidery and bits of lace. In originality, in beauty and meaning, nothing else in the whole world's needlework compares with American patchwork.

Yet for more than a hundred years American students of folk arts did not notice it; they were admiring the Old World's peasant crafts. Only recently have curators of American museums seen American needlework.

Yet in 1776 its spirit of freedom was nearly two centuries old.

For more than a year British ships had blockaded Boston and British troops had occupied the hungry city. Americans had fought and died at Lexington, at Concord, on Breed's Hill and at Charleston. The Green Mountain men had taken Ticonderoga. British armies were coming down the Hudson and a British war fleet with troopships was nearing New York harbor when at last, losing all hope of freedom with peace, the gentlemen of the Continental Congress soberly risked their lives, dipping a quill pen in an inkhorn and signing their Declaration.

"We hold these truths to be self-evident, that all men are created equal, that they are endowed by their Creator with certain unalienable Rights, that among these are Life, Liberty and the pursuit of Happiness. . . . We, therefore, the Representatives of the United States of America . . . appealing to the Supreme Judge of the world for the rectitude of our intentions, do, in the Name, and by Authority of the good People of these Colonies, solemnly publish and declare, That these United Colonies are, and of Right ought to be Free and Independent States."

They denied the Old World's ancient, traditional, never-before-rejected belief that human beings are born members of classes, low class to work or upper class to rule. With nothing but certainty of this truth, they faced the oncoming military forces of the British Empire, strongest of the world's Great Powers. They had no ally, no army, no money; in the scattered colonies the people lacked gunpowder for their muskets. They had not even a flag. They were devising their symbols of freedom: the Pine Tree flag of Massachusetts; Carolina's Rattlesnake coiled under its defiance, "Don't Tread on Me"; New York's Beaver. The Continental Congress appointed General George Washington to raise and command the Continental Army. An army in battle must have a flag.

In Philadelphia three rebel leaders hurriedly conferred: General George Washington, the planter; General George Ross, the prosperous merchant; Robert Morris, the rich financier. General Ross thought that his nephew's widow, Mistress Betsy Ross, might make a flag. They walked to her little upholstery shop on Arch Street.

She never had made a flag, she said; of course she would try. She studied their hasty sketch and said that, for her part, she would not choose six-pointed stars; five-pointed stars would make a pattern more to her taste. They thought that five-pointed stars were too difficult to make.

Mistress Betsy took a bit of paper, deftly folded it, and with one snip of her scissors made a five-pointed star. General Washington accepted it with no more words. The gentlemen said they would send her a colored sketch at once.

A breathless messenger brought it, drawn and colored by the renowned artist, William Barrett. Mistress Betsy threaded her needle and made the flag. She made it of patchwork: thirteen five-pointed stars set into a blue square, thirteen strips of red and white sewed together. Clear, gay colors, white for purity, red for courage, blue for faith; stars for light, and straight lines to ripple strong and free against the sky. This was the tradition of American patchwork, and this is what Mistress Betsy's grandchildren and their grandchildren, and theirs, would tell of the making of the star-spangled banner.

In the tradition of American patchwork she made the flag that stands today, with its fifty stars, for the inalienable liberty and human rights of every human being, the flag of the Revolution that already has carried the New World far around this earth and some day will help banish the last tyranny and free all mankind.

Embroidery

Wreath of Flowers: From a wool-embroidered picture. [PENNSYLVANIA FARM MUSEUM OF LANDIS VALLEY, LANCASTER, PA.]

MBROIDERY is a universal artcraft, and certainly the oldest. Of all known people who ever have lived, only the totally naked aborigines have lacked embroidery. Evidently Eve (or Adam) thought of Eve's embroidering the first fig leaves ever worn and all their descendants have been elaborating the art.

Through the ages whole areas of it have been broken off, to be independent artcrafts: crewel work, cross-stitch, candle-wicking, the needlepoints *gros* and *petit*. Embroidery blends with other needlework, too, forming part of designs in patchwork, knitting and crocheting (crib blankets, afghans, sweaters) and all the laces (brides' gowns and veils of embroidered laces).

Still embroidery holds its own wide field with a vast variety of stitches and thousands of effects created by applying threads of all kinds to all kinds of cloth. The most versatile of needlework, embroidery is akin to many other arts. We draw with outline stitches as with a pen or an etcher's point, and with chain, satin and long-and-short stitches as with charcoal; we paint with colored threads as with an artist's brush. Heavily padded satin-stitch is sculpture in bas-relief. Counted-thread or eyelet embroidery makes sheer fabrics into lace.

Yet embroidery is only bits of thread added to fabrics. Your thimbled finger pushes a needle through cloth to leave a stitch where you want it to lie; that's all. Whoever can sew a neat seam by hand can do any embroidery she likes, as simple or as elaborate as she pleases. It will express herself as plainly as her handwriting does, for the almost limitless variety of embroidery comes from the almost infinite variety of human beings, no two of us identical in minds, characters, or circumstances.

Ages before anyone spun a thread or pierced a fishbone to make a needle, women were doing beautiful embroidery, and in all that primitive art you see the inertia, the absence of energy, of change, of invention, of progress, characteristic of the special communalism in which all known human history began.

When Europeans first came to America they found communalism as perfect here as it had been in Egypt four thousand years earlier. In Mexico and Peru, as in ancient Egypt, everyone believed that their human ruler was God Incarnate, owning "all things grown, made, or begotten" in his realm on earth. His sacred agents inspected every new-born child and, if they permitted him to live, gave him a number. Over every ten numbers an overseer was set, and every numbered subject of the Great King lived, toiled, married and bred as his overseer ordered him to do. From these tens, certain girls were selected, trained, and kept in workshops, busily embroidering patterns of brilliant feathers on robes for the Divine Ruler and his priests.

North of Mexico there was no government at all. Here was a worthless land of sunless forests, deadly swamps, arid deserts and mountains.

The simple tribal communalists who inhabited it, the American Indians, had exhausted its poor means of subsistence. Fewer then than now, they were often hungry; and many died in famines. Their God was a Great Spirit, invisible. Their law was the tribe's traditional custom. They had no cloth nor thread nor needles, but from the Abenaki of (now) Maine to the Zuñi of New Mexico they did have beautiful embroidery. Every tribe had its traditional embroidery patterns, abstract, symbolic, full of meaning for the tribesmen and for any alien who had been taught their meaning. The women embroidered these designs on soft white doeskin, with quills.

Through the summers the women gathered quills of birds and porcupines, and dyed them yellow or brown or purple with juices of herbs, roots, berries and barks. They cut off the sharp points, and by pushing the smaller end of a quill into the larger hollow end of another a woman linked several quills together. She chewed them soft, pressed them flat, and stored them in her embroidery bag. So she accumulated short lengths of colors.

In the smoky dim community house, during the winter days, she settled down to embroider by the firelight. For needles she chewed the ends of sinews, twisted them to points, and let them dry hard. While she embroidered she kept the sinew chewed, wet and pliable, and she worked with quills soft and warm from her mouth.

Laying a quill on the leather, she fastened it in its place with a stitch of sinew; then she folded the quill back over the stitch and across her pattern, and held it there with another stitch. The colored quills, hiding the stitches, lay shining on the white doeskin.

The sinew's point would not pierce the leather; it hardly went under the soft surface. When it would not do that, she used a splinter to pierce a little hole for it. She stitched into her tribe's patterns bits of pearly abalone shell, or dyed seeds, or flakes of colored stones, or—on New England's coasts—white and purple wampum beads laboriously chipped from the inmost coil of a quahog shell, dyed, and polished between stones.

So patiently working, in time she adorned her daughter's bridal gown, her husband's and sons' shirts and belts and moccasins, with handsome embroidery; she added rich fringes of knotted leather strips. From the Floridas to the Potomac, from the Alabamas' town Mobile to the Ozark plateau, and from the Rio Grande to the Kansas' river, the Spanish explorers found their cordial hosts dressed splendidly.

Meanwhile, far away in an old Roman town in France, the oldest known piece of European embroidery was unrolled once a year and hung in the nave of Bayeux Cathedral. Centuries older than the printing press, this strip of linen 231 feet long and 20 inches wide records in seventy-two embroidered pictures the history of the Norman conquest of England in 1066 A.D. It is the only record of some events in that war which so changed the world that it still affects all our lives.

Gentle ladies worked these pictures in outline, satin, chain, long-and-short and darning stitches, with eight colors of linen threads and woolen yarns. The materials date the work in the eleventh century, and perhaps William the Conqueror's wife, Matilda, and her ladies did it. But it is not signed, so nobody knows. Some experts believe that Bishop Odo had it done in some French convent, to commemorate his mighty deeds.

For nearly a thousand years (excepting only 1871 and 1940–45 when treasures were hidden from invaders) this embroidery has been shown in Bayeux Cathedral. On the age-browned linen, now under glass, you see today the coronation of Harold, last of England's Saxon kings; his journey across the Channel and his efforts to negotiate peace with the relentless Normans; the building of Hastings castle, and its storming and burning; William the Conqueror rallying his knights to charge the British spears; Bishop Odo in the thick of battle lustily breaking heads with his bloody war mace.

In the thirteenth century the English embroideries were renowned throughout Europe. In the sixteenth century Henry the Eighth, his wives and courtiers, were gorgeous in embroidered robes, and Queen Elizabeth's ladies sat encased in gowns stiff with embroidery, working masses of flowers in tambour stitch and petit point on tapestries, bed curtains, coats, waistcoats, capes and skirts and slippers.

White-on-white counterpane using bullion stitch, French knots and buttonhole stitch, made about 1825. [Cooperstown Museum, Cooperstown, N.Y.]

Hand-woven linen table cover, about 1800. 5¼" square cream blocks embroidered in blue, assembled with 2½" blue strips embroidered in cream. Blocks and strips sometimes pieced together of small scraps of linen. [ART INSTITUTE OF CHICAGO, CHICAGO, ILL.]

So the first refugees in America were not ignorant of embroidery. The well-born ladies among them had done it, all had seen it. But it was a long time before they knew such luxury again. They came from wars and massacres in lands reeking with legal torturing and slow roasting to death of thousands of Catholics, Protestants and the Devil's own witches, and they came to a wilderness where at first they starved and most of them died.

Stranded and lost on Virginia's sea island, forlorn by the Matanzas River in Florida and by the Kennebec in Maine, finally by the James in Virginia and on Cape Cod in Massachusetts they tried to survive and failed.

They died until, in the last extremity, Captain John Smith said ruthlessly to hungry men, "He who does not work shall not

eat," and beyond hundreds of miles of unexplored wilderness to the north, Governor Bradford abolished communal sharing. Each one was left to rely upon himself, and self-reliance saved all their lives.

So began the world revolution that, as John Adams wrote later, was not the War of Independence, but the change in men's minds. The survivors discovered a fact never before known to so many: that liberty is as real as human life itself, that individual freedom is practical. Their actions announced the discovery long before their descendants declared that all men are endowed by their Creator with liberty, as with life.

Weaving wool from their sheep and flax from their fields, driving their axes into the King's pines, sailing traders' ships along the coasts from Maine to the Caribbean and back, for nearly two centuries they were denying any ruler's Divine Right to control and be responsible for their lives. Fifteen years after the Pilgrims landed on desolate Cape Cod, Virginians drove the King's Governor from Jamestown and burned his house. Before anyone thought of throwing tea into Boston harbor, almost all the talk that a boy heard from his elders "related to the tyranny of Government," so "I thought I should do what was right in my own eyes," Ebenezer Fox wrote when he was an old man, recording his memories of childhood and of the late war with England for his grandchildren.

Each man's responsibility for himself was making such prosperity as common men had never known before. Travelers were astonished to see no beggars in the colonies; everyone had food and even the lowest workingmen were decently clothed in clean homespun. The King's tariffs were so high that only the upper classes wore imported cloth, but imported steel needles and crewel wools were offered for sale in fine shops. And though the Kings of England and of France, to protect their guilds' monopolies, prohibited importation of *palampores* (our "Indian prints") from India to the colonies, the fact is that ladies in the Governors' courts were embroidering designs cut from *palampores* onto appliqué patchwork. Looking at rare pieces of this work now in museums, you might not suspect that they meant, in time, muskets at Lexington, hunger at Valley Forge, and fifty stars in a flag over Alaska and Hawaii. But they did.

There was small sale for the heavily taxed imported yarns; most women spun and dyed wool from their sheep. The indigo tub was in the kitchen; the dye pot hung over the fire in the backyard, and Grandma had learned her skill from Indian women. A brew of black walnut husks dyes brown; pokeberries yield purple; in spring the tender young butternut shells produce a light green; for yellow, boil onion skins or goldenrod; and indigo, of course, is raised for blue.

You get the tones from light to dark by simmering the skeins a shorter or longer time; different colors come from redyeing. Use alum or salt to set the colors. Try putting yellow-dyed wool into indigo; maybe you'll get the green you want. There is no end to experimenting and learning.

Ladies and commoners alike were embroidering American flowers on homespun linen in crewel patterns airier and freer here than in Europe. Prim little girls in neat pinafores, daughters of ordinary workers with shillings to spend for them, were going to Dame schools to learn to read and write and stitch their samplers.

All the European patterns and stitches had been brought here. Ships' captains and common sailors brought exotic designs from far Cathay. Generations of immigrants taught them all to each other while from coast to coast they transformed the obstinate land, the sunless forests, malarial swamps and arid desert, into the United States of America.

So when you see a piece of eighteenth- or nineteenth-century American embroidery you know its origin, English or French, Italian or German or Finnish or Slav, Persian, Indian, Chinese, but you say at once, "This is American work." It's difficult to say how you know that; you just know it. There's an indefinable something, a spontaneity, a personality, a feeling of movement and space, an assurance.

In the late nineteenth century fortunes were made from embroidery. Venturesome little companies began to sell good materials, good designs, and they grew like Jonah's gourd. In my youth they were growing to be big industries. They were havens for flocks of artists and they poured out envelopes containing underwear, little dresses, aprons, tablecloths, bedspreads, stamped in beautiful designs for all kinds of embroidery. You could buy them anywhere, and teen-age girls did buy them, of course; a girl who didn't embroider was unheard of. Unconsciously we learned from them the elements of good design, so when we wanted a pattern that we couldn't find for sale, we drew it, and it was good.

That pervasive cultural influence waned and vanished for a while. I suspect that the Binet tests caused the loss. A ten-year-old's score of twelve on the Binet scale indicated that he was as advanced as the average twelve-year-old, and samplings of American children showed that many ten-year-olds averaged a score of twelve, a high level of intelligence for their years. But the Binet theory was that we have all our intelligence in our teens and do not develop it thereafter, so a notion spread that the average American adult is mentally only twelve years old. You'd hardly expect influential men to believe that, but of course they do not regard themselves as average, and many did believe it. The statement became a cliché, everywhere repeated for several years.

This wave of contempt for Americans was disastrous in many ways and incidentally injurious to our embroidery. The mammoth producers of its materials offered us only hideous designs which retarded children could do in the crude colors. I myself protested to the manager of one huge company and he replied decisively, "This country isn't Europe; most Americans have the minds of twelve-year-olds."

We did not buy the trash and slowly everywhere the needlework departments dwindled and the little shops closed. Still we embroidered. We copied good designs in museums or drew new ones. Costly books pictured some of the creative work which such artists as Mrs. Theodore Roosevelt were doing. A few lingering specialty shops imported good materials and designs from the European branches of the big American manufacturers.

There was no longer the widespread stimulus to this needle art, but everywhere American women were embroidering. Thrown again on their own resources, they made do with what they had, and that

was a good thing. In the Kansas dust bowl's barren desolation of the 1930's I stopped for gas at a lonely filling-station lunchroom, scorching in the merciless heat, and saw on the wall behind the lunch counter an embroidered mural. It was a charming composition worked perfectly in clear blues and greens, the only coolness in miles of dust and mirages glittering under the sun. There was no ice, the drinking water was warm and tainted with alkali; the parched wooden walls had sweated out all their sap and the girl behind the counter was heat-worn, but she had made that beautiful thing herself, and looking at it she said, "It always makes me feel good."

So women in all these States went on embroidering, unnoticed and not encouraged but not discouraged until now, in mid-twentieth century, the pressure of our demand for good designs and materials is reviving the supply. The cities' big stores are expanding their needlework departments again; new little specialty shops are being opened in cities and towns, offering a wealth of patterns, wools, and silks. Some of the best embroidery ever done in our country is being done now. If you aren't doing it yet, your friends are.

Truly good, self-expressive embroidery requires only simple skill with a needle and those moral qualities of discrimination and self-reliance which every successfully housekeeping woman has. There is inexhaustible pleasure in embroidering, and a deep satisfaction comes from a quiet hour spent stitching your own idea into tangible reality.

Even a frivolous bit of embroidery is delightful. Moths once dined on my favorite sweater, and after irrepressible wails I darned every hole with yellow silk, added small colored petals, green stems and leaves, and had the prettiest embroidered sweater I've ever seen. Of course, it was no such work of art as a wall hanging or a screen may be, but even such a little bit of spontaneous embroidery is a joy.

A Dictionary
of Embroidery Stitches

ARROWHEAD STITCH

For lines or light filling. Bring needle up at top left corner; insert it below and to right, and bring out to the right on top line. For second part, insert needle back close to center of stitch and bring out close to spot where thread emerges.

BACKSTITCH

For lines, outlines, and a foundation for other stitches. Work from right to left. Bring needle up a short distance from start of line to be covered; insert it at start of line. Bring out an equal distance ahead along line; draw needle through.

BACKSTITCH—THREADED

For outlines or borders. Work a foundation of backstitches. Then thread another color or weight of yarn through these stitches. A cordlike effect is produced by this single threading. Weave still another thread in and out for a different effect. Threading can be tight or loose depending on the effect you want.

BASKET FILLING STITCH

Alternate four vertical satin stitches (*see page 33*) with four horizontal.

BASKET STITCH

For solid lines and borders. Work from top to bottom. Bring needle up on left line; insert it lower down on right line and bring out directly opposite on left line. Then insert needle on right line above stitch just made; bring out on left just below point where thread first emerged. Insert needle on right line below lowest stitch there and bring out exactly opposite. Take a stitch as shown, working in same holes into which other stitches were worked. Repeat last two steps. The needle takes a step forward and backward alternately.

BLANKET STITCH

For covering a turned-over edge, for outline or, when worked in a circle, to form flowers. Work from left to right. Bring needle up on lower line. Hold thread down with left thumb. Insert needle a little to the right of starting point on upper line; bring out directly below on bottom line; draw needle through over loop of thread.

Right: Cotton homespun bedcover embroidered with worsted yarns, believed to have been made in Texas before its admission to the Union in 1845. Note the stylized leaves and the wreath motif. The border is woven. [WITTE MUSEUM, SAN ANTONIO, TEX.]

BRAID STITCH

For borders. Work from right to left. Bring needle up on lower line. Make a loop of thread as shown in diagram; hold down with thumb; insert needle through loop and in fabric at top of line; bring out on lower line. Pull loop on needle tight; draw through over thread.

BRAID STITCH—EDGING

Worked along a hem or turned-over edge. Work from right to left. Bring needle to right side underneath edge. Loop thread as shown, insert needle through loop, then behind fabric. Bring out a short distance below edge and over working thread. Pull thread through and away from you.

BULLION STITCH

For thin petals and, by overlapping to form a circle, for rosebuds. Bring thread up to right side of fabric; insert needle back the distance of the stitch desired, bring up in same spot thread first emerged. Do not draw needle through. Wind thread around point of needle. (Six or seven times is usual, but the number varies according to the length of stitch required.) Place thumb on twists; draw needle and thread through the material and the twists. Pull needle and thread to the right and tighten by pulling working thread. Then insert needle through to the back as shown. Occasionally bullion stitches are very long and may have to be tacked in the center to hold them in place.

BUTTONHOLE STITCH

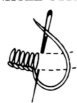

For buttonholes, scallops, cut-work, lines, and borders. Work same as blanket stitch but work stitches closer together.

BUTTONHOLE STITCH— CLOSED

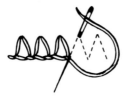

For decorative borders and hems. Work same as blanket stitch but have the needle enter fabric at the same spot for each pair of stitches.

BUTTONHOLE STITCH— CROSSED

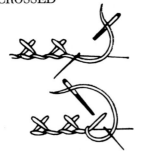

Work same as blanket stitch but cross each pair of stitches.

BUTTONHOLE STITCH— EYELET (also called BUTTONHOLE EYELET)

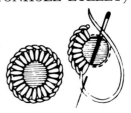

Draw circle on fabric. Work running stitches around it. Cut out center. Then work buttonhole stitch all around the circle over running stitches.

CABLE-CHAIN STITCH

For lines or borders. Bring needle up at top of line to be covered. Holding thread down with thumb, pass needle from right to left under thread held down; twist needle into vertical position, thread twisted around it. Insert in fabric the desired length and draw it through over working thread.

CABLE-CHAIN STITCH— ZIGZAG

For borders and zigzag lines. Work same as cable-chain stitch but work each stitch at right angle to the last stitch.

CHAIN BAND—RAISED

For borders. First, work a foundation of straight stitches spaced evenly apart. Work from top to bottom over the foundation stitches and do not pick up fabric. Bring needle up just above first foundation stitch; pass needle over and under this stitch, bring out toward left; then make a stitch as shown in diagram. Pass needle over and under next foundation stitch and repeat.

CHAIN STITCH

For lines and outlines. Worked in close rows, it is used as a filling stitch. Bring needle to right side of fabric. Hold thread down with thumb. Insert needle as close as possible to spot where thread emerges, bring out a short distance below. Draw needle through over loop.

CHAIN STITCH—BROAD

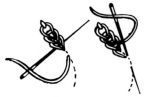

For lines, borders, and stems. Work from top to bottom. Bring needle up at top of line. Make a small straight stitch and bring needle out below. Pass needle back under straight stitch without picking up fabric; insert in same place it last emerged; bring out below. Make stitches in same manner, passing needle back under last chain stitch made.

CHAIN STITCH— CHECKERED

For borders and decorative lines. Work with two colors threaded in same needle. Work same as chain stitch, but when needle is ready to pull through, place dark thread over needle and draw needle through over light thread. Reverse for next stitch.

CHAIN STITCH—DOUBLE

For wide borders. Work from top to bottom. Bring needle up at A; insert at B and bring out at C. Place the thread over to the left and insert needle at A; bring out at D and work a similar stitch. Then insert needle at C and work a similar stitch. For fourth stitch, insert needle in second stitch. Alternate stitches in this manner.

CHAIN STITCH—HEAVY

For lines, borders, broad stems. Work from top to bottom. Make a small running stitch at top of line to be covered. Bring needle out a little below this stitch; thread under running stitch; insert needle in fabric where it last emerged. Bring out below this point and thread it again under running stitch; take it back into fabric where it last emerged. Each chain is made by working back under the 2 previous loops.

CHAIN STITCH—KNOTTED

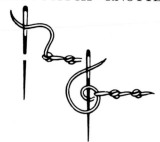

For lines and borders. Work from right to left. Bring needle up at end of line. Make a small vertical stitch on line toward left (a small slanted stitch is formed). Hold working thread down with thumb; slip needle under slanted stitch from top to bottom (do not pick up fabric); pull thread through until a loop is formed; pass needle through this loop; pull thread away and toward left.

CHAIN STITCH—OPEN

For borders, wide lines, and casings. Work from top to bottom. Bring needle out at A. Hold thread down with thumb; insert needle at B, bring out a little below A, draw thread through over working thread. Leave loop just formed a little loose as next stitch is inserted in it. Work next stitches as shown in diagram.

CHAIN STITCH—TWISTED

For lines and borders. Work from top to bottom. Work as chain stitch but take a slanting stitch as shown and do not work back in previous stitch.

CHAIN STITCH—ZIGZAG

Work from right to left. Work as chain stitch but make each loop at an angle to last. Place needle through thread of last loop so stitch will lie flat.

CHESSBOARD FILLING

For filling. Make groups of four satin stitches. Make a cross-stitch over each group, then make a small stitch in center where stitches cross.

CHEVRON STITCH

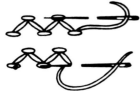

For lines, borders, and light filling. Work from left to right. Bring needle up on lower line; then, still on lower line, insert needle to the right and bring out in center of stitch being formed. Make a stitch to the right on top line (first step in diagram). Then, still on top line, insert needle to the right and bring out in center of stitch now being formed (second step). Continue in this manner.

CLOUD FILLING STITCH

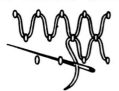

For filling. Make a foundation of tiny stitches as shown. Then lace through these stitches, first top row, then bottom to end of row. On next row lace stitches so loops meet under the same stitch as shown.

CORAL STITCH

For lines, outlines, and filling. Work from right to left. Bring thread up at end of line to be covered. Hold down with thumb, then make a tiny slanting stitch along line and draw needle through over thread as shown.

CORAL STITCH—ZIGZAG

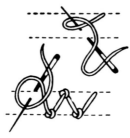

For borders. Work same as coral stitch but alternate stitches on an upper and lower line. Work over loops of thread as shown.

COUCHED FILLING STITCH

For filling, especially where a lattice effect is desired. Often used in flower centers. Work long horizontal stitches evenly spaced across area to be filled. Then work vertical stitches across these. Work a cross-stitch at each intersection. A different weight or color is usually used to work crosses.

COUCHING STITCH

For outlines, lines, and borders. Place one or more threads along line to be covered; hold down with thumb. With another thread, work small even stitches over these threads to hold in place.

COUCHING STITCH—BOKHARA

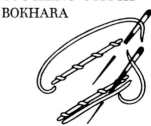

For filling. Worked same as couching but the same thread is used for the ground and the tying-down stitches. Carry thread across space to be filled from left to right; then work back as shown, making small slanting stitches at even intervals over this thread. The tying-down stitches should be close together and pulled tight.

COUCHING STITCH—RUMANIAN

Worked same as Bokhara couching but when working back over thread the stitches are longer and more slanted.

Sunflower spread with herringbone·stitch embroidered over quilting, and an appliquéd center. [PRIVATE COLLECTION]

Two wall hangings, both farm scenes. LEFT: *Worked by Mary Rees in New England in 1827.* [ABBY ALDRICH ROCKEFELLER FOLK ART COLLECTION, WILLIAMSBURG, VA.] RIGHT: *John Appleyard estate as it appeared in the 1850's. Designed from memory by his daughter Ellen in 1867 and worked in seventeen different colors of silk yarn on perforated paper.* [NATIONAL GALLERY OF ART, INDEX OF AMERICAN DESIGN, WASHINGTON, D.C.]

CRETAN STITCH—OPEN

For lines, borders, or filling. Work from left to right. Bring needle up on lower line. Make a small vertical stitch on top line as shown. Then with needle pointing up, make a similar stitch on lower line.

CROSS-STITCH

Usually worked with transfers or on fabric where threads can be counted, since crosses should be even. Make a row of slanting stitches over an equal number of threads of fabric. This forms a row of the first half of each cross. Work back over these stitches as shown. You can work cross-stitches individually and in any direction, but they must all cross in the same direction.

DIAMOND STITCH

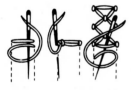

For borders. Work from top to bottom. Bring needle up on left line. Insert on right line and bring up directly below. Hold thread toward left; pass needle under the two threads as shown; draw needle through over working thread (knot made on right side of first stitch). Make a similar knot on left side of same stitch. Insert needle next to knot just made; bring out below.

Make a knot in center on lower of two horizontal stitches. Make a stitch on right line; make a knot, then make a knot on left. Insert needle next to knot just made, bring out below. Then make knot in center.

ERMINE FILLING STITCH

For filling or as a border when worked in rows. Make a long straight stitch for center, then work an elongated cross-stitch over center stitch.

EYELET HOLE

For cutwork embroidery. Draw circle on fabric. Work running stitches around it. Cut out center. Then overcast all around circle over running stitches.

FEATHER STITCH

For lines, borders, outlines, fernlike leaves, and light filling. Work from top to bottom. Bring needle up a little to left of line to be covered. Hold thread down with thumb; make a slanting stitch to the right and a little below this spot with needle pointing to the left; draw needle through over working thread. Carry thread to left side of line to be covered and make a similar stitch a little below this spot with needle pointing to the right; draw needle through over working thread.

FEATHER STITCH—CLOSED

For borders and lines. Work from top to bottom. Bring needle up at A; insert at B, bring out a little below. Draw through over working thread. Insert needle just below starting point and make a similar stitch on left side (shown in diagram). Repeat, making stitches on right side and then left; make stitches close together so an almost unbroken line is formed at outer edges.

FEATHER STITCH—LONG-ARMED

For lines, borders, and filling. Work from top to bottom. Bring needle up at top of line to be covered. Insert to left and a little lower down; bring out in center; draw needle through over working thread. Make a similar stitch to right. Continue alternating stitches.

FEATHER STITCH—SINGLE

For lines, irregular outlines, and smocking. Work from top to bottom. Bring needle up at top of line to be covered. Hold thread down with thumb. Make a slanting stitch as shown and draw needle through over working thread.

FERN STITCH

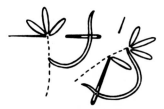

For leaf veins or fernlike leaves. Work three straight stitches all radiating from same center hole.

FISHBONE STITCH

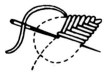

For filling. Make a short stitch at top of area to be filled. Bring needle up on left margin; insert it a little below first stitch and just across center line; bring out on right margin. Make a similar stitch inserting needle to left of center line and bringing it out at left margin. Each succeeding stitch should slant and cross at the center.

FISHBONE STITCH— RAISED

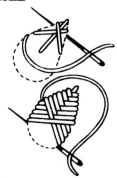

For padded filling. Make three stitches at top of area to be filled. Insert needle on right margin, bring out on left margin exactly opposite as shown. Insert

needle on right margin just below lowest stitch as shown in second step; insert needle again as shown in first step; repeat these two steps.

FLY STITCH

For light filling or borders. Bring thread up at top-left side of stitch; insert needle exactly opposite and bring out in center below; draw through over working thread. Make a small stitch to tie down loop. This tying-down stitch can be made any length for different effects.

FRENCH KNOT

For flower centers, light filling, and anywhere the effect of a single dot is required. Bring needle up at point where knot is to be made. Wind thread two or three times around point of needle; insert in fabric as close as possible to spot where thread emerged (but not in exact spot) and pull to wrong side, holding twists in place.

HEMSTITCH

A decorative way to finish off hems. First pull horizontal threads out of fabric the desired width. Three or four threads is an average amount. Turn hem up just to the edge of drawn threads. Baste in place. Work stitches from left to right. Bring needle up a little below opening; then work stitches as shown, catching hem in back at same time. Diagram shows working around three threads but you can vary this amount.

HEMSTITCH—ITALIAN

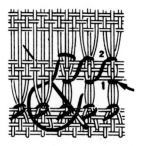

Work regular hemstitch just above hem. Leave three or four horizontal threads of fabric above this, then pull out more horizontal threads equal in number to those pulled in first row of hemstitching. Now work from right to left. Catch thread at arrow; bring needle up at 1 and insert just below arrow. Bring up at 2, then around same three threads in upper opening. Then take a stitch as shown in diagram. Continue across.

HERRINGBONE STITCH

For borders, wide lines, and as a foundation for other stitches. Work from left to right. Bring needle up at A; insert at B, bring out at C; then insert at D, bring out at E.

HERRINGBONE STITCH—TIED

For borders. Make a foundation of herringbone stitches. Then work coral stitch over them, making a knot over intersections without picking up fabric.

HOLBEIN STITCH

For lines and outlines. Often combined with cross-stitch. Assisi work and Rumanian embroideries use Holbein. It is best worked on fabric where threads can be counted, as stitches must be of equal length. Work running stitch along line to be covered, having equal spaces between. Then work running stitches back over this line, filling in the empty spaces.

KNOT STITCH

Worked along a hem or turned-over edge. Work from left to right. Bring needle to right side at fold. With needle in vertical position, insert needle to right through hem and bring out below hem over working thread (do not pull tight). Take another stitch over this loop and pull into a knot.

LADDER STITCH

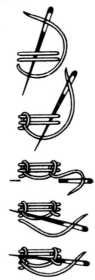

For wide borders and filling. Sides are usually straight, but an interesting effect can be achieved by expanding width of ladder as you work. Work from top to bottom. Make two horizontal stitches the desired width. Then pass needle under these horizontal stitches as shown. Do not pick up fabric. Make a similar loop stitch on right side (2nd step in diagram). Then insert needle on right margin; bring out on left margin (3rd step). Insert needle between second and third rungs of ladder, pass it under both threads of left-hand loop, draw through without picking up fabric (4th step). Work under right-margin loop in same manner (5th step). Repeat steps 3, 4, and 5. Pull thread slightly to left after making left-hand loops but leave it a little loose when making right-hand loops. This will keep stitches even.

LAZY-DAISY STITCH

For flowers and light filling.

Bring thread up in center of "flower." Hold thread down with thumb; insert needle close to or in exact spot where thread emerged and bring out desired distance below; draw through over working thread. Then tie down with a tiny stitch made over loop as shown. Make similar stitches to form a circle around same center point. Diagram shows them separated for clarity, but they can be made in same center hole.

LAZY-DAISY—LONG-TAILED

Worked in same manner as lazy-daisy but loop is smaller and tying-down stitch is longer and made toward center.

LONG AND SHORT STITCH

For filling and shading. Work same as satin stitch, but stagger long and short stitches over area to be covered. The irregular line formed by these stitches is especially good for shading colors.

LONG AND SHORT—SURFACE

Used to conserve thread. Worked same as long and short but needle does not travel so far underneath fabric.

OUTLINE STITCH

Also called stem or crewel stitch. For outlines, stems, and any fine line. Work from left to right. Bring needle up at end of line to be covered. Insert needle a short distance to the right and bring out a little way to the left at a slight angle. Keep thread above needle.

OVERCAST STITCH

For stems, outlines, monogramming. Work a row of running stitches across line to be covered. Then work small close stitches across these stitches. Pick up smallest amount of fabric possible.

PEKINGESE STITCH

First make a row of backstitches. Without picking up fabric, lace second thread through these stitches.

ROMAN STITCH

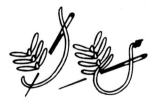

For borders or filling. Work from top to bottom. Bring nee-dle up on left line; insert exactly opposite on right line; bring out in center. Then make a tiny stitch over this loop and bring needle out on left line (second step). Stitches can be made slightly curved as shown or perfectly straight.

RUMANIAN STITCH

For borders or filling. Work from top to bottom. Bring needle up on left line; insert exactly opposite on right line; bring it out about halfway back toward left line, draw through over working thread. Then tie this stitch down with a slanting stitch as shown.

RUNNING STITCH

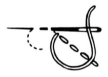

For outlines, foundations for other stitches; for filling when worked in close rows. Work from right to left as shown.

SATIN STITCH

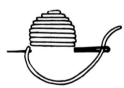

For filling where background fabric is to be covered completely. Bring needle up at one edge of area to be covered, insert needle at opposite edge and return to starting line by carrying it underneath fabric. Make stitches close enough together to cover background fabric com-pletely. Satin stitches should not be so long that they look loose and untidy. You can divide large areas to be covered into small sections.

SATIN STITCH—SURFACE

Used to conserve thread. Worked same as satin stitch but needle does not go all the way underneath area to be covered. Take a tiny stitch at edge; then take a tiny stitch at opposite edge.

SCROLL STITCH

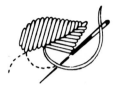

For borders. Work from left to right. Bring needle up at end of line to be covered. Make a loop of thread as shown. Insert needle in center of loop along line to be covered and pick up a small amount of fabric; pull loop tightly under point of needle, then draw needle through.

SEED STITCH

For light filling of large areas such as flowers, leaves, and backgrounds where a solid effect is not desired. Make tiny straight stitches in any direction. The stitches are not worked in a regular pattern but should be of equal length. They can be made single or double as shown.

SHADOW STITCH

Work on sheer fabric so under part of stitch shows through in a shadow effect. Work from right to left. Make a small back-stitch on one side of area to be filled, slant needle to other side of space, make another back-stitch. Shadow stitch is worked on right side of fabric but main part of stitch appears on wrong side so that X's show through fabric while parallel rows of continuous backstitches are on right side.

———

SHEAF FILLING STITCH

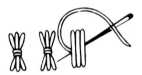

For filling. Make three vertical satin stitches. Then bring nee-dle up beneath them at center and bring out at left side; wrap thread around center twice without picking up fabric and insert where thread emerged.

———

SPLIT STITCH

For outlines, stems, and lines. When worked in close rows, it is used for filling, and by work-ing rows in different colors, for shading. Work stitch like out-line stitch but with thread be-low the needle; then split work-ing thread close to its base when you bring needle out.

STAR STITCH

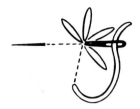

Work simple straight stitches as shown. Diagram shows six spokes, but any number can be made.

———

STAR FILLING STITCH

For light filling. Work a cross-stitch; then work another of equal size across it. Finally, work tiny cross-stitch in center over intersection of the first two.

———

THORN STITCH

For stems and leaves. First make a long center stitch, then work diagonal stitches over cen-ter from bottom to top.

———

VANDYKE STITCH

For borders and lines. Bring needle up at 1. Insert at 2 and bring out at 3. Then insert at 4 and bring out at 5. For next stitch, insert needle under cen-ter-crossed stitches and without picking up fabric draw needle through. Insert needle in right margin below last stitch, bring out directly below on left.

WAVE STITCH—OPEN

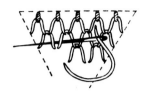

For filling. Work a row of small straight stitches from left to right across top of area to be filled (shaded stitches on dia-gram). Bring needle up on right margin below these stitches. Slip needle under first straight stitch and, without picking up fabric, draw needle through. Make a tiny stitch below and on line where thread last emerged; then work under next straight stitch. The third and following rows are slipped under the bases of two stitches of previous row as shown.

———

WHEAT-EAR STITCH

For borders, stems, and wheat-like stalks. Work from top to bottom. Bring needle up on line to be covered (1); insert at 2; bring out at 3. Insert close to spot where thread first emerged and bring out a distance below. Then without picking up fabric, slip needle from right to left underneath the first two stitches (first step in diagram). Insert needle in spot where thread last emerged and bring out to left as shown in second step. Insert needle at bottom of loop and bring out above and to the right; insert again at bottom of loop and bring out a distance below.

How to Embroider

BACKGROUND FABRICS

Embroidery may be worked on almost any fabric: linen, wool, cotton, silk, or a synthetic fiber. Your choice will be dictated by the effect you wish to achieve and the type of embroidery you wish to do. The pieces illustrated were made when many households had their own looms and not only wove much of their own fabric but often spun their own thread. Synthetic fibers were unknown, and if an especially luxurious effect was desired, rich silks and velvets imported from Europe were purchased for that special piece of embroidery.

THREADS

On early American pieces, fine worsted yarns were used to ornament hand-woven cottons, linens, and woolens. Linen threads, too, were used to embroider many pieces, as flax was often raised, spun, and dyed at home. Silk threads from Europe were used almost exclusively on the luxurious imported silk fabrics. Today you may use any suitable thread. Crewel wool, an all-wool, 2-ply yarn sold in many colors, creates a beautiful texture and may be used for bold effects. The regular 6-strand cotton embroidery floss is most readily available. All six strands may be used at once, or it can be separated for finer work. A heavier cotton thread with a definite twist and silk or rayon may be used where a shiny effect is desired.

NEEDLES

The best needles for any type of embroidery are called crewel needles. They have a slender eye but are only about 1¾″ long. They run from size 1 to 12; the larger the number, the finer the needle. Select a size that is slightly larger at the eye than the thread you use.

HOOPS

It is necessary to use an embroidery hoop to obtain the best results since it holds work taut. Hoops of both metal and wood are made in many sizes and in round and oval shapes.

PREPARING DESIGNS FOR USE

If the design you wish to use is already drawn full-scale, trace it onto tracing paper (if design is heavily detailed, trace outline only and use original as a guide for inside stitches). If it is smaller or larger than the size you want, reproduce it on graph paper or on wrapping paper ruled into one-inch squares, and then trace it onto tracing paper. Pin in place on fabric over a piece of dressmaker's carbon, and go over outline carefully and firmly with pencil or knitting needle. Check to see if design is visible on fabric; if it is not, bear down harder.

LEFT: *Originally black satin, the background of this wreath of pastel flowers has now mellowed to a golden brown. A mid-nineteenth century firescreen delicately worked in silk threads.* [HENRY FORD MUSEUM, DEARBORN, MICH.]

RIGHT: *Elaborately embroidered satin apron with a design of grapes, grape leaves and tendrils, made about 1850.* [NEWARK MUSEUM, NEWARK, N.J.]

Directions for Wreath of Flowers

See full-color photograph on page 16.

SIZE
Embroidered area is 11½" in diameter.

MATERIALS
⅝ yard 39" velvet; 3-ply fingering yarn or crewel embroidery wool (colors listed under Embroidery).

NOTE: Original piece was the center of a large framed picture. This design can be used as a pillow cover or a picture to be framed.

TRANSFERRING DESIGN
Trace outline of design on tracing paper, joining the two parts, and transfer to fabric.

EMBROIDERY
Follow diagram and stitch key. Lightweight lines indicate direction of stitches. Use yarn single, double, or even triple to create different effects.

TO MAKE DOUBLE LAZY-DAISY STITCH: Make a lazy-daisy stitch, pulling thread tight so that lengthwise threads lie close together. Make another lazy-daisy stitch over top of first stitch, spreading lengthwise threads so that first stitch shows between them. TO MAKE LOOPED STITCH: Make 4 lazy-daisy stitches on top of each other, having the tying-down stitch very loose so loops look fluffy.
COLORS: On original, leaves and stems were in shades of green; flowers in shades of red, pink, lavender, yellow, orange, white, and blue; most centers were yellow.

STITCH KEY

Outline Stitch ——————

Lazy-daisy Stitch

Double Lazy-daisy Stitch

Star Stitch

Satin Stitch

French Knot

Looped Stitch

Crewel Work

Linen bed hangings, mid-eighteenth century, embroidered with brightly colored crewel yarns in a variety of stitches, including satin, Rumanian, outline, French knot and couching. Hung over a brilliant blue quilted bedspread. [FROM THE CREWEL WORK COLLECTION OF COLONIAL WILLIAMSBURG, VA.]

O FORM of embroidery is more delightful than American crewel work. Though it is rarer than needlepoint and even more beautiful in its freedom and grace, its stitches are simple and so varied that they are never monotonous. Almost anyone who can baste a collar neatly in place or smoothly darn a sock can make most intricately designed American crewel work and enjoy every minute of it.

The easiness and speed are American. Crewel work itself is an antique needle craft; nobody knows how old. In Exodus you have read about the embroidered curtains of the tabernacle, the embroidered robes of the priests; crewel work, historians say. Centuries upon centuries later when young Augustus Caesar was founding the Roman Empire, the sails of Tyre's trading ships were embroidered in crewel work.

Another thousand years passed. Then Christian Kings and Knights were riding across and beyond their known world to fight for the Holy Land, while their ladies left behind them sat shivering in drafty castle towers, with chilly fingers embroidering pictures of their crusading lords in crewel work to hang on the cold stone walls.

In colder convents the cloistered nuns were stitching altar cloths and coffin palls in crewel work.

Five hundred years later at Leyden in Holland the Pilgrims talked of venturing across the perilous ocean to the unknown other side of the earth. And ladies lately of Elizabeth's court sat at their embroidery frames, discussing her life and death and still working at their crewel-work bed curtains. The East India Company took these Tudor patterns to India to be printed there on cotton cloth for sale in England; and they returned exotic, subtly Orientalized, with lotus, pomegranate, pineapple, blooming with them on the Persian-Indian Tree of Life. This tree grew from India's symbol of Mother Earth, and strange Eastern birds stood on its branches.

Such was the crewel work that the English Pilgrim women and that pretty little French Huguenot, Priscilla Mullins, had seen before they knelt praying on deck as the Mayflower put to sea. That was the noble ladies' needle craft in the homelands that they would never see again. Their children's children would be doing crewel work in the new American way.

So here arises the confusion of tongues, like that at Bab-el, which always exists between the Old World and the New. What is crewel work? In the old terms, it is embroidery solidly done with crewel wools, which are loosely twisted, fine yarns of uncertain origin, perhaps first spun in and named for an English town: Crewel. But in America the women no more followed the old way with a needle than men and women followed the old way of reverent subjection to rulers.

The first thing that the women did to crewel work was to stop covering cloth with woolen yarn. When they had sowed and weeded and reaped flax, and soaked and beaten and broken the stems, and washed and combed and spun the fibers, and threaded the loom and wound the shuttle and flung it back and forth through the web of warp until at last they held in their hands a length of creamy linen, nubbly smooth to stroking fingertips, they did not hide it under stitches. They adorned it delicately with crewel work, in a new way.

In the Old World they had dared to read the forbidden Bible; they learned from it that God gives life and liberty to every person. Accepting that responsibility, they must choose death or exile. They left the known world. Multitudes of them crowded miserably on the rolling and tossing little sailing ships to cross the ocean. In the ten years of the 1630's two thousand men, women, and children reached Massachusetts Bay.

In the savage wilderness they learned, as Captain Smith's and Governor Bradford's few pioneers had learned here, that on this inhospitable planet man must, in fact, earn his bread; each must survive by his own effort or perish.

They survived. In hunger and danger they roused strength and courage, they discovered new abilities in themselves, and from achievement they got new satisfaction. Self-reliant, they thanked God for life and liberty and earned His blessings. When they gathered a harvest, they feasted joyfully in thanksgiving to Him who rewarded man's and woman's labor with food now and hope for the future.

Winter days are short in New England; evenings are long. In firelight the spinning wheel whirred, the loom clacked, and an older sister sat by the candle, self-indulgent for once, stitching colors on linen. In dire

Side chair. [AMERICAN WING, MET-
ROPOLITAN MUSEUM OF ART, POWERS
FUND, 1925, NEW YORK, N.Y.]

*Knitting pocket, worn under a lady's
hoop skirt. Note the thistle and the
maple leaf.* [MUSEUM OF THE DAUGH-
TERS OF THE AMERICAN REVOLUTION,
WASHINGTON, D.C.]

Wing chair with crewel work. [PHOTOGRAPHED BY SAMUEL CHAMBERLAIN AT ASHLEY HOUSE, OLD DEERFIELD, MASS.]

want she had learned to be self-reliant and inventive, and probably she did not own a tambour needle. Certainly she did not cover the beautiful linen with monotonous loops of yarn.

With the precious needle that she owned and would use all her life, she made swift and airy stitches: feather stitch, herringbone, couching, seed stitch, outline, French knot. (Did saucy Priscilla, well-born in France, who in a new world refused a captain and married a plain carpenter, bring the French knot to America? I wonder.)

The colonial women not only did crewel work with any thread they had, on any cloth they wove; they gave the old patterns space and gaiety. They discarded all traditions of the craft but one: they kept its basic principle of design.

At first their only dye was indigo, so they did the first American crewel work in blue

on bleached-white linen. Nothing is lovelier than its cool grace, and it is wholly American. Two hundred years later, when a group of women in Old Deerfield revived that early blue-on-white crewel work, one of them, inspired, outlined each blue figure with a half feather stitch in white. This gives her work the delicacy of frost on a windowpane.

Then they made dyes from the woods. Doubtless the Indian women taught them the walnut-husk browns, the pokeberry browns and purples, the yellow saffron that they mixed with indigo to get shades of green. They dyed their threads with all these, and when later they could get cochineal reds, their crewel work began to glow like jewels.

By this time they were weaving cotton cloth. So they embroidered it, too, as well as their linen and woolen, with wool or linen or cotton. They used what they had; they

broke all rules but one, and already they had made American crewel work quite different from European.

The one rule that they rarely broke was that of crewel-work design. It isn't so much a rule as a way of looking at things. It is seeing the fundamental shapes of things that makes crewel work unique and distinguishes it from all other embroidery.

Look, for example, at the crewel-work apple tree and the cherry. Either is a tree bole (often rising from rounded breasts of India's Mother Earth) with two or four flat branches, a few flat leaves, and some circles. How do you know that one tree is apple, the other cherry? The line of those branches tells you.

The trees are no more subtle than the crewel-worked Scottish Thistle or English Rose. The thistle is a circle with a fragment of a larger circle protruding from its circumference. It has a thick stem and near it are one or two long, twisted shapes. The rose is a circle surrounded by semicircles, one or two or three rows of them. From between the curves of the outer row some narrow, pointed shapes extend.

Now embroider these forms with any color that harmonizes or contrasts with colors near them, to please your eye. Blue, perhaps, or brown. Go around the circle with a rapid chain stitch (our version of the tambour). Scatter little backstitches on its center; or

crisscross its center with long stitches and catch them down with short stitches where they cross. Outline-stitch around the semicircles and around the pointed or the twisted shapes; or buttonhole around them; or edge them with long and short stitches, as you like. Put a few seed stitches on them or not. Or do half of one of them in satin stitch, the other half in outline filled with seed stitches. Outline or long and short or satin stitch will make that protruding part of the thistle.

The result does not look like any thistle or any rose that ever bloomed. Yet when you see them you know what they are.

Well, how do you know that any flower is what it is? The real flower distracts us by its own color, its scent, its petals unfolding, but we always know what flower it is. Actually our eyes recognize its basic form. And basic form is the age-old characteristic of crewel work.

Every object has a simple, fundamental shape and we always see it, even when we don't know that we do. Every child sees it and draws it when he draws a house: straight lines for walls, slanting lines for roof, curling lines for smoke. Or a man: round head, oval body, straight legs.

Crewel work is older than known history. The art of China, Persia, India is so old, so childlike still, that its makers see the basic shapes of things. Oriental artists carved them on stone four thousand years ago. Abraham's wife Sarai may have brought them westward from Ur. Certainly ships brought them up the Red Sea to ancient Egypt and imperial Rome, and Europeans have copied them ever since then.

The Tree of Life was there, and Oriental birds and flowers and fruits: the peacock, the parrot, the lotus and pineapple, pomegranate, artichoke. There was the urn, too, with flowers growing from it, that makes gardens in countries where no flower rooted in the ground can survive summer's arid heat.

British ladies added the English oak, the English rose, and their royal emblems: the lion of England, the thistle of Scotland, the three feathers of the Prince of Wales. Women from all Europe brought them to North America and here they added the new wonders: American birds and flowers, corn blade and tassel, wild grapevine.

The pewter platter guided a bit of charcoal in drawing the vine's wandering curves; then it was easy to sketch the broad leaves and the triangular masses of thimble circles hanging down. The same thimble served for fruit on the apple tree and the cherry. And who cannot draw the pine tree's pyramid?

The tall pines' dense shade seemed to cover the unknown continent to the unreached Western Sea. Already Americans denied the King's ownership of those pines and were defying the King's men who marked the best of them for the masts of the Royal Navy. When another century had passed and was ending, the Pine Tree flag would fly from the masts of America's fighting ships through the first long war for individual liberty and property.

That war, as its leaders knew and John Adams said so well, was not the Revolution. Long before the farmers' muskets spoke at Lexington, the world revolution had begun in the minds and spirits of Americans. It was in the spirit of those women living precariously between the vast ocean and the Red Man's wilderness, farther from civilization than the most remote South Sea island is now, and quietly with their needles revolutionizing the world's oldest needle art.

They had never heard of abstract design, but they had no trouble with it. One had only to look at God's visible world with her own eyes, as a child does, to see the beauty of its infinitely various forms. She had only to be true to herself, trusting and relying on truth that she saw and knew, to express herself beautifully with needle and thread.

Sometimes one wavered from pure abstraction into a naturalism as charmingly naive as primitive painting. This artlessness is heartfelt. You look at the fawn whose legs do not quite fit, the lady sitting uncomfortably on air, the parrot whose tail is confused with its wing, and you know they were stitched with love; the untaught artist communicates her feeling and you echo, "How darling!" Always around these touching figures, in true crewel work, is crewel work's abstract design; and always in American crewel work the single abstract form is self-reliant, whole in itself, free and gay in space.

Anything that you see with a child's simplicity is a motif for American crewel work. Draw its basic form as you see it, use any stitch in any way that pleases you, on any cloth with any thread. True American crewel work is as much your own as your handwriting is. You do it by seeing and liking shapes and colors, and using fabric and threads to show them as you see them.

Copy the early patterns if you like; a needle in your hand will express yourself as surely as a pen will, and in a far future experts will study your stitches and anxiously say, "Twentieth century, don't you think?" I beg you, don't bequeath such headaches. For kindness' sake, stitch your name, small but plain, into your crewel work, *and the date*.

Eighteenth-century-American crewel work. [National Gallery of Art, Index of American Design]

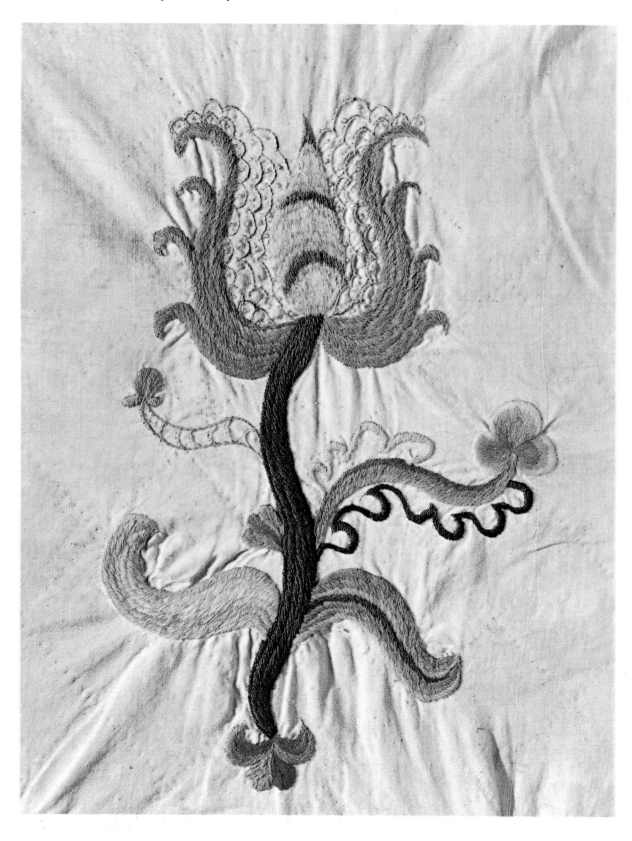

ABOVE: *One of several variations on a tulip motif from crewel bed coverlet shown on opposite page. From Vallett homestead in Montville, Connecticut. Mid-eighteenth century.* [NEW YORK HISTORICAL SOCIETY, NEW YORK, N.Y.]

How to Do Crewel Embroidery

STITCHES

The embroidery stitches most often found in crewel work are Blanket Stitch, Chain Stitch, Outline Stitch (or its variant, known as Stem Stitch or Crewel Stitch), Satin Stitch, Surface Satin Stitch, Long and Short Stitch, French Knot, Running Stitch, Seed Stitch, Feather Stitch, and Couching Stitch (see pages 24-34).

BACKGROUND FABRICS

You can work crewel embroidery on almost any fabric; cotton, wool, burlap, linen, or mixtures, so long as it is of good quality. Your choice of fabric will depend on the item you are making and the tone and texture you want to achieve in relation to the thread you are using. Traditional crewel work was done on unbleached linen or wool; the unbleached tone made a sympathetic ground for the dull finish of crewel wools.

THREADS

Crewel wool, an all-wool, 2-ply twisted yarn, comes in many colors and creates a beautiful texture. But you can use any thread: the regular 6-strand cotton embroidery floss is the most readily available. It can be separated so that a finer thread may be obtained. A heavier cotton thread with a definite twist or silk or rayon floss will produce a shiny effect. If you are working large designs on a heavy linen or burlap, you might use tapestry wools.

NEEDLES

The best needles for crewel work, as for most embroidery, are called crewel needles. They are short, about 1¾" long, and have a slender eye. They are numbered 1 to 12, the higher the number the finer the needle. Select a size that is slightly thicker at the eye end than the thread you are using.

HOOPS

Embroidery hoops are necessary for neat work because they hold the fabric taut. They come in two shapes: round and oval; in different materials: wood and metal; and in many sizes.

TRANSFERRING DESIGNS

With pencil, on tracing paper, trace or copy (enlarging to scale, if necessary) the outlines of the designs you wish to use. Pin your design in place on the fabric over a piece of dressmaker's carbon. Then carefully, but firmly, go over design with pencil or any sharp object such as a knitting needle. Check to see if design is visible on fabric; you may have to bear down harder. When the outline has been transferred, you are ready to start embroidery.

Directions for Crewel Motif

See full-color photograph on preceding page.

SIZE

Overall area of motif is 8" x 11½".

The original motif was one of several variations on flower themes. This design can be used alone or in combination with other crewel motifs for a wall hanging, chair cover, pillow, bedspread, curtains, apron or picture to frame.

EMBROIDERY STITCHES

Only four stitches were used on this motif. They are indicated on the drawing as follows: double lines—outline stitch; dots—French knots; all other areas are worked in satin and long and short stitch or surface satin and surface long and short. Use long and short or surface long and short in larger areas or when shading colors (see pages 32-33).

Follow lightweight lines on drawing for direction of stitches.

Colors are indicated by letters on the drawing. Medium-weight lines indicate color separation; when this is a zigzag line, colors should blend into one another instead of being sharply separated.

49

COLOR KEY
C   *Light Green*
F   *Light Blue-Green*
G   *Dark Blue*
H   *Medium Blue*
I   *Light Blue*
K   *Medium Brown*
L   *Light Brown*
M   *Tan*
N   *Dark Red*
O   *Medium Red*
P   *Light Red*
S   *White*
U   *Medium Yellow*
V   *Light Yellow*
X   *Flesh*

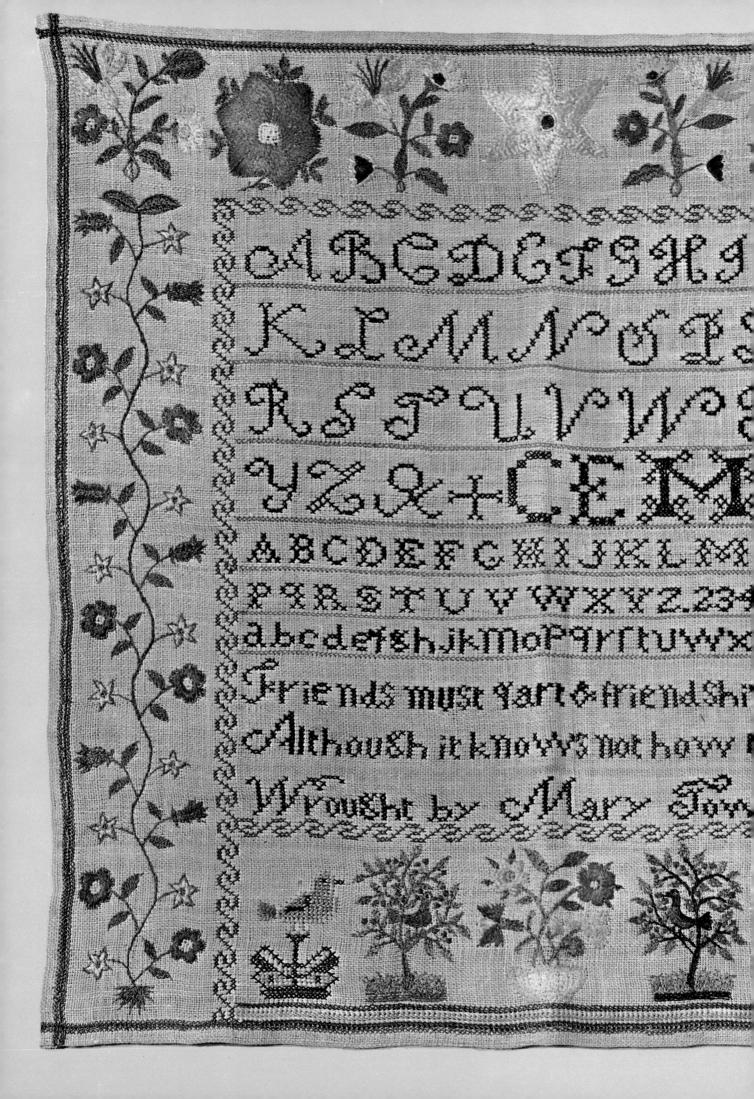

A B C D E F G H I
K L M M N O P
R S T U V W S
Y Z & + C E M

A B C D E F G H I J K L M
P Q R S T U V W X Y Z . 2 3 4
a b c d e f g h j k m o p q r t u v w x

Friends must part & friendship
Although it knows not how

Wrought by Mary Tow

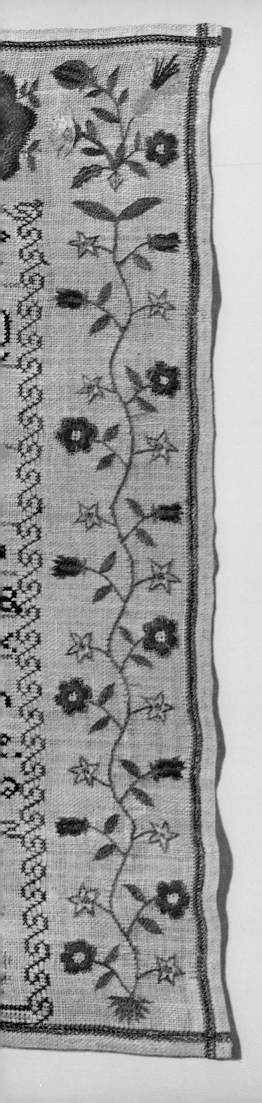

Cross-Stitch

Mary Towne's sampler on natural linen: brightly colored flowers within a graceful border. [OLD STURBRIDGE VILLAGE, STURBRIDGE, MASS.]

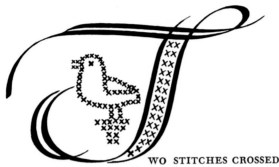

WO STITCHES CROSSED at their middles are all there is to the embroidery named, with a Simple Simon's candor, cross-stitch. Still it may show us that simplicity, in things as in persons, has more values than appear at first glance.

In the days when all properly brought up little American girls stitched their samplers, as all little boys did their chores, they wrote verses in each other's Autograph Albums to record the eternal friendships of first days in school. Their careful Spencerian penmanship is faded now on the brittle pages where you read two verses often repeated, the first usually signed by Abner or Joseph, the second by Eliza or Phoebe:

When Duty whispers low, "Thou must,"
The youth replies, "I can."
And
Straight is the line of Duty,
Curved is the line of Beauty.

Dutiful those little girls were required to be, silently repressing their rebellion while they did their daily "stint" of stitching that must be done before they would be allowed to play. And the beauty of their work is in its four-square character, strictly faithful to the straight line. Yet it is a gentle beauty, for in the beholder's eye the straight line becomes the curves of vines and flowers, of woodland bird and rabbit and deer and of the darling dog and the long-tailed mouser on the hearthrug.

So those grim hours of duty unexpectedly produced the deep joy of work well done, a triumph earned by difficult self-discipline.

Once felt, that triumph is always wanted again, and more and more; few joys on earth equal it. The children who did their stints, at first unwillingly, became men and women whose lives were rich in that happiness. The American Declaration had said that God gives every person an inalienable right to pursue happiness, and it was the happiness of self-disciplined achievement that they pursued and enjoyed while they were creating these United States of America, our inheritance.

Only a few of the many cross-stitched samplers that the little girls made are safe in museums now. (In passing may I say that every one of them still in an old trunk should be given or lent to a museum at once, to keep it safe from mice and moths, flood and fire and careless heirs.) These samplers are merely samples of a child's needlework. Mothers and Dame-School teachers set a child to making them, partly to teach her to use a needle skillfully, more to develop her character by making her discover the joy of finishing a task thoroughly and well.

Therefore these samplers are precious Americana and charming needlework, but their charm is primitive. In the nineteenth century American women made quantities of more sophisticated cross-stitch; where it is now I don't know. The dainty white-on-white lawn underwear must have worn out years ago. The tablecloths and napkins, dresser scarves, cushions, curtains, rugs must be surviving somewhere (I hope), not yet antique, only old-fashioned. I can't be the only American woman making cross-stitch now, either.

Still in these primitive samplers are the same elements of cross-stitch needlework that we use in the most skillful designs: the precisely crossed stitches of precisely equal length, laid exactly on the straight lines of a fabric's warp and woof. Many motifs, too, will move from these simple pieces to be as chic as plate glass and plastic in a modern room.

Look at the curve-handled urns with those anonymous, blue-stemmed plants so exuberantly growing from them, which Anzolette Hussey, aged nine in 1821, made so perfectly. That urn is as old as Persia and as new as tomorrow morning. Magnify it a dozen times, do it in silky, heavy white on coarse white, or in colors on color, and there's a conversation piece for tomorrow's room.

Anzolette's birds perched on her pine trees are delights, too. And there are countless uses for her border of graceful curves which really are not curves but seem to be because they are blunted angles. That is a border to do in no time at all on checked gingham. A small daughter could do it herself on dimity for her very own room, her very own bedspread and curtains. What Anzolette did, can't a little girl do now? Indeed she can, and more.

Anne Anthony, who was born in the fearful days when the Redcoats were coming with guns and Congress couldn't decide what to do, finished her sampler when she was ten years old. The war had stopped then, but grownups were more worried and gloomier than ever; they said the Redcoats did not go, their Redskins would be taking scalps, enemy agents were creeping and crawling everywhere, and Americans were fighting Americans; the United States were not United. On hot August mornings Anne worked with sticky thread, trying to keep the lines straight; they wobbled, but she did make the words plain:

> Tho Mercy is his darling Grace
> In Which he Chiefly Takes Delight
> Yet Will he all the humane Race
> According to their Works requite.

Above this truthful statement she had drawn and worked the figures, we must suppose, of Father, Mother, brother, and sisters or aunts, perhaps little Anne herself in her lavender gown, all in a shady grove of three trees. Above these, her Colonial home, blue walls, brick steps, door and windows in their rows, brown roof. Beside this, in beautiful clothes, Mother and Father as tall as the house, brother and big sister or aunt again, with the little pet dog jumping, two birds flying over their heads and a handsome tree on either side. An ambitious little girl, was Anne. She added two alphabets, block letters

Eliza Ann Edwards centered her cat and its kitten in her sampler, into which she also stitched an array of animals and people, birds, baskets and her home. [THE BROOKLYN MUSEUM, BROOKLYN, N.Y.]

and script, and enclosed all in a most elaborate border of large flowers and leaves and birds. The flowers and leaves are crewelwork designs transposed into cross-stitch, and one bird is an American cardinal. No doubt you know more about birds than I do, and will recognize the others.

When Anne had fastened the last stitch and snipped the thread, with what a huge sigh of expanding satisfaction she must have smoothed out the finished work under her hands. Ten years old on a day in May of 1786, and her whole life was before her, now that her sampler was done!

More than a hundred and seventy-five years later, here is her sampler like a message to us. Someone has said and many repeat that we are living in an Age of Anxiety. Anne Anthony was born when the colonies were besieged, invaded, the people aroused like nests of hornets, and any day the house might be burned over her cradle. She lived through six years of desperation, chaos, want, hunger, while all the news was of Washington's army retreating from defeat to defeat, and inflation made her father's money "not worth a Continental." She finished her sampler in the lull, while hope of secure independence was failing so that even Washington despaired. Then the States were

united in a new Constitution, but their union was so weak and times so hard that leaders of the eastern States and the Republic of Vermont were talking of giving them back to England. But British ships blockaded American harbors, the British-allied Indians were threatening the Mohawk and Hudson river valleys and raiding into Kentucky, while in Congress the western War Hawks pleaded and shouted for war to defend the little Republic's very existence. In that war battle after battle was lost, the Federal Capitol was lost and burned; only the war in Europe and America's seamen desperately fighting on the Great Lakes and the seas preserved the United States.

Those were the years of Anne Anthony's generation. She would be a lace-capped lady, thirty-nine years old, when John

ABOVE: *Jane Treale started her sampler with careful attention but grew lazy after a while.* [NATIONAL GALLERY OF ART, INDEX OF AMERICAN DESIGN, WASHINGTON, D.C.]

LEFT: *Ten-year-old Anne Anthony framed pictures of her home and family with an elaborate border of birds and flowers.* [MUSEUM OF FINE ARTS, BOSTON, MASS.]

RIGHT: *Anzolette Hussey's sampler resembles a child's slate, with its alphabets marked in neat rows against the dark background.* [SMITHSONIAN INSTITUTION, WASHINGTON, D.C.]

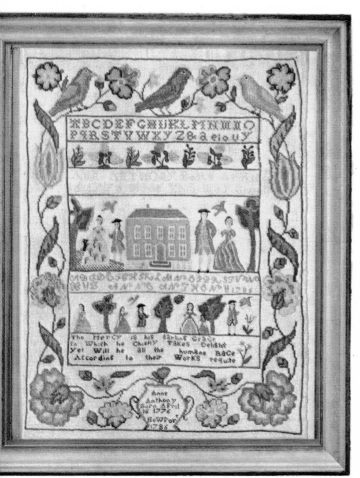

Quincy Adams's skill won the Treaty of Ghent and after forty war-torn years her country's, our country's, independence was secure.

Now in our time we have our anxieties and our hopes, and her sampler earnestly saying:

> Yet Will he all the humane Race
> According to their Works requite.

So here are samplers from the happier nineteenth century, the century of the Indian wars, the Minnesota Massacre, the Far West, the Nauvoo, and the Mountain Meadow Massacres, the Mexican War, the horrible War between the States, Lincoln's assassination, while Americans on foot got their ox wagons over the mountains into the land that Spaniards had explored and abandoned as worthless, that the English had consigned forever to Indians and fur traders. They went into a wilderness of sunless forests, their way blocked by the fallen trees of thousands of years, by treacherous malarial swamps and flooding rivers, and all the way to the Great American Desert they built cabins, roads, towns, cities by (as they said) "main strength 'n' awkwardness."

Already in 1826 Eliza Ann Edwards was more fortunate than little girls farther west would be in the 1870's; she had a cat and a kitten, and she lived in a two-storied house (smaller than the more important cat) with birds as large as the chimney tops perched on its roof. Swans swam on the lawn, too, where a watchdog did not bark at a deer.

You see in Eliza Ann's sampler that cross-stitch is more elaborate now. She adapts more designs from other needle crafts, works them more solidly and uses more colors. Here are the urn and the pine tree again, here also the Whig Rose and the Lemon Star. Archaic griffons appear with naturalistic beehives and sailboats and those tiny dogs with the perky tails and racing legs of pet

black-and-tans. An almost bewildering variety of animals and people, birds and baskets, fruits and flowers are set inside the colorful, wide border, with no confusion or crowding. Because each is complete in itself, set apart and free in space, the whole effect is clear, airy, and serene. Eliza Ann took pleasure in it.

At the same time, Jane Treale was a very different little girl and her sampler shows that the idea of proper bringing-up was changing. Jane didn't finish her sampler till "the 14th year of her age, 1832." She was not required to do a daily stint and do it well. Her elders, doubtless well-meaning, were too self-indulgent and lazy to make her learn the satisfaction that comes from doing a disliked task thoroughly.

Jane draws a large house, badly. Her alphabets are well begun and poorly finished. She works part of a solid border, abandons it and pieces it out with an easier one. It is also prettier; it is a charming pattern made with a few stitches, but Jane does it carelessly. Then, tiring of cross-stitch, she works the treetops in galloping satin stitch. A great girl, fourteen years old; shame on her!

I fear that while Eliza Ann was dutifully sewing a fine seam, Jane was romping and climbing trees with her brothers, often forgetting her sunbonnet and running bareheaded while her cheeks freckled and her braid came undone. She may even have whistled tunes, though many times warned:

> Whistling girls and crowing hens
> Always come to some bad ends.

Then one day she joyfully married, and she did not repent, for later she worked her new initials beautifully on that disgraceful sampler to record that Jane Eliza Treale was now Mrs. S. Not a bad end at all. You never can tell.

Those satin-stitch treetops were harbingers of a change that appears fully in Mary

Towne's work. She did not date it, so when she did it is anybody's guess; and I hope that's a lesson to you. I'd guess the 1890's, because I was then embroidering such flowers myself.

The 1890's were an age of desperate anxiety. After seven years of little rain had made a dust bowl of the prairie States, a world-wide depression (then called a Panic) stopped trade, shut factories, closed banks. Foreclosed mortgages dislodged farmers from the land. In endless lines of covered wagons they traveled the roads, east and west, north and south, seeking a chance to work for food. Coxey's Army rose in Ohio and from a dozen other places. From the Pacific coast its hordes swarmed toward Washington, seizing, crowding, and running trains wildly, stopping only to terrorize towns and ravage stores of food. Federal troops guarded all government buildings. Eastward from the Mississippi for a hundred miles, dispatchers cleared all trains from the tracks, so that Coxey's western armies trudged on toward Washington footsore, robbing and begging for food. I was riding in a covered wagon that summer. That winter, by stealth, I scantily embroidered a pincushion for my mother's Christmas present and somewhere, I think, Mary Towne was stitching her sampler.

You'll go far before you see more graceful borders than Mary Towne's. In the delicate inner ones she achieves a perfection of flowing curves; notice that she did it by perfect accuracy in making the straight lines and precise squares of cross-stitch. The outer borders and the motifs across the top are the new development; samplers have become samples of all the stitches that little girls knew.

We knew many, for though times were hard, they were modern times. Progress surely could go no farther. Some ministers preached that it had gone too far in worldly ways; grandfathers said that Americans were

growing soft. Railroads and telegraph wires were clear across the country to the Pacific Ocean; wood stoves were in almost all kitchens; kerosene lamps were commonplace; the new washtubs were galvanized iron much easier to lug than wooden ones, and there was Gold Dust Soap, powdered. There were rubber-tired buggies in the cities, where streets were paved and gaslighted at night and glossy teams pulled streetcars. Even in small towns the Boston Racket Store had colored embroidery flosses and packets of needles, and Santa Claus might even bring a good little girl the rapture of a wee thimble that fitted her finger.

Mary stitched contentment into those climbing-rose borders; what charming effects she got with simple outlines and satin-stitch leaves and petals. She may have had several needles, threaded with different colors and stuck into the emery strawberry which kept needles sharp and bright. Then she could complete each motif without wasting bits of thread by rethreading a needle. "Waste not, want not," mothers said, and now there were plenty of needles. The days were gone when my great-aunt used her needle for twenty-six years and, when the threads wore through the eye, put on it a rose made of sealing wax and wore it as a stickpin for the rest of her life.

Well, this is an Age of Anxiety. Of course all ages are. In an Age of Anxiety nothing is more tranquilizing than a quiet hour of needlework, especially needlework as precise and monotonous as the little crisscrosses of cross-stitch. If conscience tries to reproach you for idling when there is so much to do, it is silenced when you reply in surprise, "I *am* doing something. Look." Truly you are, for while your hands are creating beauty that will last longer than this age of ours they cannot be restless or hurrying, and peacefulness comes from them to you. It isn't possible to be agitated while doing needlework. You are still; you rest and are refreshed.

How to Do Cross-Stitch

Although American cross-stitch was most widely used in samplers, it was also worked on tablecloths and napkins, curtains, cushions and rugs, and on ladies' underwear. Any cross-stitch design can be worked on an even-weave or squared fabric or worked over Penelope canvas, which is basted on to the foundation material and pulled out when the work is done. Penelope canvas comes in various stitch sizes, usually 7, 9, 11, and 13 meshes to the inch.

CROSS-STITCH

A completed cross-stitch is composed of a stitch like / and a stitch like \ , adding up to X. You can make each X by itself or do all the strokes in one direction, then come back and fill in those in the other direction. You can move either straight ahead, sideways, or diagonally, the only rule being that in any run of X's they should all be crossed in the same direction. The stitches on the back should be parallel to the threads of the fabric and not form X's, except where necessary to jump from one part of the design to another. For samplers, work cross-stitch over two threads of linen. Some other sampler stitches are: Outline Stitch, French Knot, Herringbone Stitch, Satin Stitch, Long and Short Stitch (see pages 31-33).

If you make an error and a few stitches must be taken out, it is easy to unthread the needle and pull out the thread. However, if you have ever examined handmade samplers, either old or new, you will have noticed that more often than not there was a slight variation somewhere. So don't be concerned about a small error if you have passed it, unless it really disturbs the symmetry of the design.

HOW TO READ CHARTS

Most graphed designs can be used in cross-stitch. The thickness of the embroidery floss or wool should be adapted to the background material. Each small square is one cross-stitch (unless otherwise specified). For thread-count samplers, each square equals two threads of linen.

Follow color key symbols for each color. For the chart on pages 60-61, fill in areas banded by black lines in cross-stitch unless otherwise specified, but do not embroider black lines. The color for the whole area is indicated with the color key symbol in a circle.

SAMPLER CROSS-STITCH

The motifs and letters on museum samplers were copied from pattern books or drawn by the young embroideress with the aid of her teacher. Then, following her chart, she embroidered each cross-stitch evenly by counting the threads of her background fabric precisely and working every stitch over the same number of threads. This is called thread-count embroidery. We have written the directions for the sampler using this method of working cross-stitch. It might seem a little difficult at first, but as you count threads you will find your eyes adjusting to the work and the needle almost automatically working over the right number of threads.

MATERIALS

Even-weave linen with 30 threads to the inch. You can use dress linen with about 31 threads to the inch. However, because the threads vary in size and the weave is not even (there are not the same number of threads in each direction) your stitches will not be uniform and the finished size of your sampler will vary slightly from the original. It is also more difficult to count the background threads of dress linen. Six-strand embroidery floss (*see color key*); blunt tapestry needle; embroidery hoop.

Use an embroidery hoop to hold fabric taut. Divide six-strand floss and work with only two strands of floss throughout.

TO PREPARE FABRIC

To keep edges from fraying while handling, whip around them with sewing thread. Make stitches about ½″ apart and ¼″ deep. Fold fabric in half lengthwise and baste a temporary guide line with dark sewing thread, following the thread of material. Fold crosswise and repeat. This will mark the center for you and help you in counting.

PLANNING PLACEMENT

Remember to allow enough linen on all sides of your sampler for mounting or turn-under. Note arrows indicating vertical and horizontal center of design, and key these to your guide lines. If center lines are not indicated on a chart, it is a good idea to mark them yourself before starting work.

FINISHING AND FRAMING SAMPLER

After embroidery is finished be sure to add your name or initials and the date.

Since samplers are washable, they can be finished simply with a ¼″ hem and hung on the wall without any mounting or fram-

ing whatever. A double-pointed steel knitting needle or curtain rod slipped inside the hem at top and bottom will help it hang evenly. If a sampler is to be framed, either with or without a mat, it should first be mounted on cardboard.

A carefully designed and balanced sampler worked by a teenage girl in 1837. [NATIONAL GALLERY OF ART, INDEX OF AMERICAN DESIGN]

Directions for Brick House Sampler

See color photograph on page 59.

SIZE
9¾″ x 12¾″.

WORKING METHOD

Work border first. Short straight lines around border indicate center line of border motifs (use as a guide for border placement).

All motifs are worked in cross-stitch except the following: lettering at top—green satin stitch; little birds in a row and flowers in urns—satin stitch (follow color key); row of blocks across sampler—yellow satin stitch outlined with red outline stitch; little lines connecting blocks—red outline stitch.

House is worked in red cross-stitch, then lines to indicate bricks are worked in white outline stitch. Windows are worked in white cross-stitch, then lines are worked in green outline stitch. The name and date are worked in green cross-stitch. Using the alphabet and numbers, draw in your name and the date and embroider.

COLOR KEY

- ● Green
- ⊠ Dark Red
- · Red
- ◉ White
- ⌃ Yellow
- ⊂ Orange
- ∴ Gold
- ⌐ Pink
- ⌐ Brown

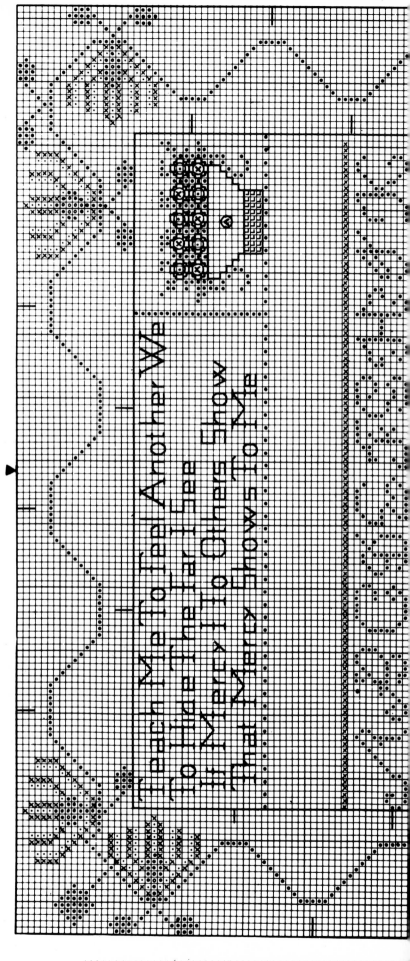

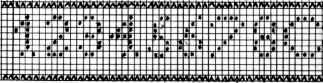

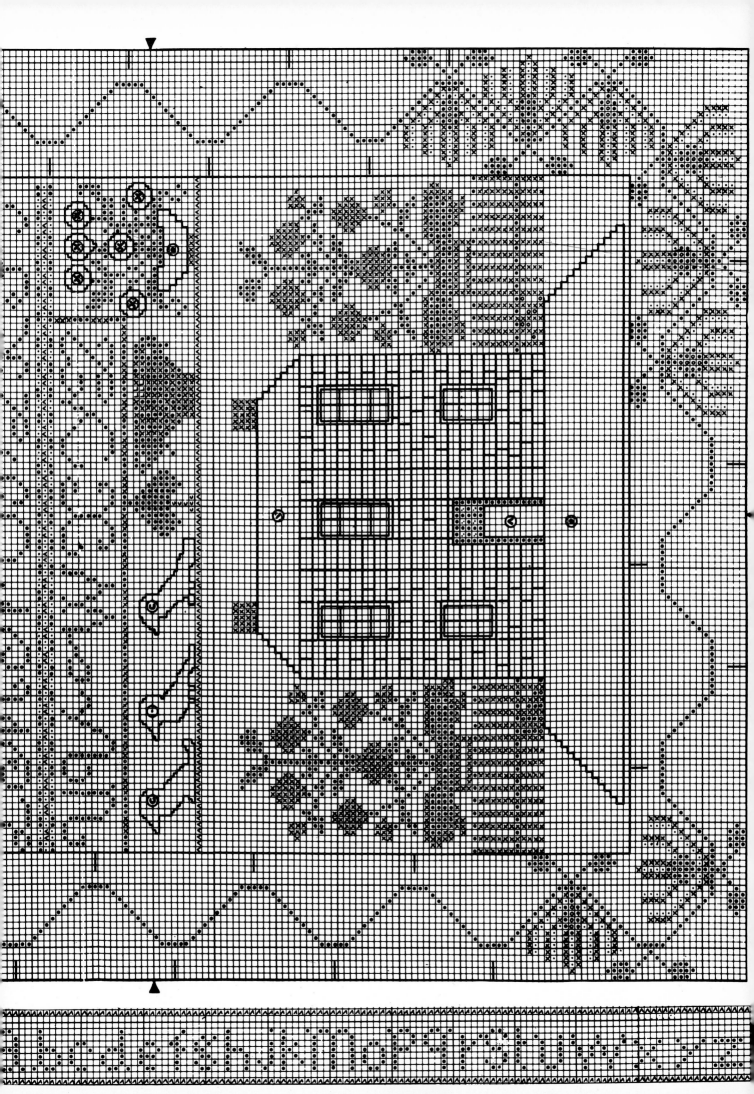

Needlepoint

Firescreen panel, with allover floral design. Original cross-stitched in tapestry yarns on double-mesh canvas.
[METROPOLITAN MUSEUM OF ART, NEW YORK, N.Y. GIFT OF MRS. RUSSELL SAGE, 1909.]

EEDLEPOINT is an old embroidery and it has been in America since the days of Good Queen Bess, but American needlepoint is hardly more than a century old. In fact it is the newest, the youngest of American needle arts.

Nobody knows where or when, or above all how, needlepoint originated. Howard Carter, the archaeologist, found a bit of it in an ancient Egyptian tomb; it was no more primitive than the most sophisticated piece now in an embroidery frame. Eight hundred years ago Chinese were doing fine needlepoint, the tiniest possible stitches in silk on silk; but nothing more came of that, or indeed could, and that perfection is lost now.

The first colonists in Virginia knew sixteenth-century English needlepoint and it was then what it is now: woolwork done on square meshes of stiff canvas woven especially for it. Queen Elizabeth preferred it to all other embroideries, and she and her ladies worked it on tapestries, rugs, bed curtains and bellpulls and waistcoats; they covered chairs and benches and stools with it, and stitched pictures of it, until nothing more could be done in English needlepoint. They perfected it, and beyond perfection there is nowhere to go. So English needlepoint is still the tapestry stitches and figures and the repeated small designs that Queen Elizabeth knew.

English rulers brought it to England's crown colonies, and here it remained English, as English colonial rulers always did. There is no colonial American needlepoint, because needlecrafts are art, art expresses a culture, and American culture is the first to be created by and for everyone—not merely by a few artists for a ruling class.

The colonies here were Crown colonies; they belonged to the monarchs ruling Britain, France, and Spain by Divine Right, and their Governors came from London, Paris,

Floral bouquet of lilies, roses, carnations, irises and pansies. Worked in wool and silk about 1850. Canvas is still tacked to the wood frame that kept it taut. [PENNSYLVANIA FARM MUSEUM OF LANDIS VALLEY, LANCASTER, PA.]

and Madrid, bringing their entourages and their culture with them. By their Kings' orders, the bureaucrats of France and Spain selected their colonists carefully, making sure of their loyalty, morality and religion; they gave them food, seed and tools, planned the village and mapped the village's fields to be made in the wilderness, and sent soldiers whose Commandant governed the people well.

The British colonies were melting pots. British rulers gave the land to Companies of capitalists who expected to make profits from it. Their agents sent shiploads of people from all Europe: low- and middle-class refugees from religious persecutions, workers, adventurers, ne'er-do-wells, hunters, fishers, slaves. The capitalist Companies got no profits, and failed. More than one British Governor, hoping to get rich quick and go home, consorted with pirates and shared their bloody loot. From Quebec to New Orleans the well-governed French and Spanish colonists contemptuously pitied the uncared-

Child's carriage robe with center decoration of family pet and wreath of ivy in needlepoint on background of afghan stitch crochet. [New York State Historical Association, Cooperstown, N.Y.]

Bird and foliage, worked on canvas basted on wool. The canvas strands were pulled out after the picture was com-
pleted. [Witte Museum, San Antonio, Tex.]

for, unruly, turbulent people along the Atlantic coast.

Culture remained aristocratic in New
France and New Spain. In the British colonies, expert craftsmen made the colonial
forms of English and French furniture, architecture, pottery, and women began developing American cooking and needlework,
while they were learning from experience
a world-revolutionary understanding of the
real nature of man.

English needlepoint (Elizabethan, Jacobean) came to America with the British rulers. Some two centuries later it stayed, as a

few of them did, in the world's first classless
society. Martha Washington worked one of
the first examples of needlepoint to be called
American; indeed, she worked ten of them,
seats for drawing-room chairs for her newly
remodeled home, Mount Vernon. With an
eager diligence that any woman under-
stands, she worked all ten in one year.

Now Mrs. Washington's revolutionary
convictions were as firm as her husband's.
Through the times that tried men's souls,
while hope seemed hopeless in the winter at
Valley Forge, she held to them with a quiet
courage supporting his. Still she was English

ABOVE: *Doorstop—a box weighted with pebbles, then covered with fabric and needlepoint.* [WENHAM HISTORICAL ASSOCIATION AND MUSEUM, WENHAM, MASS.]

RIGHT: *Pincushion, about 7½" square, made by a niece of Washington Irving, mid-nineteenth century.* [SLEEPY HOLLOW RESTORATIONS, TARRYTOWN, N.Y.]

gentry, born and bred. Her chairs were imported from England, and she worked the needlepoint seats for them in an English shell pattern.

Needlepoint was never at home with the thrifty patchwork, the braided rugs and woven coverlets in modest houses where the spinning wheel whirred and knitting needles flashed in firelit evenings. Who can see it now in America's family-room kitchens where children romp and hot dogs broil? Other embroideries may frolic on aprons and pot holders, dish towels and baby's bib; needlepoint is more formal. It has qualities once believed to be exclusively those of a ruling class: dignity, decorum, elegance.

In fact these always were common human qualities. The simple savage Redskin had them. The oppressed, thwarted, brutalized "working classes" of Europe needed only freedom to express them. While Mrs. Washington presided in her drawing room, illiterate hunters and trappers along the Western Waters, wearing fringed deerskins and beaded moccasins, were doffing their coon-

skin caps and "making their manners" to weary women as gallantly as satin-and-lace courtiers kissing Madame's hand in Versailles, and much more sincerely.

Already the words "lady" and "gentleman" were acquiring their unique meanings in the new American language.

Still there was no American needlepoint. The reason was simple: the materials cost too much. Back East in the States almost any thrifty woman could now hook a rug or sew a patchwork quilt top from materials in the rag bag; she could embroider homespun linen with homespun wools. Needlepoint required costly imported canvas and a blunt needle useless for anything else.

So needlepoint is our youngest embroidery. The Republic was hardly more than fifty years old before American women began to develop it, and still their greater interests were creating new patchwork designs and American lace. The needlepoint of those days has a *Godey's Lady's Book* air. Perhaps we might call it American Victorian. The colors are gayer than the Good Queen might have chosen and American flowers and birds are in the designs, but the cushion top and the chair seat are primly conventional, made for the parlor that was opened only when company came. The gentlemen's needlepoint slippers and braces (Americans called them suspenders) were Christmas or wedding gifts, to be worn only on Sundays.

Needlepoint is not necessary. It isn't thrifty. It has no utility; its value is beauty alone. And three generations of the Old World's emigrants, at last free, worked and saved for a long century before they abolished the hungry poverty in which their ancestors lived for six thousand years. The nineteenth century was growing old before homekeeping women in all the thirty-five States could afford to create an art purely for its own sake.

Our grandmothers began to make American needlepoint, and few examples of it are

in museums yet. Many more are in homes, and countless numbers are in embroidery frames. Recently scores of such artists as the late Mrs. Theodore Roosevelt, Jr. have been working original American designs and hundreds are making them now. The characteristic American freshness, originality, freedom, are in them. If you are not working one yourself, you see them in your friends' homes and you can find in libraries a few books showing pictures of this new American art.

The first needlepoint that I saw may have been an early example of it. My mother

BELOW: *Chair cushion with a shell motif, one of ten embroidered by Martha Washington at the age of 69.* [MOUNT VERNON LADIES' ASSOCIATION, MOUNT VERNON, VA.]

Swatches, surprisingly modern in design although embroidered over a century ago, found in a work basket at Sunnyside, home of Washington Irving. [SLEEPY HOLLOW RESTORATIONS]

made it when she was a girl in Dakota Territory, during the Hard Winter of 1880–81. It was a bookmark worked in silk on a strip of perforated paper. The design was free and lively, spaced on the paper and unframed. My mother said that she "thought it up" herself and worked it in half-cross-stitch to make the thread go farther.

I believe the paper came from Germany; it was a precious thing on those prairies west of the Mississippi. Today some friends of mine are making needlepoint bookmarks on strips of plastic screening, using its misty soft green as the background of the designs.

My mother didn't know, then, that the half-cross-stitch is a thrifty version of the traditional needlepoint Tent stitch (once used to sew skins together for tents?). In *petit point* you work it over one horizontal thread and one vertical thread; that is, diagonally across on open mesh of the coarse, stiff canvas. The basis of all needlepoint is the geometric square; needlepoint is one of the counted-thread embroideries.

Can you, quick now, name another one? The others are woven drawn work and some elements of hardanger, but somehow I never think of drawn work as embroidery. To me, needlepoint is alone.

You work the Tent stitch diagonally across the canvas, square by square. The wool completely covers the canvas. Nothing in embroidery is easier to do than Tent stitch, or, to my mind, more unbearably monotonous.

The monotony must be restful to women who are buying the quantities of ready-made designs now in the shops, and covering the background with Tent stitches. The designs are usually good and the final achievement justly admired. But there is so much more fun, so much more variety, to be enjoyed in making needlepoint.

First, there are all the other traditional stitches. The upright Gobelin is only Tent stitch done over two horizontal threads instead of one. Monotonously, it merely makes

a coarser texture, but something can be done by using both stitches in developing a design. Then there are cross-stitch, double cross-stitch, long-legged cross-stitch, and seed stitch and knotted stitch; and why not invent a few stitches?

What women have done, we can do, and then some, I hope. There are many more than seven ways of crossing a line over squares and any stitch based on needlepoint's squares and repeated over an area is a perfectly respectable needlepoint stitch. Mrs. Theodore Roosevelt's superb design of lean monkeys swinging on vines across (and, you feel, into and out of) her tall, three-leaved screen is needlepoint full of original stitches.

Then there is endless variety in wools and many other fibers now, variety in both color and texture. Nor need they be woolly. Highlighting a design in silk may startle you with delight. A flower's curled-over petal, the light on a bird's breast, shine out in silk and enliven the whole design.

Adventurous spirits improvise more daringly. One Tuesday evening Mrs. Robert Coleman Taylor of New York saw Galahad, her Scottish terrier, dreaming. You have watched your own pet's ears prick, nose quiver, tail stiffen in the excitement of a dream, and you may have guessed the dream from the paws' twitching. Mrs. Taylor made a needlepoint picture of green meadows spreading over gentle slopes to a distant horizon, and nearby two impudently placid white rabbits sitting before the alert, motionless Scotty. She worked his portrait in his own black hair. This delightfully humorous work of art, entitled Galahad's Tuesday Dream, deserves its honored place in your public library's costly books picturing such masterpieces. And doesn't your own pet deserve as much?

Nothing prevents you, of course, from doing modern, abstract, "nonrepresentational" work in needlepoint, if you like. Many needlewomen are doing that.

There are few books and, as yet, not one Museum of Modern American Folk Arts to show us how truly rich our country is in such original work. Only its creators' friends see the many ways in which they are filling needlepoint's technical form with their own personalities, their own memories and fancies, the unique occasions or familiar scenes of their own lives.

This is not as difficult as you may suppose if you are not doing it. A child can build a house of blocks, and needlepoint canvas is a series of square blocks. All the lines of your house are straight, and no one else sees it with your eyes. Draw it as you see it, work it in needlepoint, and you have something wholly your own, always precious to you. Grandma Moses did not think that she was an artist, either. When her eyesight grew too dim for embroidery, she simply painted what she liked because she liked it, to please herself.

Such self-reliance is an American characteristic. Most Americans are heirs of men and women who crossed a perilous ocean to conquer an unknown continent, saying, "Nothing ventured, nothing gained," and "I'll try anything, once." We are experimental, inventive, creative in meeting every little difficulty of our daily lives, and we put these characteristics into our needlework.

American women are creating American needlepoint, now. They are making it a new needle art, fresh, vigorous, gay, restrained only by its basic technique and the good common sense that is a sense of proportion, of beauty and humor. It is as varied as the tastes, the interests, the lives of its creators. It is all original, individual, homemade, and it is wonderful. When it is old enough to be the proud curator's envied prize, displayed in museums, its rich variety will startle next century's artists.

How to Do Needlepoint

CANVAS
Many types of canvas are available; they are woven of single or double threads and come in several widths with a varying number of meshes. Changing the number of meshes per inch will change the over-all size of your piece, making it larger if there are fewer meshes per inch than specified, or smaller if there are more meshes per inch.

YARN
Many types of yarns and threads can be used for needlepoint. The most popular are 2-ply crewel and 4-ply tapestry yarns, made of extra-long fibers that wear well and are easy to work with. For delicate work, strands can be separated to make finer stitches.

NEEDLES
Blunt tapestry needles are especially suited to needlepoint, for the tips glide easily through the canvas without snagging the yarn. They range in size from 18 to 24; the larger the number is, the finer the needle. Select a size with an eye slightly larger than the yarn you expect to use.

FRAME
You may use a frame if you wish, but generally it is easier and more comfortable to work without one.

PREPARATION
Whip the edges of the canvas to keep it from fraying while you work, or cover them with bias tape or masking tape.

STARTING AND ENDING YARN
A good working length for yarn is about 18". If too long a strand is used, the yarn may weaken from being drawn through canvas continually. Make running stitches through several meshes outside working area before starting work. A knot is not necessary, but if one has been used, snip it off when thread is secured. Knots left in work will cause bumps and may work through the surface. End yarn by making running stitches through several meshes

outside area just worked. Start and end yarn in middle of work by weaving it in and out of the wrong side of completed stitches.

FOLLOWING CHARTS

Each square on a chart equals one mesh on canvas. Charts are usually keyed with color symbols, so as you work, simply count squares to find number of meshes to be worked in each color. Always work the design first before filling in the background. To assure center placement of your design, mark the exact center of both chart and canvas. (Baste lines horizontally and vertically on canvas.) When you begin work, count squares and corresponding meshes from the center mark as you go along. If several colors are involved, thread a needle for each color, keeping all yarn and needles not in use in back of work until needed for design.

REPEAT DESIGNS

If you are adapting a motif that will be repeated several times, first determine the horizontal and vertical center of your canvas and plan your work so that you will be able to center one of the motifs exactly in the middle of the canvas. Then plan all other motifs in relation to that one.

BLOCKING

Blocking will straighten canvas that has become crooked through handling and may even help hide uneven stitches. Sponge wrong side of needlepoint until yarn and canvas are thoroughly and evenly wet. Stretch needlepoint into shape and tack on a board face down, using rustproof tacks spaced ¾″ apart. Let dry thoroughly. (It may take several days.) Press on wrong side with damp towel and hot iron. Do not allow iron to touch face of work.

A Dictionary of Needlepoint Stitches

BYZANTINE STITCH

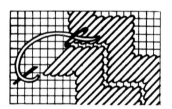

For covering large areas to produce the effect of a brocade or woven fabric. Work satin stitches diagonally over four vertical and four horizontal threads of canvas and form steps as shown.

———

CHAIN STITCH

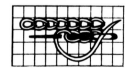

Used in multicolored designs for a softly shaded effect. Work same as chain stitch on material, making a stitch over each mesh of canvas.

CASHMERE STITCH

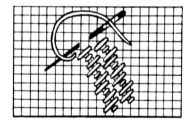

Produces a woven fabric effect. Work one stitch diagonally over one intersection of mesh, then two stitches over two vertical and two horizontal threads. Repeat these three stitches. On next row change position of short and long stitches as shown.

———

CHEQUER STITCH

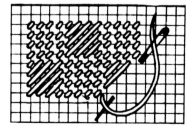

Arrange stitches in squares, the first square having sixteen small stitches, the second, seven graduated stitches. See diagram for number of threads to work over.

———

CROSS-STITCH

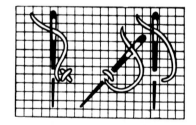

One of the easiest and most widely used needlepoint stitches. It is sometimes called gros point. You can work over a single intersection of canvas threads as shown or over two or more vertical and horizontal threads, depending on the thickness of thread and mesh. Always complete one stitch before going on to the next. All stitches must cross in the same direction.

CROSS-STITCH—DOUBLE

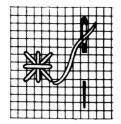

Make cross-stitch; then another diagonally over it.

HALF-CROSS-STITCH

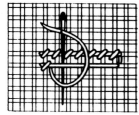

This stitch is worked from left to right, working diagonal stitches over single intersections of either single- or double-mesh canvas. The half-cross-stitch looks like the tent stitch on the surface, but the back of the canvas is not completely covered; it requires less yarn than the tent stitch.

DIAGONAL STITCH

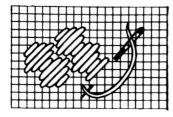

Work in diagonal rows from top-left corner to bottom right. Make stitches over two horizontal and vertical threads of canvas, then over three, four, three, and then two again. Alternate stitches on next row so a large stitch falls next to a small one.

DOUBLE STITCH

Make oblong cross-stitches worked over one horizontal and three vertical meshes alternated with a cross-stitch worked over one intersection.

EYE STITCH

Usually a canvas stitch but can be worked on any fabric where threads can be counted. Work sixteen straight stitches all into the same center hole. This stitch is often finished with an outline of backstitches worked around the square, making each backstitch over two threads.

FERN STITCH

For double-mesh canvas. Make a diagonal stitch under mesh as shown, then another diagonal stitch from A to B. Repeat.

FLORENTINE STITCH

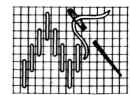

Forms zigzag patterns known as Florentine work. Work straight stitches over four threads of canvas rising or falling two threads above and below the last.

GOBELIN STITCH— ENCROACHING

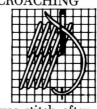

A canvas stitch often used for shading. Work stitches over five horizontal threads and slanted diagonally over one. The next row overlaps the last by one thread of canvas.

Pair of pillows, both with floral motifs, photographed on a window seat in Washington Irving's study. [SLEEPY HOLLOW RESTORATIONS]

GOBELIN STITCH— UPRIGHT

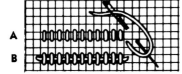

Work stitches over two horizontal threads of single-mesh canvas as shown at top of diagram. Sometimes a thread is laid across meshes first and stitches worked over it as shown.

HUNGARIAN STITCH

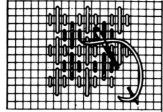

A canvas stitch worked either in one color or contrasting as shown. Make groups of three upright stitches, working over two, four, and two horizontal threads of canvas. Alternate rows so all spaces are filled.

JACQUARD STITCH

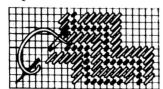

Make rows in steps, one row worked over two vertical and two horizontal threads of canvas; the next row short stitches worked diagonally over one intersection.

KNOTTED STITCH

Make one long slanted stitch over one vertical and three horizontal threads of canvas, then tie down by working a small stitch across it. Rows overlap each other by one thread of canvas.

MILANESE STITCH

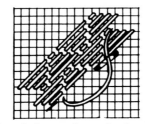

This stitch consists of triangles composed of four stitches of graded length. The triangles are set so they point alternately up and down. Make backstitches as shown. For the first row the backstitches pass diagonally over one, then four intersections of canvas. Second row passes over three, then two intersections; third row passes over three and two, and the fourth row over one and four.

MOORISH STITCH

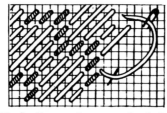

Work diagonal rows of stitches over two, four, six, and four intersections. Work next row over two intersections.

PARISIAN STITCH

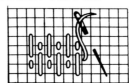

Make upright stitches alternately over one and three threads. Alternate rows so a long falls over a short stitch.

PLAIT STITCH

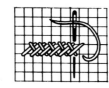

Make diagonal stitches, one forward and then one backward.

RICE STITCH

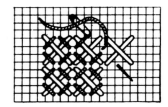

First cover background with large cross-stitches worked over four vertical and horizontal threads of canvas. Over corners of each cross-stitch, make small diagonal stitches at right angles to each other. Background stitches are often worked in a heavier weight.

SCOTTISH STITCH

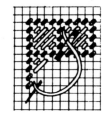

Squares of stitches worked diagonally over one, two, three, two, and one intersections. Outline with stitches worked over one intersection.

TENT STITCH

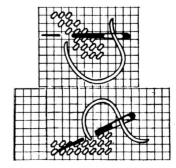

Often called petit point. This stitch can be worked over single- or double-mesh canvas. The rows may be worked diagonally or straight across canvas, always making the stitch diagonally across a single intersection. Work from right to left. This stitch covers the back of the canvas as well as the front, making a stronger, more durable piece, but requires more yarn than the half-cross-stitch.

Directions for Shell Motif from
Martha Washington's Chair Cushion

SIZE
Shell measures 5″ across by 4″ high.

MATERIALS
Double-mesh canvas with 10 meshes to the inch; tapestry yarn (colors listed with color key for chart).

WORKING METHOD
Entire piece was worked in cross-stitch. Use all four strands of tapestry yarn. Follow chart for stitches and photograph for placement of shells, working enough of them to cover the top of your chair. You can finish off by making a plain gusset in the same wool as your background shade or, if the chair is fairly square, by leaving 4 ninety-degree sections empty at each corner and mitering the canvas so that the one top piece covers the sides as well.

```
┌─────────────────────┐
│     COLOR KEY       │
│                     │
│   ⊠  Red            │
│                     │
│   ⊡  Mustard        │
│                     │
│   ⊘  Gold           │
│                     │
│   ☐  Tan            │
│                     │
└─────────────────────┘
```

See full-color photograph on page 69.

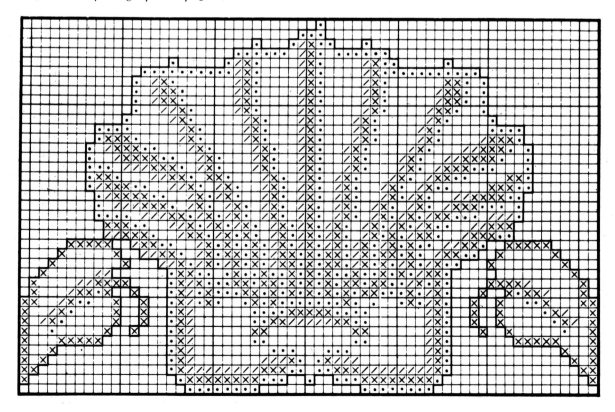

Patch-work

Mariner's Compass, a nautical theme traditionally worked in blue, red and white. [Shelburne Museum, Shelburne, Vt.]

ATCHWORK is the American folk art; women invented it here. It is uniquely American; the Old World created nothing like it. And in its patterns American women have recorded the whole history of these multiplying States, from Philadelphia in 1776 to Hawaii this morning.

Oh, patches are nothing new. They must be nearly as old as clothes. No doubt, in bitter winter weather, a cave woman somehow patched her small son's bearskin. As soon as women began to weave they must have sewed pieces of cloth together to make a large piece, too. They did it in ancient Egypt; they did it in Medieval France and Spain. I am told that in seventeenth-century England they made bedcovers in that way. "Crazy quilt," my grandmothers called the haphazard mosaic, with slight respect, but my young aunts made "crazy-quilt throws" of scraps of silk and velvet, embroidering them and feather stitching the seams. These elegant "throws" were draped on pianos, to Queen Victoria's taste. Today they are quaintly interesting; I wouldn't throw one away, but I would not call it patchwork. True patchwork is designed; it has meaning in every line.

Its origin was the most extreme poverty. Women created this rich needlework art who had not a penny to spend or a half-inch bit of cloth to waste. I sing no praise of poverty—I have had plenty of it and I thoroughly detest it—but no one can deny that, in freedom, poverty is stimulating. During the war scarcity of the 1940's I saw women creating beautiful patchwork.

We were Dorcas members meeting in our abandoned little country schoolhouse. From a bale of woolen mill ends we were to make knee blankets for war-wounded men in wheel chairs. Our task was merely to sew the scraps together; nobody suggested patterns, but one after another we picked out scraps that made pictures: a curve of blue for a lake, green strips for its bank, dark pointed pines, streaks of sunset colors in blue sky. Or a gray road, blue stream and covered bridge in autumn woods. When our bundles had gone to the Red Cross, someone displayed that patchwork in a Main Street shopwindow before it went to express our care for them to the unknown wounded.

That was only a little incident among countless others, for in this spirit American women created patchwork and are creating it now. The cost is not money. New patterns come from wanting to express some meaning with shapes and colors. Traditional patterns are innumerable. The loveliest of quilts, coverlets, cushions, aprons, borders, may cost no more than thread to sew them, for who hasn't worn-out clothes that will yield dozens of perfectly good small pieces of cloth?

You have a choice of methods, for there are two kinds of patchwork. The earliest was made by sewing bits of cloth together in patterns now named "Geometricals." The seams are almost always straight, for only the Dutch women of Manhattan and Long Island and the German women in Pennsylvania and Ohio had the superb skill to sew a perfectly curving bias seam. I wouldn't attempt it myself.

A century or so later Americans were so prosperous that they could spare bits of cloth merely for ornament. Then women who wanted a pattern of curves (and were not Dutch or German) cut out curved pieces of cloth, laid them on cloth, and hemmed down their turned-under edges. Women from France may have done this first, because when patchwork is cloth applied to cloth it is named "applied" in French: appliqué.

So there were two developments of American patchwork. The appliqué is perhaps more graceful, but it shall come later; we'll consider the geometricals now. They are older and to me much more interesting. Also, they are far easier to do.

If you use a traditional pattern you needn't even think about it after you've cut out the pieces. You cut out dozens of them, using sharp shears and a stiff pasteboard pattern piece; you stack the colors neatly in piles. Then you thread a needle and settle comfortably in your chair. The needle runs easily back and forth through soft cloth while nerves relax and useless worries fade away. Smoothing out a finished block, you have a pleasant sense of achievement. You are making a thing of beauty that generations to come will prize.

Or, brisk and busy, you may hum while you feed long strips of patches through the humming machine. Snip them apart, set them together and run them through again. You may make a whole quilt-top in a surprisingly short time. This will horrify some, but I was a pioneer child; I know how pioneer women welcomed the marvelous machine, incredulously admired its swiftness and its perfect stitching, and thanked God for easing women's work. Whether your tool is a needle or tamed electricity, your patchwork is your own; you can express yourself in pattern and colors and way of working.

If you want to understand patchwork, you will find in the nearest library some clues that will lead you into an exciting adventure

Robbing Peter to Pay Paul. An obviously skilled needlewoman worked the curved seams of this pattern. [BROOK-LYN MUSEUM, BROOKLYN, N.Y.]

in culture. It can take you to rich collections in museums, but if you can't visit them, never mind; nearly every little town and county in these States has some treasures of old patchwork. An interest in it takes you far from libraries and museums, into the living culture of our country. When you know patchwork patterns you know all American history, the backgrounds and characters of all the people who came here to be this nation of all mankind; you know much more than is written in books. There is no end of learning more from patchwork patterns.

For only one example, look at the Lemon Star. This eight-pointed star came to America when Louis XIV claimed this continent from Quebec to the unknown Western Sea and from the Arctic to the Gulf. Nobody knows why an eccentric Frenchman came from France, traveled into the farthest Cana-

dian wilderness, and there built a castle on the shore of the St. Lawrence River opposite Montreal. His family name was Le Moyne; his crest was an eight-pointed star, and he gave his seven sons, born in the castle, the titles of Lords.

In 1699 the King's Governor-General sent two of those sons, the Sieur d'Iberville and the Sieur de Bienville, to govern Louisiana from the old village of the Alabama Indians, Mobile, on the Gulf coast. Louisiana was unexplored but vaguely it extended from the Great Lakes to the Gulf and from the Floridas and the headwaters of the Ohio River to the Western Sea.

The King shipped colonists from France, and in 1718 Jean Baptiste Le Moyne, Sieur de Bienville, settled some of them by Lake Pontchartrain and named the settlement New Orleans. Farther up the Mississippi he placed settlements in (now) Louisiana, Arkansas, Missouri, Illinois. Beside the river in Illinois he built Fort de Chartres, that great stone fortress then the strongest in New France south of Quebec. (The Mississippi tore it down later; it is restored now.) Where Grand River runs into the Missouri he built Fort Orleans, on an island that the rivers have totally erased. He brought from France the fabulously rich financier, Philippe Renault (Reno), who imported six hundred slaves to work the old iron mines in Missouri and shipped iron to Cuba and Europe.

In Missouri the Sieur de Bienville's troops defeated a force sent from New Spain (Mexico) to seize the Mississippi valley. Their sons led hundreds of Sioux warriors (Missouris, Iowas, Osages, Kansas and Arkansas —Quapaws) a thousand miles up the Ohio to meet a British invasion, and at Fort Duquesne (Pittsburgh) they defeated and routed General Braddock's Redcoats and the colonials under George Washington.

In America the French held the Mississippi valley for their King, but in Europe the British were victorious. So in 1765

Colonel Stirling raised the British flag over Fort de Chartres and the French people, fleeing across the Mississippi, in one summer changed St. Louis from a trading post to a French city under the flag of Spain.

Two decades later French and Americans defeated the British at Yorktown, and Great Britain ceded the western Mississippi valley to the United States by the Treaty of Paris. But British troops remained north of the Ohio River, Indians raided across it, and the few American pioneers in remote Kentucky, between mountain ranges to the east and Spain to west and south, could reach no market where furs and bear oil could buy powder and lead. Spanish agents and American traitors were urging them to secede to Spain and gain a world market through thriving New Orleans.

Desperately the United States needed a port on the Gulf. Revolution and yellow fever in Martinique destroyed the supplies and troops made ready there for Napoleon's campaign to take the Mississippi valley, so the United States might hold the West, with a Gulf port open to the Kentucky pioneers.

Odd Fellow's Patch. A geometric design combined with blocks of quilted wreaths. It has a feather-quilted border.

The square, the triangle and the diamond are the basic elements of patchwork design. Endless new patterns can be created by varying forms and changing colors.

RISING SUN, *with curved patches and triangles, is pieced in a circle, then appliquéd on a square block.*

CORONATION, *or King's Crown in early days, was later called the President's Quilt or Potomac Pride.*

CROWN OF THORNS. *A geometric sometimes known as Georgetown Circle or Memory Wreath.*

UNION STAR. *The designer of this motif probably used a plate to draw the perfect circle.*

DOLLY MADISON'S STAR *originated in Virginia in the early 1800's to honor President Madison's wife.*

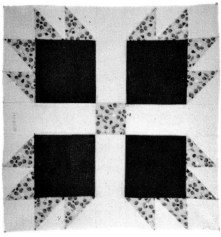

DUCK'S-FOOT-IN-THE-MUD *on Long Island, Hand of Friendship in Philadelphia, Bear's Paw in Ohio.*

THE LITTLE GIANT. *A skillful use of triangles to simulate a curve was named for Stephen A. Douglas.*

CALIFORNIA STAR *combines small nine-patch center blocks edged with a delicate feathered star.*

MISSOURI PUZZLE *may refer to a troubling political situation before Missouri became part of the Union.*

MISSOURI STAR *no doubt expressed the joy of the people when, in 1821, Missouri became the 24th state.*

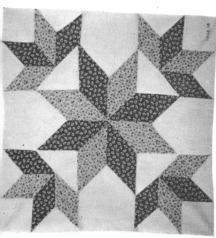

LEMON STAR, *named after Jean Baptiste Le Moyne, is the basis for many lily, tulip and peony designs.*

KANSAS TROUBLE *recalls the gay Delectable Mountains, but the darkness of the patches is ominous.*

MOUNTAIN PINK, *a delicate pattern. Much of the pattern's beauty depends upon precise workmanship.*

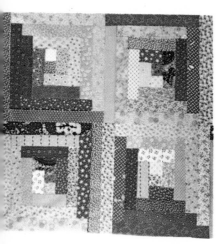

LOG CABIN. *Other arrangements of rectangles are Windmill Blades, Straight Furrow, Barn Raising.*

LUCINDA'S STAR *from Indiana. An eight-pointed star illuminated with 96 small and twinkling triangles.*

PINE TREE, *a colonial favorite. With variations, it is Live Oak, Temperance, Paradise and Christmas Tree.*

Congress appropriated $2,000,000 to pay for the port, and President Jefferson sent James Monroe and Robert Livingston to France to buy it. Their offer was not warmly received; diplomacy was slow, clogged by smiling indifference, until suddenly the Emperor sent for them and abruptly said that he would sell all Louisiana now, at once, or nothing. Price, $15,000,000. They had no authority to spend such a sum, no time to communicate with Washington; they bought unmapped Louisiana for $15,000,000.

When Talleyrand, aghast, asked Napoleon, why, the Emperor replied, "I need the money." He added, in effect, that since he could not take the continent from England, he would raise up a power there that someday would destroy that hated enemy.

And when at last all men were free to trade on the Mississippi, Kentucky's frontiersmen floated their loaded longboats down the treacherous river to New Orleans, and their womenfolks found a new patchwork pattern. It was the eight-pointed Le Moyne Star, crest of Sieur de Bienville who had founded New Orleans nearly a century earlier.

That crude settlement had now become a brilliant center of French culture, a city of stone and lacy ironwork and flowering parks, where ladies and gentlemen wearing the latest Paris fashions were carried to and fro in painted sedan chairs borne on the shoulders of slaves. Most Americans on the Mississippi were woodsmen and boatmen in deerskin breeches and jackets and coonskin caps. Their wives did not know French; the best that their tongues could do with Le Moyne was Lemon; but they knew what to do with the Lemon Star.

One thing they did was to make six upstanding points in red, two lower ones in green, then add stem and leaves in green and call the pattern "Pineys." So simply they changed the Sieur de Bienville's Star into the homely peonies whose roots they had

brought all the way from an English garden.

Look for the Lemon Star when you see patchwork. It has hundreds of variants and every one of them has a meaning. In strong yellow with brown center it is Kansas Sunflower; in glowing red with round white center and triangles radiating from it, it is Rising Sun; cut in half and given stems it is Bouquet of Tulips; set in a pattern of squares and arrowheads it is California Star. Doubtless somewhere in these States now it is Telstar.

An old variation is the Feathered Star. The Prince's Feather is from the crest of the Prince of Wales; it came to America in crewel work and became appliqué in the South, and stuffed quilting. Nobody knows the origin of the Feathered Star; it looks as though a woman, thinking of the Prince's Feather, cut out little triangles to feather-edge the Lemon Star. If so, then after wars between France and England had devastated Europe for generations and had burned villages and killed settlers in America, an American woman combined the symbols of England and France to make one of the loveliest of old patchwork patterns.

Modulating old patterns into new ones is the art, and the joy, of patchwork geometricals. Their elements couldn't be more simple: the square, the triangle, the oblong, the diamond. Anyone can cut them out and their combinations are endless, the seams are short and straight.

More than a hundred years ago a woman lived in New Jersey, poor, sick, bedridden. Her solace was one book, *Pilgrim's Progress*. No doubt it eased her to think of the pilgrims who escaped from Doubting Castle and Giant Despair and "came to the Delectable Mountains—behold, the gardens and orchards, the vineyards and fountains of water."

She made a patchwork pattern of pointed oblongs, clear red on white; she set the bright peaks around square beyond square in ranges that keep the eye climbing upward as mountains do. She named it The Delectable Mountains, and it is an outburst of joy. Only this quilt itself can give its effect. At sight of it, every face brightens.

How can a few notes of music, some paint on canvas, mere pieces of cloth sewed together, have this power to lift the human spirit? No one can explain this; it is the mystery of art.

This mysterious power chills you when you see these same oblongs set whirling, at odds with each other; you feel a dread uncertainty before you know this pattern's name: Kansas Trouble. It speaks of the years of night raids, burning cabins, murder and massacre in Bloody Kansas before John Brown came from them to raid Harpers Ferry and kindle war's atrocities from Canada to Mexico.

Let's look at these two patterns, Lincoln's Platform and Little Giant. When the self-taught backwoodsman, rawboned Abraham Lincoln, met the cultured gentleman, Stephen Douglas, in forthright controversy over principles of American political philosophy, their ardent partisans made these patchwork patterns.

Lincoln's Platform is four-square, bluntly candid; the Little Giant, as firmly decisive, is elegant and subtle. The lines in both are straight, but in Little Giant they frame the solid center in what seem to be gentle curves. Patchwork's triangles never have been used more skillfully.

You cannot exhaust the uses of triangles. Simply following each other in rows they have such vitality in motion that on the Atlantic Coast they are named Ocean Waves while farther west the inland women named them Birds in Air or Wild Goose Flight.

Set triangles above triangles in widening rows, appliqué a bias strip for a handle, and you have Flower Basket, a "modern" design nearly two centuries old. Set triangles into triangles in colored circles blazing out from a round center and you make Rising Sun, or

in hotter colors the western desert's Blazing Sun. Or split the circles to let the colors run in waves of tones to brilliant points; this is the Star of Bethlehem, or the Lone Star of Texas.

Square bits of cloth, cut across into triangles, oblongs, diamonds; with these scraps saved in the rag bag thousands of forgotten women expressed their interests, beliefs, fears, and hopes; they created an art and made a record of American life, American history. Only listen to the names of the patterns: Coronation, King's Crown, Whig Rose, Bear's Paw, Tomahawk, Log Cabin, Pine Tree, Birds in the Window, Union Star, Potomac Pride, Martha Washington's Flower Garden, Dolly Madison's Star, Mountain Pink, Lemon Star, Oregon Trail, 54-40 or Fight, Kansas Sunflower, Cactus Rose, Lone Star of Texas, Kansas Trouble, Lincoln's Platform, California Star, Press Gently, Island Garden. Only a few of so many, and how much they mean, all the way from London to Hawaii, all the years from 1608 to 1963.

Let us remember, too, that "when Freedom from her mountain-height unfurled her standard to the air," that standard was a patchwork pattern of thirteen stripes, red and white, and a blue patch that once held thirteen stars and now holds fifty.

That standard was raised by poor and hungry people who had come, or been shipped like cattle, from all the lands of the Old World to live in the edge of a wilderness if they could. Let us remember that they found freedom here and fought to defend and preserve it, and that in freedom they made our country from nothing at all but bare hands and unconquerable spirit.

So let us treasure as part of American culture the inexhaustible variety of patterns in old patchwork that record gallant lives, and honor as culture bearers the thousands of women who are preserving and still enriching this heritage.

Star of Bethlehem, an eight-pointed star composed of hundreds of diamond-shaped patches sewn by an expert. A wide chintz border and appliquéd motifs from the chintz complete this quilt. Also called the Lone Star of Texas. [THE BROOKLYN MUSEUM]

How to Do Patchwork

QUILT TOP

Use closely woven fabrics with soft textures such as calico, percale, or muslin. Be sure fabrics are colorfast and preshrunk. It is best not to combine partly worn goods with new materials because the latter will outlast the former.

MATERIALS

To estimate the amount of materials needed, first decide on the amount of each color needed for the individual block or unit. Multiply this by the number of blocks or units required for the quilt you are making. It is wise to have enough material to allow for possible waste in cutting.

INTERLINING

Use cotton quilt batts or a lightweight preshrunk blanket.

BACKING

Use a good grade of sheeting which comes as wide as 90" or use regular 36"-wide muslin and join strips to form the proper size. A muslin backing is easier to quilt than percale. Backing should be preshrunk.

PREPARING PATTERNS AND CUTTING

Trace pattern piece onto tracing paper and then cut permanent pieces from cardboard, fine sandpaper, or blotters (use sandpaper rough side down when tracing on fabric and it will not slip). Lightweight linoleum can be used to make patterns. Replace patterns from time to time as the edges wear. Place patterns on wrong side of fabric, allowing at least ½" in between each. Pencil around patterns, being careful not to pull or stretch fabric. This pencil line will serve as your sewing line. Cut out, allowing ¼" all around from pencil line. Separate the patches according to size and shape.

PIECING

Assemble all the pieces for one

unit or block of quilt. If the pattern is very intricate, pin or baste pieces together. With right sides facing, join pieces with a small running or back stitch, following pencil line exactly. Clip seams after sewing curved pieces.

APPLIQUÉ

This is the sewing down of pieces on a background, fully described in the next chapter. See directions on page 105.

SETTING

This means the assembling of blocks or units of quilt top and adding strips or any borders. Join blocks or units from the center out to insure a smooth, unwarped effect. Press all seams. It is best to press both seam edges to one side instead of pressing them open.

QUILTING DESIGNS

When quilt top is completed, mark it for quilting designs. See quilting chapter, pages 112-123.

Sunburst, sometimes called Rising Sun. Each motif has 64 triangular pieces surrounding the center. The quilt has a very handsome appliquéd swag-and-bow border. [THE BROOKLYN MUSEUM]

Delectable Mountains, a pattern of bright peaks set in ranges that keep the eye climbing upward as mountains do. [NEWARK MUSEUM, NEWARK, N.J.]

Directions for Patchwork Blocks:
Mountain Pink and Crown of Thorns

QUILT BLOCK DESIGNS
Here are two individual blocks to use in designing your own quilt. See general directions, page 86, for making quilts. These may be alternated with plain blocks or edged with borders. If a whole quilt is too ambitious a project for you, use the designs for pillow covers, curtains, aprons, and even sports clothes.

An assembly diagram and pattern pieces are given for each design. Diagrams are marked with the size of the finished block; the pattern pieces are given for each design. The pattern pieces on diagrams are shown in black, white, and gray to indicate color changes (see blocks on color pages 82 and 83).

Each pattern piece is marked with the number to be cut for one block. Pieces are shown actual size and can be simply traced for your patterns.

Mountain Pink is pieced to form a circle which is appliquéd to a square block.

CUT 5 E
CUT 5 REVERSED F

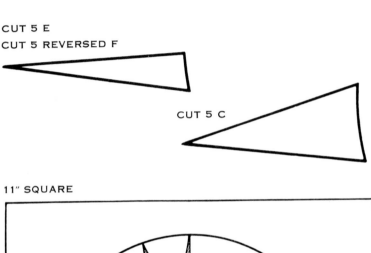

CUT 5 C

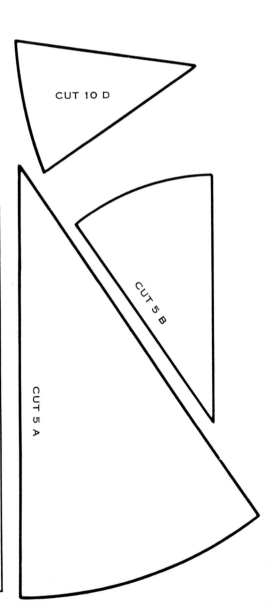

CUT 10 D

CUT 5 B

CUT 5 A

11" SQUARE

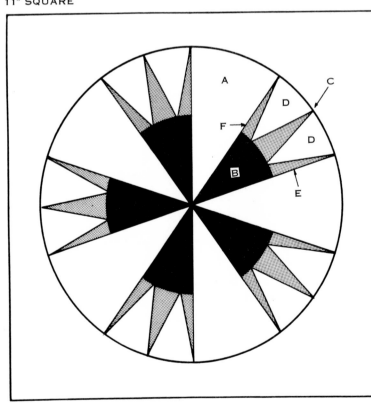

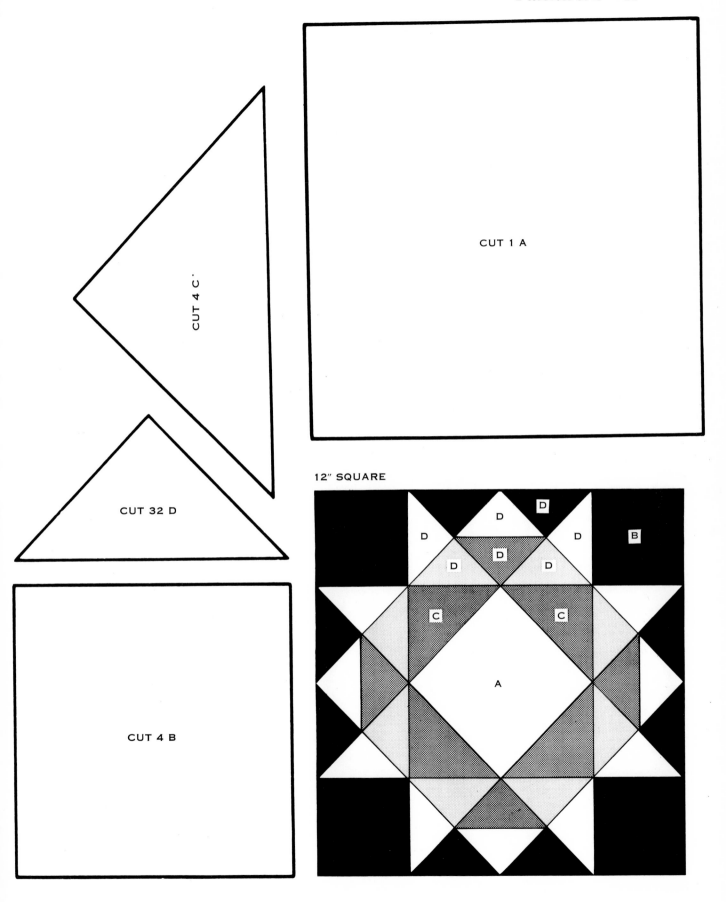

CUT 4 C

CUT 1 A

CUT 32 D

CUT 4 B

12" SQUARE

Album Quilt for Amanda and William Porter, April 3, 1849. [MARYLAND HISTORICAL SOCIETY, BALTIMORE, MD.]

MERICAN APPLIQUÉ is a wholly native folk art; nothing like it thrives anywhere else. It is a gaily carefree and extravagant child of American pieced patchwork, as I suppose is only natural, because appliqué has never known really hard times. Not until after a hundred years of saving and working in this land did colonial women actually have cloth to spare. Then they began to hook rags into unnecessary rugs, and to cut good parts of worn-out garments into ornaments of new cloth.

In appliqué their fancies escaped from the straight-seam limitation of pieced patchwork, so appliqué became less symbolic, more naturalistic. Its lines are completely free and its pattern can be as intricate as you like. The technique lends itself to graceful curves of flowers and foliage, to the natural shapes of butterflies, birds, and animals, even to the figures of people. Any scene that an artist can paint on canvas, an artist can put on cloth in appliqué, and many thousands of homekeeping women have been and are artists. If you think you aren't one of them, you may surprise yourself with a bit of appliqué.

Nearly every woman has the materials, the tools, and the skills that appliqué requires. You need to be able to cut cloth with shears, to press it with an iron, to hem it down neatly; that's all. For background you need a piece of good cloth as large as you please; a muslin or percale sheet may be transformed into an entrancing bedspread. Nowadays it can be a lovely, fadeless color, too. Or you can make any appliqué in blocks; a block is easier to handle and goes anywhere in a handbag.

Now the design should be your own. You don't know half the joy of needlework until you create something wholly yours. Then whether it is as subtle as an arabesque or as naïve as a child's drawing, it is honestly your own idea, your design, your satisfaction; it is a work of art. It will not be original because nothing is; it will be unique because you are.

You need not be able to draw a line (though probably you are; nobody knows if you haven't tried). Wherever you look you see shapes and colors; take what you please where you find it. If you plan a bedspread or curtains or a cushion, the motifs you want may be in the wallpaper you chose. Or cut them out of magazines and seed catalogues; enlarge them from snapshots; buy patterns from museums; but arrange them to please yourself and work them in colors that sing to you.

Must you buy new cloth for your design? You will be more interested and your work will always be more interesting if you use what you have as our thrifty grandmothers did. The dress that you wore on a memorable day but will not wear again, the pieces left from the sunsuit you made for the baby, the remains of the apron that a little girl made for your Christmas present, all such things have values that are not sold in shops. "Making do" with them in your appliqué will stimulate your ingenuity surprisingly; they suggest charming ways of utilizing their patterns and colors, and the memories stitched into your work will always enrich it.

Certainly all kinds of American women have made all kinds of appliqué in all kinds of ways, for this artcraft is so completely free that its possibilities are limitless.

One way in late-colonial days used the *palampores* which New England's sea captains brought home from their daring two-year voyages around the Horn to the fabulous East Indies. The exotic fabrics, richly hand-blocked and painted in the strange forms and gorgeous colors of India's Tree of Life, and peacocks, jungle hens, Persian pears, pineapples, lotus blossoms, were rare as emeralds in the homespun linsey-woolsey colonies. They were forbidden, too. For people wanted them so eagerly that, to protect their own weavers' guilds, the British Parlia-

ment strictly prohibited their importation, while Louis XIV and the Regency issued no less than thirty decrees of death by torture to any trader bringing one of them into France.

Of course these efforts to suppress liberty did not succeed; as always, they merely changed useful traders to smugglers and bootleggers, making them criminals and setting the police after them. In America the colonists were thriving mainly from forbidden weaving and trading, and obviously they paid no attention to Parliament's order because now in our museums are entrancing examples of appliqué made from India's seventeenth-century *palampores*.

Colonial women cut out their designs, applied them to hand-woven linen and highlighted a fantastic flower with buttonholed edges, softened an outline with half feather stitching. Did they cut the precious stuff only after it was worn shabby? Or to hide a loving husband's fearful crime? Or because they preferred their own design to the Indian's? Nobody knows. They called their work, in French, *broderie Perse*, Persian embroidery. They left us works of art, and an idea still inspiring.

For today we have such a wealth of beautiful designs, machine-made, that every department store is more richly colorful than

any Oriental bazaar. Beautiful designs are commonplace to us; we are so rich that we don't know how rich we are. Think what can be done with a mill end from a bargain sale, or an old chintz curtain. These large designs, printed or woven, are wonderfully adaptable to appliqué. Center one on a coverlet, scatter smaller bits around it, border the whole with swags and tassels, or scallops, or bands, add a touch of embroidery, and you have a mid-twentieth-century version of early eighteenth-century American *broderie Perse.*

The impulse to embroider these ready-made designs is almost irresistible. Not too much; only a little is enough. Emphasize a petal's curl with solid buttonholing; soften a leaf's edge with feather stitching; French-knot a rose's center; satin-stitch only the curve of a bird's breast. Understate all other edges by invisible hemming. Touches of embroidery, no more than light touches, highlight the values of all appliqué work and are traditional.

Another traditional form of appliqué is the Friendship Medley. This charming custom combined the announcement of a girl's engagement with a shower for her. It was popular in all thirty-five States less than a century ago; its revival now would be hailed as a most original idea. Of course every well-brought-up girl then had twelve quilt tops in her Hope Chest, and after she was engaged these were quilted before her marriage; her bridal quilt was made then, too. But the Friendship Medley was another thing.

For that, a mother invited all her daughter's friends. Early in the afternoon the young ladies came, with quilt blocks in their workbaskets, and we all know how they chattered while each one finished her appliqué block and stitched her name or initials on it. All must be done before sunset, because then the young men came for the quilting-party supper and dance.

Sometimes the girls "set" the quilt top;

Friendship Medley. Dated 1876, each block is a different design. Made by young ladies to celebrate the engagement of a friend. [NEWARK MUSEUM]

more often the happy fiancée and her mother later arranged the blocks and set them together with bands of calico print or their own patchwork. These gave unity to a coverlet in which no two blocks are alike, though each one is interesting.

When the Friendship Medley was put into the frames, the young ladies came again to a quilting bee, and the young men to the evening's party. And two generations of those young men gaily whistled the popular song, " 'Twas from Aunt Dinah's quilting party I was seeing Nellie home."

Mothers saw to it that sons had their quilts, too, made in the same way. These were Freedom Quilts, celebrating a son's twenty-first birthday. Since children owe to their parents all that they have, even life it-

Prince's Feather and Rising Star (also known as Princess Feather or Ostrich Plume and Rising Sun) made in New Jersey about 1850 by Catherine Fitzgerald and her sisters. Feathers are appliquéd, stars pieced. [NEWARK MUSEUM, NEWARK, N.J.]

self, a girl worked at home till she married and a young man's labor belonged to his parents until he was twenty-one years old. Then his father "gave him his time," and thereafter he could work for himself. A generous and prospering father gave him more, perhaps a team and wagon. His young lady friends made the blocks for his Freedom Quilt and later quilted it, and they all danced at the quilting parties.

Many Friendship Medley and Freedom Quilts must still be in old trunks and attics;

a few are in museums. (And more should be.) Shadows of the customs linger; in my own Connecticut neighborhood we still "tie a quilt" as a wedding gift to every son and daughter of every member of our Dorcas Society.

Another interesting use of American appliqué is the family records. Each of these has the family's name, of course. As a family takes years to grow, so a family-record quilt takes years to make; no needlework is more leisurely. Every block is a picture, dated, and

Black and white quilt, with appliquéd willow, oak and snowflake. Each block has a large snowflake and four oak leaves. The border design is of weeping willows and oak trees. Pre-Civil War. [SHELBURNE MUSEUM, SHELBURNE, VT.]

Charter Oaks and Eagles with Rose Wreaths heavily padded and stuffed. Mid-nineteenth century. The roses are out-lined with buttonhole embroidery. [SHELBURNE MUSEUM]

signed by its maker. Such a quilt may have in its center a large block on which the homestead is appliquéd, the house with its chimneys, gables, windows and door, the trees around it, the lawn and path and flower beds, father, mother, the children and their pets, the pony and carriage. (What fun to appliqué the new car, next year's model. How quaint it will seem someday.)

Around this central block are set smaller ones, some made and signed by aunts and cousins. Each records a memory: the trip to Niagara, the son in his regiment's uniform, the daughter's wedding; or some familiar sight such as the washerwoman at the tub, the oysterman calling his wares, the sturdy dappled-gray polka-dotted pony, the portrait of the President.

From such a quilt I learned recently that the daughter of the President of the Confederacy stood firm for the Union. This was news to me. In appliqué they faced each other, standing on a scroll reading *Jefferson Davis and Daughter, 1861*, he in tall hat, blue tailcoat, and striped trousers, she in prim bonnet, tight basque buttoned with French knots and trailing skirts modishly hunched over a bustle. She held the Stars and Stripes, but both were fondly smiling.

Mrs. Ralph Sutton of Chappaqua, New York, has refused $5,000 for that quilt; her great-grandmother (and family) made it. Of course it is worth more than money. But a century ago it was valued no more than a quilt being made today. All that we do becomes a legacy that time increases, for good or ill.

Such family records are versions of the Album Quilt; its name describes it. A devoted gardener keeps her flowers in appliqué on her blocks; a bird watcher's Album pictures her favorite birds; a thinker stitches the Great Seal of these United States. A grandmother once made an Album of every animal mentioned in the Bible. A small granddaughter who watched her, herself a grandmother now, said the other day, "She'd cut one out and hold it up and say, 'What does this look like? Does it look like a bear?' It was fascinating when she finished it. I suppose they'd call it a child's quilt now. She called it an Album."

Since Album Quilts express their makers' interests at the time, they are as up to date as current news and almost as old as American history. The Lincoln Quilt, for instance, an Album in Vermont's Shelburne Museum, graphically tells us what some women thought of the Lincoln-Douglas debates, at the time.

The Album and the Medley are combined in many variations. Perhaps the most popular was the Friendship Quilt. This is an expression of the spontaneous, voluntary co-operation, possible only in freedom, with which Americans so quickly transformed the dark forests and burning deserts of 1789 into these States as they are now. The house raisings, corn shuckings, quilting bees, the mass production and mass distribution of every good we are enjoying, are wholly new in human history, and they are typically American.

The Friendship Quilt means what an American word means; the word is "neighborliness." It has no equivalent in any other language. Neighborliness is not love, not friendship; it may be less than liking. It is the mutual helpfulness of human beings to each other, an unforced, voluntary co-operation springing from a sense of equality in common humanity and human needs. The

15 antique appliqué blocks

ROSE OF SHARON, *one of many designs with this name.*

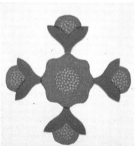
CALIFORNIA ROSE, *also called Combination Rose.*

WREATH OF PANSIES. *Flower wreaths were popular designs.*

OHIO ROSE; *dates from about 1850.*

MISSOURI ROSE, *also Ros Tree and Prairie Rose.*

WHIG'S DEFEAT, *appliquéd and pieced.*

ORIGINAL ROSE *or Indiana Rose.*

RADICAL ROSE; *dates from Civil War period.*

CHARTER OAK, *inspired by the historic Connecticut tree.*

PINEAPPLE, *simple versio of a popular motif.*

Abraham Lincoln spread, 1865. The 49 squares, each signed, are of homespun linen or cotton, appliquéd in both wool and cotton. [SHELBURNE MUSEUM]

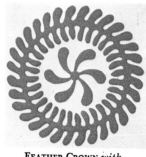

AK LEAF, *a New England design.*

FEATHER CROWN *with Ragged Robin center.*

PRIDE-OF-THE-FOREST *requires painstaking work.*

THE REEL, *oldtime favorite.*

OAK LEAVES *and Cherries.*

journeys into the unknown and unpredictable, the American settlements, churches, schools, towns, factories, all began in neighborliness; all grew from that new spirit into this country of all mankind today. Neighborliness is the meaning in history, of these United States, the first successful league of States on earth. And modestly, in its small way, the Friendship Quilt expresses neighborliness.

This quilt was always made for neighbors in distress, usually for neighbors going West, sometimes to honor a minister, a teacher, a hero. Each neighbor gave a block, and all met to "set" the top, do the "putting in" (to the frames), the quilting and binding. When fire destroyed my parents' tree-claim "shanty" in Dakota Territory, as a matter of course the neighbors gave them a Friendship Quilt.

Appliqué patterns are not symbolic as patchwork's geometrical patterns are. There cannot be a pattern for *broderie Perse* nor for a Friendship Medley, a Freedom Quilt, an Album. These are traditional American appliqué and they express meanings eternal in human life, but the meanings are personal, the patterns as new as sunrise. Like painting, appliqué is a technique, a way of expressing meanings.

Pieced and appliqué patchwork complement each other, and many needlewomen combine them. A strip of pieced triangles emphasizes the fluid grace of appliquéd flowers; a pieced Sunburst is a firm center for airy Prince's Feathers in appliqué. Piece four points of the Lemon Star in white, two lower points in green, appliqué them on blue, and you have water lilies. Or piece the upper points in colors, set them on leafy stems in appliqué, arranged in an appliqué vase, and you have a bouquet of flowers. Or piece a basket of triangles and fill it with a riot of appliqué flowers or fruits, and bees and butterflies or even birds may hover (appliquéd) above them.

Appliqué takes patterns from pieced patchwork as it takes them from all the arts and from all nature, and transforms them into fresh designs pleasing their maker. In appliqué you find an endless variety of patterns, each unique, the only one like it: a Persian-Indian Tree of Life bearing American flowers and fruits for American birds; a Yankee clipper ship; a French Aubusson carpet transformed in Virginia; a Southern Colonial house amid Louisiana's cypresses dripping Spanish moss. You find Midwestern farmhouses and fields, horses and cows behind board fences; California's lupine-purple and poppy-golden hills.

Newest of all American appliqué are Hawaii's intricate, wholly original patterns. Nothing at all like them has ever been anywhere else. For on those islands dreaming in sea and sun, abruptly the New World overlapped the Old World's beginning and the islands' people have the strangest of all history.

Over their immemorial sea horizon came men from an unimagined world, bringing the nineteenth century abruptly upon the artless Sandwich Islanders and, perforce, three generations of those Stone Age people lived through four thousand years of human progress. A deluge of unheard-of opinions, ideas, customs, things, came upon them: clothing never needed, hymns to a new God which they transformed into their own music, wheels, tools, books, steam engines, cities, electric lights, motorcars, bulldozers, roads, at last even the atom's terrible power, quicker than thought erasing a solid island from existence.

The naked Sandwich Islanders were at home, wise and competent in the Stone Age. Did the sudden destruction of all they knew overwhelm them? Not at all. Today their grandchildren's children are flourishing in the twentieth century's civilization, at home and equally competent in its cars, its cities, its planes, its universities and laboratories,

Child's silk picture coverlet, made in Kentucky in 1866. Appliquéd and embroidered quilt blocks with birds, flowers and animals. Notice the blocks depicting Little Red Riding Hood's adventures and the story of the fox and the sour grapes. [National Gallery of Art, Index of American Design, Washington, D.C.]

Appliqué. Pictures and stylized motifs worked with cloth on cloth, created by color and the simple hemstitch.

The Gossips, a humorous picture, 11" x 12", appliquéd in silk about 1830 by Eunice W. Cook. [NATIONAL GALLERY OF ART, INDEX OF AMERICAN DESIGN]

Wall hanging. [ABBY ALDRICH ROCKEFELLER FOLK ART COLLECTION, WILLIAMSBURG, VA.]

Album Quilt (see pages 90-91). Blocks combine motifs shown elsewhere on these pages.

Oak Leaf Coverlet. Signed and dated E. H. Broth

Bridal counterpane with hearts and flowers and lavish swags of leaves and blossoms. [THE BROOKLYN MUSEUM, BROOKLYN, N.Y.]

...bruary 21, 1853. [NEWARK MUSEUM]

Eagle quilt top. Note the gay tail feathers appliquéd in narrow strips of bright calico. [HENRY FORD MUSEUM, DEARBORN, MICH.]

contributing citizens of the latest of the United States of America. No achievement of individual self-development ever has surpassed this feat, accomplished so swiftly by so many persons. The fact that all men are created equal needs no better demonstration.

Small and unnoticed in the torrent of novelties came American patchwork; missionaries' missionary wives brought it. They brought, too, steel needles and pins, and woven cloth. Traders brought these marvels for sale; they brought whole bolts of this magically made cloth, blazing red, yellow, orange, green. The islanders never had made a loom, never thought of weaving; the first woven cloth they saw had come whirring from power looms to cross the vast ocean in traders' ships.

So Hawaiian appliqué owes nothing to poverty but a germinal idea. It bloomed from suddenly overwhelming plenty. On their summer islands the people never had needed clothes; in groves of bananas, breadfruit, coconuts, where thousands of birds nested and the ocean teemed with fish, they never had lacked food. Now, among countless new ideas, there was the idea of earning money, there was the idea of patchwork, and at the trader's were piles of marvelous cloth, to be had for money. The island women combined these ideas with the fact, and created Hawaiian appliqué. It is their own, original, unlike any other.

Its technique is an intricate appliqué. The designs are highly stylized forms of the islands' flowers and foliage, so highly stylized that you may not recognize them; I don't. The characteristic colors are strong reds, yellows, oranges, almost violently contrasted in each piece, though I have seen rare designs of sea currents done in clear blues and greens.

This is the latest American appliqué. Its earliest dates are late nineteenth century and its fullest development is going on now —going on into tomorrow. You'd know that it is up to date and then some, if you knew

only one thing about it: it wastes cloth, lavishly. It wastes new cloth.

To make a piece of this newest appliqué you must have originality, time, patience, skill, perfect accuracy, and two whole pieces of cloth of the same size, the size of quilt or coverlet, if that is what you plan to make. The first piece will be background, the second will be the design applied to it; their colors should contrast sharply.

Designing a quilt is a major undertaking. No trifling qualities of mind and character, no faulty co-ordination of thought and hand, create this masterpiece of contemporary American needlecraft, original, unique, as everlasting as anything on earth can be.

I would not put so much of my time and self into working a design that was not wholly my own, though I might waste reams of paper before I made one worth the sewing. I see no reason why this living needle art need stop anywhere, and as Hawaiian women have adapted Early-American patchwork to their sea-island lives, so I would adapt their new technique to my own in Connecticut. A maple leaf, a snowflake, a hemlock's drooping bough, can be stylized as beautifully as banyan or bougainvillea.

Still, an authentic Hawaiian design is well worth making, and having it to enjoy and bequeath will be worth more than the making. Two patterns with their variations (and you might want to vary the colors) are preferred in the new island state: Press Gently and Garden Island. Perhaps Press Gently has a wistful meaning not without pathos. To Hawaiians, Garden Island represents the untouched loveliness of one of their small islets.

Wherever, whenever, there is appliqué patchwork, whoever creates it, this graceful needle art is for women who catch today on the points of their needles and hem it down, to tell new centuries who we were and what we had and admired and loved and how we lived, and how very quaint it all was, long ago.

How to Appliqué

MATERIALS

Use closely woven fabrics with soft texture such as calico, percale, or muslin. Be sure fabrics are colorfast and preshrunk. It is best not to combine worn fabrics with new ones because the latter will outlast the former.

CUTTING

Cut actual-size pattern pieces from cardboard, fine sandpaper, or blotters. (Use sandpaper rough side down when tracing on fabric and it will not slip.) Replace patterns when their edges wear. Place patterns on wrong side of fabric and pencil around them, allowing at least ½″ between each piece, being careful not to pull or stretch fabric.

NOTE: In cutting pieces for appliqué, some people prefer to have the pencil line on the right side of the fabric as a sewing guide. Cut out, allowing ¼″ seam allowance all around. Separate the pieces according to shape and color. A good way of doing this is to stack all identical motifs in one pile and run a thread through the middle, leaving the knot under the pile. Lift off a motif from top when needed.

Appliqué is the process of applying one material to another by sewing. The neatest method is to turn the seam allowance over the pattern piece and press (see illustration). Slash edges on curves to make them lie flat. To be sure of accurate placement, you can trace around your pattern piece on the foundation. Then follow these lines when basting appliqué pieces in place. This is especially helpful if design is intricate. Place the appliqué with edges turned under on your foundation and baste in place. There are a variety of stitches to use in sewing appliqué pieces. The one used most is a regular hemming stitch. You can also use a blind stitch or even a buttonhole stitch. The main thing is to make neat, even stitches. Use thread in a color matching the piece you are sewing. Sometimes decorative stitches are worked on edges after appliqué is completed. Feather stitch or blanket stitch makes a pretty edge. When bias strips are used on a curved line, baste the inside edge first. The material can then be stretched until it lies flat along the outer edge. If you are an experienced sewer or after you have practiced awhile, you may use short cuts such as pressing under seam allowance with your thumb and forefinger or simply pinning your appliqué in place and turning under the seam allowance as you sew. It is when you use such a short-cut method to appliqué that the pencil lines on the right side of the piece are helpful. To enrich certain areas of design, appliqué is sometimes padded. To do this, leave a small section open when sewing; stuff cotton batting in opening, pushing it under the appliqué piece with a knitting needle until it is firm and even. Finish sewing down piece.

PIECING

Piecing is the process of sewing pieces of a design together. With right sides facing, join pieces with small running stitch or backstitch, following pencil line exactly.

SETTING

Setting is the process of assembling the blocks or units of a quilt top and adding any strips or borders. Join blocks or units from the center out to insure smooth, unwarped results. Press all seams. It is best to press both seam edges to one side instead of pressing them open.

QUILTING DESIGNS

You can quilt a top or leave it plain as you prefer. If you decide to quilt the top, mark it for quilting designs when it is completed. See quilting chapter, pages 112-123.

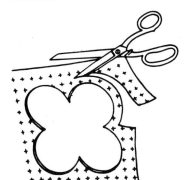

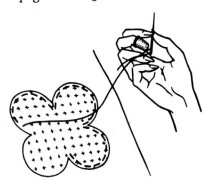

How to Do Hawaiian Appliqué

Hawaiian quilts differ from traditional early American appliqué in several ways. The designs are large motifs, usually repetitive, since several layers of fabric are cut at once to make the appliqué. Often these designs are worked out by a folded-paper cutting method. They reflect their tropical inspiration: coral, vivid flowers, palms, pineapples, and the Pacific. The quilts are almost always made with one strong, bright color, usually red, blue, or green on white, or a combination of yellow and red, the royal colors.

Rather than copying or exchanging, each woman made her own pattern and named her own quilt design. If she borrowed a design, she had to change it somewhat so she could call it her own.

MATERIALS
Use closely woven fabrics with a soft texture such as calico, percale, or muslin.

DESIGNING
If you wish to design your own Hawaiian quilt, first experiment with shapes on a smaller scale.

Take a sheet of paper about 8″ square. Fold paper in half, quarters, or eighths. You can also, if you like, do the paper folding diagonally several times. Cut out sections of paper as children cut paper doilies or valentines. Unfold paper to check design; perhaps you want to cut out more to make it lacier. Try several shapes and types of designs. You can cut border designs by folding the paper as you would to cut a string of paper dolls. When you have a design you like, refold paper and make a full-size pattern of one complete section of design. You can use large sheets of wrapping paper or newspaper. Be sure to mark center.

CUTTING

Fold fabric in the same way your paper design was folded. Pin full-size pattern on folded fabric and cut out, allowing ⅛″ to ¼″ seam allowance all around. You will need very sharp scissors when cutting through several layers of fabric.

QUILTING DESIGNS

Hawaiian quilts have very simple quilting designs, sometimes just diagonal straight lines about ½″ apart over the entire top. Some designs are equally spaced lines that follow the outline of the appliqué. We call this wave quilting, the Hawaiians, *luma-lau.*

If quilting straight lines, mark your quilt top when appliqué is completed with a ruler and soft pencil. Pencil lines can be erased after quilting has been completed. When quilting by following the outline of the appliqué, it is not generally necessary to mark the lines.

FINISHING

After quilting has been completed, remove quilt from frame. Trim lining, if necessary, and finish quilt with a binding neatly hemmed down.

Breadfruit in the royal colors of red and yellow.

Maui Beauty illustrates the basic Hawaiian quilt: an intricate center medallion cut from a square of folded bright cotton and a border, both appliquéd to a white background. Wave quilting, called luma lau, follows the pattern outlines.

Kahili, symbol of royalty. The center medallion is surrounded by motifs of fern fronds and crowns.

Ke Kahi O Kaiulani, or the Comb of Princess Kaiulani, with Kahili, combs, leaves and wreath border.

Grape Vine, four square blocks joined at center, a variation of the popular grape leaf quilt design.

Koomi Malie, or Press Gently, rhythmic pattern inspired by garden flowers, leaves and branches.

Garden Island symbolizes the Hawaiian island of Kauai, known for the luxuriance of its vegetation.

Koomi Malie and Grape Vine combined with a striking border of stalks and foliage.

[ALL QUILTS ARE FROM HONOLULU ACADEMY OF ARTS]

Directions for Oak Leaf Coverlet

See color photograph on page 102.

SIZE
102″ x 102″.

MATERIALS
Quilt Top: 5 yards 72″-wide sheeting. Appliqué and Piecing: 36″-wide cotton, 3½ yards green print, 3 yards red print.

CUTTING
From sheeting, cut twenty-five 16½″ squares; cut two 9″ x 85″ strips and two 9″ x 102½″ strips for outer border.

Using actual-size patterns and adding ¼″ all around for seam allowance, cut the following pieces: From green print, cut 100 oak leaves and 40 swags; from red print, cut 100 scallops, 40 stars with tassels, and 25 centers.

APPLIQUE
Following diagram for placement, appliqué pieces to each 16½″ square.

ASSEMBLING
Sew squares together with ¼″ seams, arranging them 5 across and 5 in length. Cut and piece red and white triangles together to form saw-tooth border. Sew this border in place. Then sew outer border in place.

Following diagram and starting at a corner, appliqué swags and stars with tassels to border.

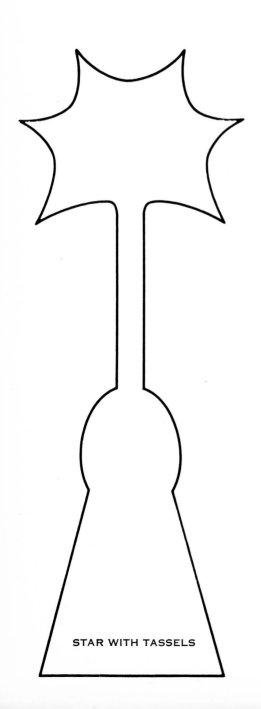

STAR WITH TASSELS

ASSEMBLY DIAGRAM

OAK LEAF COVERLET 102″ X 102″   CORNER SECTION SHOW

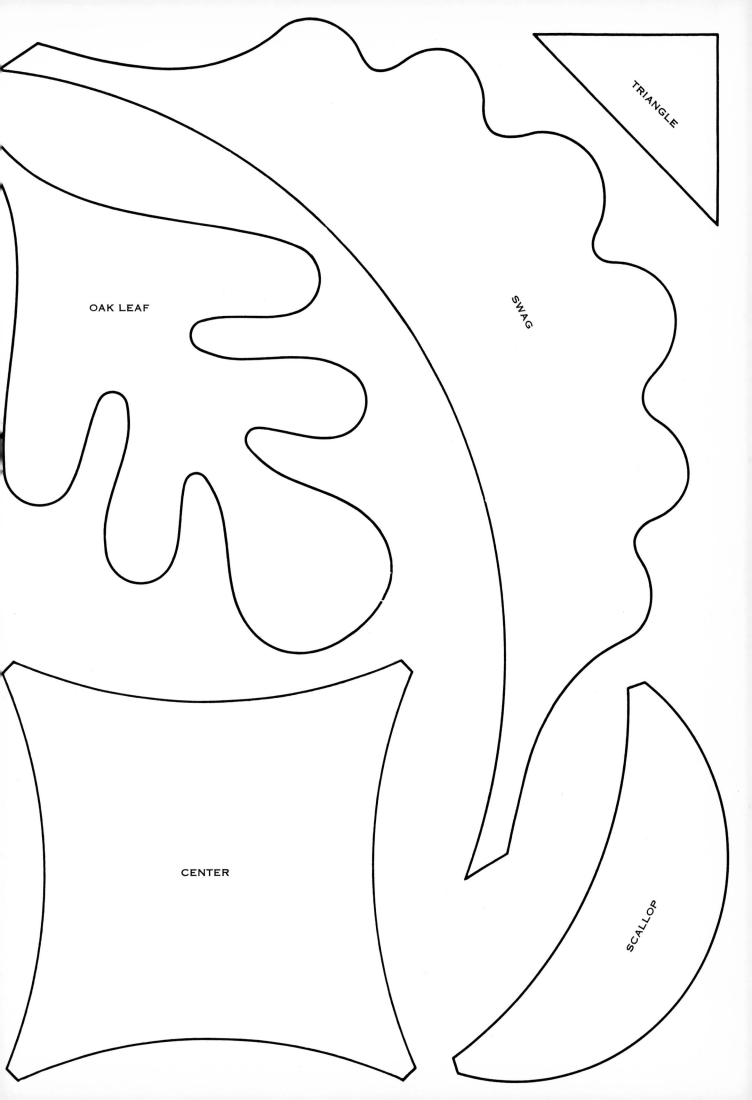

TRIANGLE

OAK LEAF

SWAG

CENTER

SCALLOP

Plain and stuffed quilting, meticulously worked on an appliquéd beige and brown bed covering in George Washington's home. Late eighteenth century. [MOUNT VERNON LADIES' ASSOCIATION, MOUNT VERNON, VA.]

UILTING came from the East long ago. Nobody knows who began it nor where nor when. Apparently the Chinese always have worn quilted garments; prehistoric women may have invented them in the bitter cold of winter on the Gobi Desert. Europeans discovered quilting some eight hundred years ago when the ignorant Crusaders invaded the rich Moslem civilization.

The Christian baron, so clumsy in a hundred pounds of hammered iron that if he fell he couldn't get up without help, encountered agile Saracen knights wearing quilted silks under chain armor as strong as iron but so airy that a whole suit of it could be drawn through a finger ring. The Moslems kept the Holy Land. The barons went home to regenerate Europe. They brought back new ideas of industry, art, bathing, and chivalry with its standards of courtesy, honor and respect for women. Incidentally, they brought back quilting.

It was strictly practical sewing. In Europe quilting held a layer of straw or tow between two pieces of covering. This was a boon to Europeans. Quilting made mattresses; they were softer than bare earth or planks, smoother than loose straw or rushes. It made warm bedcovers. Quilted hangings served better than cloth to keep icy winds from blowing through crude wooden shut-

ters and doorways to make torches flare and smoke in the manor's bare stone hall. A shirt of flax tow quilted between canvas and leather kept a knight's armor from chafing his skin raw; and on a common man, who of course must fight without armor, such a shirt might check the force of an arrow and save his life.

Thus quilting raised the standard of living, slowly through four hundred years into the sixteenth century. Then from the newly discovered underside of the earth the Spanish galleons came "rocking through the tropics by the palm-green shores" under full sail, bringing cargoes of pure gold from brutally ravished Mexico and Peru. The grandson of Ferdinand and Isabella ruled most of Europe and the courts reveled in splendor. Silk could not carry the weight of jewels that ladies wore; their gowns must be quilted. In European museums today you see their skirts and petticoats, quilted with thread of spun gold, gorgeous with pearls and diamonds, rubies and emeralds sparkling wherever seams cross.

For two hundred years such gowns were high fashion. The Spanish glory waned; the Sun King of France rose over the Continent and shone ever more brilliantly, decade after decade. His peasants ceaselessly fought and died for him in quilted shirts of canvas, tow, and leather; his courtiers glittered around

Bedcover and backdrop from home of George Washington's mother, both pieces thickly padded with cotton, eighteenth century. Photographed in a room of much later period. [MARY WASHINGTON HOUSE, FREDERICKSBURG, VA.]

him, their ladies in gold-quilted, jeweled brocades.

Queen Anne reigned in England. There gentry and prosperous yeomen slept on quilted mattresses, sometimes thick with two layers of padding; and ladies learned a new needlework evidently brought from Italy, named *trapunto*.

Trapunto is done with two layers of cloth only, no padding between them. Delicate designs of small flowers and leaves were drawn on fine white linen and quilted with outline stitching to a coarsely woven lining. Then the lady turned the work over and from the back she pushed wee bits of cotton through the meshes of the lining, to pad each tiny leaf and petal. With a little bodkin she drew cord under the lining, along each stem.

A lady of the manor, with maids and men and the work of a whole manufacturing farmstead on her hands, probably did little of this delicate needlework. It is more suited to the tedium of ladies-in-waiting at court. In *trapunto* they made many a bed suit of dainty curtains and coverlet, beautiful in summer. Indeed always beautiful, but such sheer bed curtains must have failed to keep winter's drafts from chilling the noses of sleepers.

Meanwhile far away and out of mind on the coast of that northern America which only Spaniards had explored (and they had abandoned its worthless swamps and deserts), the common wives of common men were quilting mattresses and piecing quilts for the cord beds built into corners of their one-room cabins.

It's a plausible guess that those colonial women developed American quilting from American patchwork. After making a Bear's Paw pattern and piecing it in a quilt top, no woman would like to obliterate those Bear's Paws under crisscross seams; anyone would quilt around them. Then she would find them repeated in small even stitches on the quilt's underside. These patterns outlined in stitches have the charm of understatement. Often it is hard to say which side of a patchwork quilt is the prettier.

Compromise settled the question. When colonial women had grown more flax and made more cloth, they began to make quilt tops of pieced blocks set in plain blocks on which they quilted the patchwork pattern. This was an innovation, and I suspect that it was the origin of the whole needle art that American women have been developing ever since then.

Its elements are always the same: two layers of cloth sewed together with a soft filling between them. Today the results are as various as fabrics are now, and fillings, and stitches, and quilters' wishes and tastes and characters.

The quality of this needle art is subtle. Perhaps the quickest way to understand it is to think of quilting as the obverse of embroidery. Embroidery dominates and decorates a fabric with stitches; quilting does not. Quilting stitches are so modestly retiring that you must look for them to see them. Only their effects strike the eye, and their effects are lights and shadows. And what do the greatest artists work with, but light and shadow? Quilting may be as delicate as ivory carved in China or as bold as Rodin's marble.

A quilter uses fabrics as sculptors use ivory or marble, so the choice of fabric and filling is important. Not every kind of cloth will do for quilting. Fabrics must be smooth so that light and shadow can be outlined clearly on them; you want no fuzziness. For your calm enjoyment, both fabrics and filling must be pleasantly easy to sew. Of course the thickness of the filling determines the depth of the effect you can get; also it determines the number of stitches in a needleful. In any case, I prefer a short needle, very sharp, and make sure that it is large enough to make a hole amply larger than the doubled thread it pulls behind it. Expert quilters use various sizes and kinds of thread; a beginner will be

Counterpane photographed in Washington's bedchamber at Mount Vernon, Va. Straight lines of border are worked over cord. [MOUNT VERNON LADIES' ASSOCIATION]

happier with the special quilting thread. It is especially smooth and strong and unwilling to kink. It comes in practically all colors.

Quilting is only sewing but there is so much to learn about the art that a beginner will find it worthwhile to quilt a small piece before starting a large one. A little experi-ence teaches a lot about the effects of stitches. More experience constantly teaches more, for the fascination of quilting grows. Quilters become addicts.

You'd like an accent for the living room? You need a remnant of plain cloth (cotton, linen, silk, woolen, any cloth suited to the

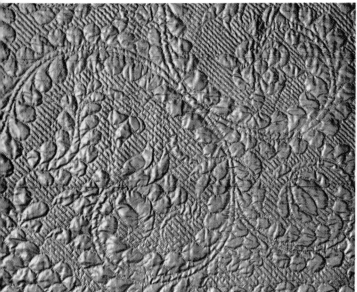

From coverlet quilted in early 1800's. [SHELBURNE MUSEUM, SHELBURNE, VT.]

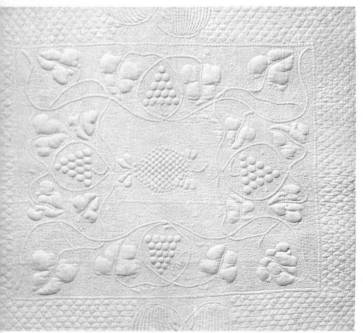

Stuffed quilting, center design of white counterpane shown on page 121.

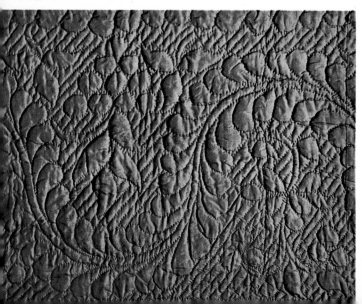

room) of precisely the right color. Transfer, or draw with crayon or hard pencil, your chosen pattern on it. Take as much cheesecloth for lining and a piece of flannel, worn-out blanket, bathrobe (almost anything soft will do) for filling. Baste or pin them all firmly and smoothly together. Clamp them into embroidery hoops if you want to; large pieces of quilting need stretching in frames, but you can do such a small piece in the hand. Thread your needle with thread matching the cloth's color, and simply sew along the pattern's lines with small, even stitches. Then crisscross all but the pattern with lines of sewing. You'll soon have a cushion top to catch every eye.

More ambitiously, and using more scraps of time you can quilt a set of unique chair seats. Or upholstery for an antique sofa. Or a coverlet and curtains. Or the skirt of an evening dress. There's hardly a use for cloth that isn't enhanced by quilting. You can quilt a baby's most charming little cap and jacket, indeed a summer or evening jacket for yourself. In China, Japan, Korea, quilted jackets are ordinary work clothes; here, one is exotic. And it is feather-light, cosily warm in chilly air conditioning or under an autumn moon.

Whether large or small, quilting patterns are simple. They must be, because we do not quilt the pattern; we quilt its background. You may quilt in any color but you are not working with color; you are working with light. To contrast with shadows, the light must lie on a smooth surface. So the pattern is the untouched surface of the cloth. It stands out in bas-relief because the light on it is unbroken. The quilting makes the background of tiny hills of cloth that break up the light with their shadows.

A good example is the Laurel Wreath. This is an early American quilting pattern,

Feather pattern from petticoat, made about 1840. [FENIMORE HOUSE, COOPERSTOWN, N.Y.]

one of those timeless old designs that are always modern. Once it was the laurels that ancient Greek artists and athletes won in their Olympics and that Roman world conquerors wore in their bloody triumphs. Julius Caesar never was seen without his laurel wreath; he wore it anxiously to hide his baldness. And the pessimist observed, as we read in our Bibles, "I have seen the wicked in great power and spreading himself like a greenbay tree" (Psalms 37:35). The evergreen laurel, ancient symbol of eternity in the eastern Mediterranean, gives us the bay leaves that season our stews and pot roasts.

No pattern is more simple than the Laurel Wreath. Its stems are true arcs, halfway around a dinner plate. Its parallel leaves are so easy to draw that the tops of countless apple pies wear Laurel Wreaths swiftly cut in the folded dough. Yet no quilting pattern is more effective than the light on those smooth slim leaves and the subtle curves of shadow around them. Break up the light on the background with a myriad of random stitches and the wreath stands out as if carved. You don't notice the quilting; you see the light on the pattern.

For uncounted centuries quilting was merely a practical way of padding clothes. In America it was the practical way of padding patchwork quilts. Patchwork itself was a niggardly practical way of using every scrap of precious cloth; American women made it beautiful. When they quilted around a patchwork pattern they were making usefulness serve beauty, again.

Then, once free from quilting's traditional monotony, they were free, too, from pieced patchwork's straight lines. They set their patchwork blocks with plain blocks and on these they outlined gracefully curving Prince's Feathers and Laurel Wreaths with simple running stitches. They added stitched feath-

Eagle with 24 stars made about 1825. [Museum of the Daughters of the American Revolution]

Cloud quilting worked in coral thread. [Shelburne Museum]

From petticoat. [Museum of the Daughters of the American Revolution, Washington, D.C.]

ers and leafy festoons to the borders.

They began to discover that plain sewing is only the A B C of quilting. You have noticed the thin lines of shadow between the little puffed squares or triangles of a machine-quilted pot holder. That is the prehistoric pattern. Probably you have the new coverlets of flowery nylon, polyester-filled, machine-quilted in a pattern of ovals above ripples of that same thin shadow. This is an early American pattern. Tired of snapping a chalked string against a stretched quilt top to stamp the same old straight lines, our great-grandmothers drew curves around a teacup.

The whole unexplored field of creative quilting opened before them when they began to play with that thin shadow, to repeat it, and widen it, and shape it and change its tonal quality. There are old American quilts that seem to have blocks or borders of crinkle-woven chiffon, so closely together the wavering tiny shadows lie. Separate the crinkles with a fingernail and you find the little even stitches that totally changed the texture of the sheer cloth. The effect is delightful; the thought of such patiently time-consuming work is staggering. Who'd do it now?

Those countless rows of stitches repeating the thin shadow were a new way of quilting. The forgotten women who did it were creating a new folk art. In time they completely divorced quilting from patchwork. They began to work intricate patterns, white on white, made wholly of the qualities of light on cloth.

This is American quilting, as free as a needle in the hand, as varied as fabrics and stitches and threads, and almost as unlimited as imagination. Its only rules are the inexorable laws of those mysteries: light and space. So far as these will let you, you make its patterns in any way you like, with any materials you choose. It is the most experimental, the most individually creative needlework, so it is the most endlessly fascinat-

ing to do. And, we Americans being what we are, we do it swiftly. (If sometimes you wish, as I do, that you hadn't done so quickly what you just now thought of, a few snips of the scissors undo it.)

For example: a massive wreath of larger and smaller flowers with stems and leaves. The flowers will be highlighted, the leaves more or less subdued, as the shadows between them are darker or lighter. You make the shadows with your stitches. Outline a petal sharply with linked backstitches; densely fill the space around it with tiny random stitches, and you lift the petal above a darker shadow. Run a line of plain sewing around it, crisscross the space with long basting stitches, and the shadow is lighter, the petal lower. Or reverse the basting, make its long stitches underneath and cross the short ones on top to make little stars scattered on the space; the shadow will be even lighter and the petal fading into it. A frame or border (of any shape) may be well filled with the old quilting, square puffs between straight lines of plain sewing; then the closer the lines, the smaller the puffs, the darker will be the border.

Of course this is no more than a hint of what you can do with a needle. A pattern quilted in white on white has all the tones of a painting. And now that we have such a wealth of fabrics in so many unfading colors, with threads to match them, the gradations of tone in quilting rose on rose, yellow on yellow, blue on blue would be something beyond our grandmothers' dreams.

Once you begin to work out a design in tonal qualities by changing the refractions of light on cloth, you understand American quilting and what fun it is. I think it is the most playful of needle arts. It is so easy to do (or hastily undo), it is done so quickly, and its variety is so inexhaustible and its surprises so many that it is never for an instant monotonous.

Also, a finished piece is a joy forever.

How to Quilt

NOTE: The following directions are for quilting coverlets. The same designs and information may be applied to quilting other pieces such as pillow tops, dinner skirts, jackets, linings, upholstery fabrics, etc. Many designs also may be used on patchwork and appliqué coverlets for quilted borders and backgrounds.

MATERIALS

You will need to estimate the amount of materials necessary for your quilting project. A full-size counterpane, used without a dust ruffle and long enough to fold over pillows, should measure 90″ x 108″. For twin-bed size, the 72″ width is usual. A special quilting thread is generally used for cotton, linen or wool quilts because it is extra strong and has a smooth finish that makes it glide easily through layers of material. If not available, mercerized thread between Nos. 50 and 70 should be used. If your coverlet is of silk or rayon, silk thread should be used. Generally the thread should be the same color as the background fabric.

QUILT TOP

Fine quilting deserves the very best materials available, whether cotton, silk, rayon, linen, or wool. Fabrics should be firmly woven, soft in texture, and of good quality. If you plan to wash your coverlet, the fabric should be preshrunk and, if colored, of a fast dye. If there is any doubt, wash a small sample before starting quilt. In the cotton family, calico, percale, muslin, or cotton satin may be used. For a more luxurious coverlet, silks, rayons, linens, or wools

are preferred. After deciding which fabric you intend to use, estimate how many lengths you will need to get the desired quilt width and multiply that figure by three for the number of yards needed for the average quilt top. If you plan to bind edges with matching fabric, add another half yard.

INTERLINING

Use cotton quilt batts or a lightweight, preshrunk blanket. If a particularly puffy effect is desired, try a Dacron polyester batt, or use a double thickness of cotton batting.

BACKING

This may be of the same fabric and joined in the same manner as the quilt top. A good-grade sheeting which comes as wide as 90″ or the regular 36″-wide muslin joined to the proper width may also be used.

QUILTING PLAN

If you are working out your own quilt, after top is assembled, plan placement of quilting designs. Using graph paper and allowing each square to equal one square inch of your coverlet, make an over-all plan. Sketch the quilting patterns that you want to use, borders, center and other design areas, in scale on the plan. This will give you an idea of how your arrangement of patterns will look on your finished quilt and whether they are in proportion. When designs are decided upon, with pins or basting thread, outline same areas on quilt as those on plan. This is the time to chart mathematically the placement of border repeats. It is generally easier to start border design at

center of each edge and work repeats toward corners so that design may be adjusted to meet attractively.

TRANSFERRING QUILTING PATTERNS

Perforate the full-size designs you wish to use with a tracing wheel, a large pin or needle, or stitch along lines on sewing machine with unthreaded needle. Following your quilting plan, place quilt top on firm surface and pin perforated pattern securely in position. Cover a small pad of cotton with soft cloth. Dip in cinnamon, cocoa, or a mixture of 1 teaspoonful of powdered ultramarine (purchased at the drugstore) to 4 teaspoonfuls of cornstarch. Pat powder over perforations to spread evenly, then rub lightly with scrubbing motion to work it through perforations, making certain that neither fabric nor pattern moves. Carefully remove pattern and blow off excess powder, then go over design lightly with a soft lead pencil. Background designs are generally marked after special designs are quilted and the quilt is still in the frame.

QUILTING FRAME

Large pieces such as quilts require a frame long enough to enclose the entire piece or a convenient working section, while a small item can be worked with an ordinary embroidery hoop. Both may be purchased through some mail-order houses or store needlework departments or shops. If you wish, you can make your own frame. It consists of four wooden strips, each about 1″ x 2″ and long enough to enclose the entire quilt, or, if not convenient, one half or one quarter of the quilt when strips are joined. Fasten strips where they cross at corners with clamps. Rest frame on supports such as chair backs, which will bring it almost to breast height for working.

ASSEMBLING QUILT

Thumbtack a 2″ strip of firm muslin securely along top edge of frame. To this pin or baste your quilt lining securely, stretching it smooth and taut. Over lining spread quilt batt. Over all place quilt top; smooth and baste layers together in diagonal lines from center to edges of quilt and around outer edges, avoiding unnecessary fullness or tightness.

QUILTING STITCH

While many old counterpanes were quilted with backstitch or chain stitch, today's quilting patterns usually use a simple running stitch. A beginner in quilting should try a small practice piece, because the thickness of the layers and the puffiness of the filling often make it difficult for the inexperienced to make short, even stitches at first. One method is to hold the needle nearly horizontal, rather than diagonal as you do for ordinary sewing, and take several stitches before drawing the needle away from the quilt. Another method that is slower but unfailingly accurate is done by making the stitch in two separate movements. The left hand is placed under the frame to receive the needle which is pushed vertically downward from the top. Then with the left hand the needle is pushed upward to complete the stitch. This method is generally used when the quilts are of heavy material or if the filling is thick. To begin, thread needle, make a knot at the end of thread and bring needle through to top of quilt. Pull gently and firmly until knot pulls through backing and disappears in batting. To fasten thread, make a backstitch and run end of thread into batting.

STUFFED QUILTING

Designs that are small in area such as leaves, petals, grapes, circles, vines, and stems are often stuffed. This is called *trapunto*. It is done by basting good-quality cheesecloth or fine muslin interlining underneath portion of design to be stuffed before attaching the coverlet backing. In such stuffed quilts no batting is used for interlining. Transfer quilting design to fabric interlining. With interlining facing, quilt design through it and top fabric. Then carefully part threads of interlining with bodkin or knitting needle and insert small bits of cotton batting or absorbent cotton between two layers of fabric into each small area. For vines,

stems, and raised outlines, two closely parallel lines of quilting are necessary. Upholstery cording or cotton rug yarn is then run through casing formed by quilting lines. Needle must be brought through interlining at curve or turn and then inserted again, leaving a small loop of

yarn. Never draw cording through to top of quilt. Stuff designs evenly and firmly so they will stand in relief on quilt top. After stuffing and cording are completed, transfer other quilting patterns to top fabric. Assemble quilt and backing, place

in frame, and quilt remainder in regular manner.

BACKGROUND QUILTING

When motifs and border are completed and while quilt is still on frame, pencil in background pattern. Use a yardstick for straight lines and cups, saucers, egg cups, even fifty-cent pieces for circular designs. Diagonal lines have always been one of the most popular of backgrounds. They are generally ¼″ to ¾″ apart. Occasionally cord is run between the closely spaced diagonal lines. On some museum pieces stitches are so close that they give a crinkled appearance to the background. Other very effective ruled patterns are squares, diamonds, and diagonal plaid designs. Egg cups or fifty-cent pieces are fine guides for drawing shell or cloud backgrounds. Interlocking circles, however, are more effective when larger circular objects are used such as saucers or bread-and-butter plates. See photographs for suggested background patterns.

MACHINE QUILTING

Although classic quilting is considered a handcraft, it may be done by sewing machine. Straight quilting lines and simple designs are most adaptable to machine work. For this it is essential that the quilt top, interlining, and backing be basted together most securely. Basting lines should not be more than 2″ apart to prevent shifting of fabric while stitching.

BINDING QUILTS

When quilting is completed, remove from frame and trim edges, making sure to remove any batting that extends beyond quilt top. Bind edges with double-fold bias tape or matching fabric cut in 1″-wide bias strips and joined to desired length.

Counterpane, a fine example of stuffed quilting, made about 1800 (see detail of center on page 116). [IN THE DAVID TOWNSEND HOUSE, PART OF THE CHESTER COUNTY HISTORICAL SOCIETY, WEST CHESTER, PA.]

Bedcover from the home of George Washington's sister, Betty Lewis. Fine quilting enhances appliqué designs of Prince's Feather and of dragons with amusing heart cutouts for mouths and eyes. Photographed in a room of much later period. [KENMORE, FREDERICKSBURG, VA.]

Directions for Quilted Ship

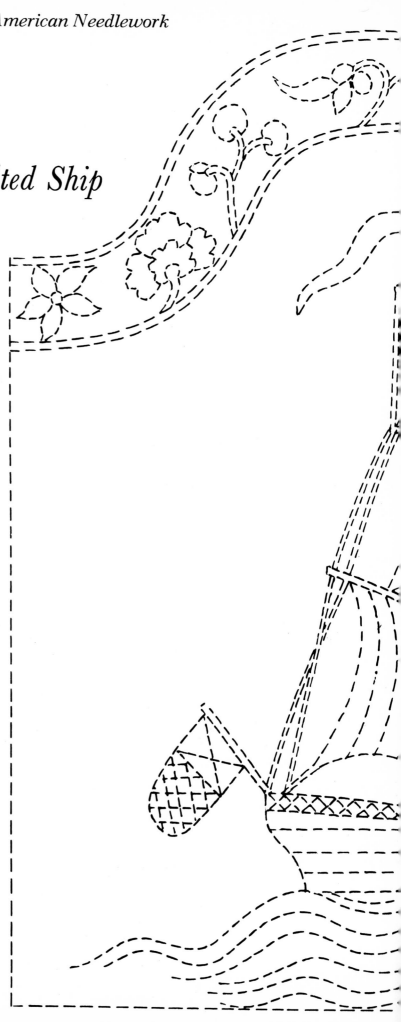

See color photograph of ship on page 117. Pages 117-118 also show background quilting.

SIZE

Minimum dimensions for the design are 12″ x 10⅝″. The design should be placed so that the point at the top of the border is on the vertical center of fabric. The arrow indicates the horizontal center.

NOTE: The pattern has been separated to make tracing easier. Link the two parts together when you trace off, then transfer design to your material, spacing it equally if you are repeating.

The original ship is on a petticoat border. You can adapt the design to a petticoat or skirt of your size; use a commercial pattern, or trace a petticoat or skirt of your own and cut interlining and backing fabric the same size. Then quilt through all layers (see "How to Quilt" for more specific step-by-step instructions). You can also utilize the ship design for a picture, a pillow or a coverlet center. (The ship might be adapted to alternate with other nautical motifs such as Mariner's Star, page 76.)

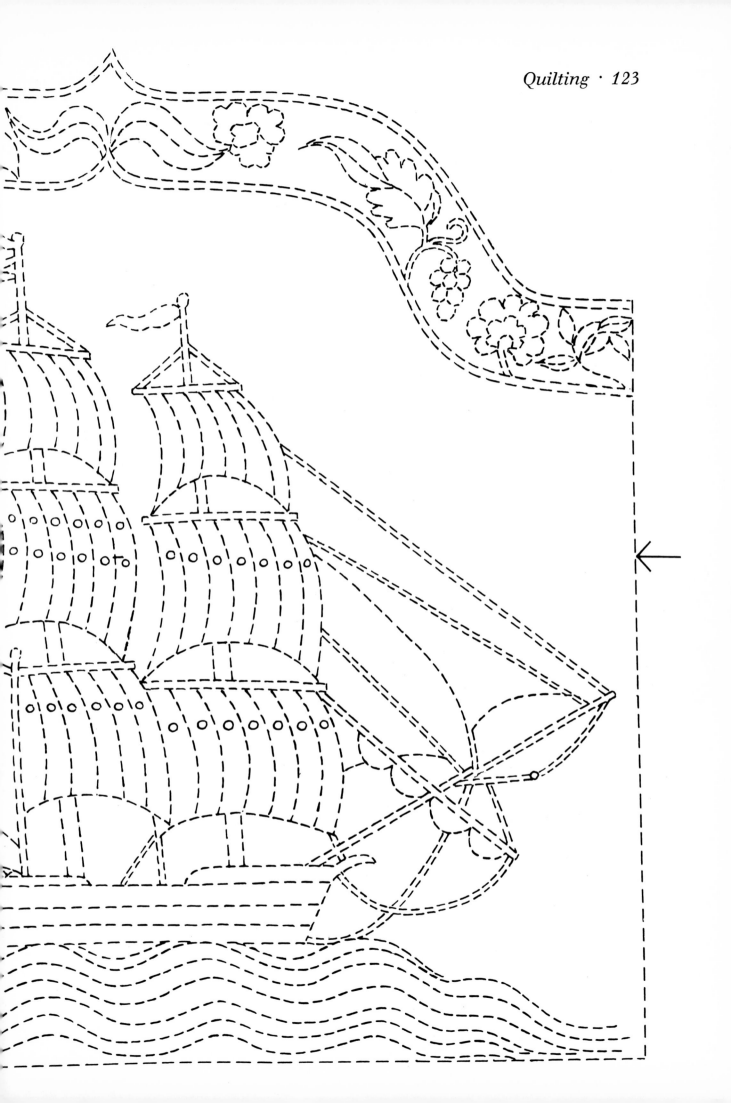

Hooking

Finely hooked rug, a deep wine red with formal center motif and wide floral border.
Made in New England about 1850. [HENRY FORD MUSEUM, DEARBORN, MICH.]

OOKING IS an old needle craft, probably little younger than weaving. Certainly its method is simple: nothing but drawing a little loop of rag or yarn through the mesh of a strong but coarsely woven fabric. This is done with the most primitive of tools: the shepherd's crook which Stone Age men carried to seize things beyond arm's reach and that we use, in tiny size, to make the American hooked rug.

When underneath the stretched burlap the fingers of your left hand lightly guide the strand to be looped up by the hook in your right hand, you are repeating an action older than history. For thousands of years seafaring men and homekeeping women did this to make mufflers and wraps and bedcovers. But hooked rugs are new. Colonial women invented them in America, not two centuries ago.

Twice since then this art has been neglected, almost lost. Incredible as it seems, through the nineteenth century the dominant American thinkers believed that there was no American culture. Culture, they thought, was European; and of the hundreds of American painters, singers, writers, architects, they noticed only those who had gone to Europe and been acclaimed there. Until lately they saw no American needle crafts. Only housewives knew those, and thought them too commonplace to interest important people.

Today there is intense interest in all these expressions of our culture, and in all the continental States hooking is a liveliest art. Young women are thronging classes in hooking. Curators are bringing out rare treasures of earlier American hooked work; librarians are meeting an increasing demand for the few books of historic and modern designs; the market is supplying a growing demand for the materials and implements of hooking. When a group of churchwomen announce an exhibition of hooked rugs, the unexpected flood of exhibits and visitors overwhelms them.

This revival of an almost lost art is a bit of the renaissance that Americans began during the 1919–1939 Armistice of the World War and are now continuing vigorously. We are all more deeply aware of our whole heritage of American principles and history, arts and culture and character. We are learning and loving American furniture, glass, china, American square dances and folk songs,

American needle crafts, because we are seeing the whole Old World that Americans left behind them and, in contrast, we know our country better and cherish its unique values.

The making of so many hooked rugs is part of the revival of personal independence and self-reliance, of individual self-expression in American life. With the little hook in your hand you make your home express yourself. Your hooked rug is the size you want, the shape you want. Its colors are your choice, its design is drawn to please you. As every woman knows, the rug makes the room; your own hooked rug makes a room your work of art. Do you believe that you can make a rug as beautiful, as valuable, as a priceless old Persian? You can.

Of course you can. You don't believe that you can't do what a peasant woman in Isfahan does?

You will not do it quickly, for hooking is not hurry-up, slapdash work. It requires precision and time. Unless you have hooked a rug, or until you do, you may not realize how patiently persistent you are; you may never have enjoyed the tranquillity of leisurely creation.

A room-size rug is a major undertaking,

for experts do a square foot of fine, perfect hooking in six hours. If this prospect daunts you, better make a small rug. Anyway, better begin with a small rug. You will learn how to make mistakes and quickly undo them. You will learn what texture does to colors and what colors do, so startlingly, to each other, and how to make them harmonize and balance in a design. The fascination and satisfaction of hooking will enthrall you. Then you will plan the large rug you want and make it perfectly as you want it to be.

For the small practice rug you can buy a pattern stamped on burlap and work it with rug yarns. If you draw loops nearly an inch long, you can clip them when the rug is done and it will have a velvety surface, soft and softly shaded. Clipped wool yarns were most popular some twenty years ago, but the first American rugs were made of rags, and today the best designers are using that traditional material.

They buy mill ends and remnants of thick woolen cloth, dye them, and cut them into strips as narrow as an eighth of an inch. (These tiny strips don't fray, as I'd expect.) They work the rugs in wee loops and produce the fine texture of Oriental rugs, which takes hard wear forever without showing it.

The first hooked rugs were thriftily made from the rag bag, for nearly all useful things were still made by hand then, so nothing could be wasted. But a century of freedom and hard work in almost uninhabitable wilderness had already made Americans so prosperous that workers everywhere else were envying them. After the first few desperate years, there never was a famine here. For the first time on earth, here was a land where famine never came. Working-class houses were snug. The windows were glass; the floors were wood; parlor floors were even painted. The cord beds were plump with feather ticks, clean homespun blankets, and patchwork quilts.

Of course every scrap of cloth was valuable, made as it was from wool on the sheep or flax in the field, but when the whole family was clad in good cloth and there were quilts to spare, what use could a woman make of saved rags?

She knew the *rugge*, that hooked wool-on-wool bedding that women from Sweden and Scotland, Holland and the Germanies, had brought to the wilderness to keep them from freezing on their pallets. It inspired her. She washed and ripped sugar sacks from the West Indies; she sewed them together and drew a pattern on them. She dyed the rags with cochineal and indigo, walnut-husk and pokeberry juice; she cut them into strips and hooked them into her pattern. Every woman knows what she felt when she laid this new thing, made with her mind and hands, on her parlor floor before the swept and redded hearth.

It was a useless luxury, an evidence of well-earned prosperity. She called it a rug and did not know that she was making a new language, too. The Swedish word *rugge*, meaning coarse, rough (rugged), was changed in England to "rug," meaning a thick cloak or wrap. The English name of what she made is still "mat" or "carpet." But she called it a rug, and so do we.

Those were troubled times. Defying the King's regulations, women were weaving

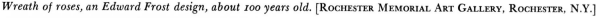

Wreath of roses, an Edward Frost design, about 100 years old. [ROCHESTER MEMORIAL ART GALLERY, ROCHESTER, N.Y.]

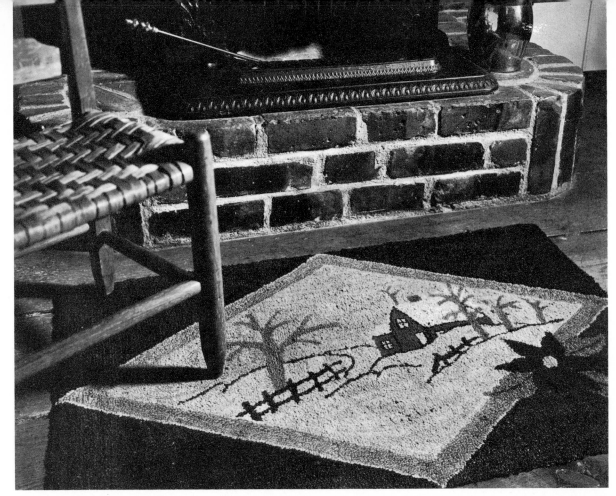

Hearth rug depicting a bright orange-red farmhouse against snow. The golden beige tree is the same color as the inside border (note the bright red poinsettia on one edge). The entire picture is set against a charcoal gray. [ROCHESTER MUSEUM OF ARTS AND SCIENCES, ROCHESTER, N.Y.]

homespun and men were cutting down pine trees, and the King's men harried them. Through the years of the French-English war the Indians burned villages, killing and scalping men and carrying away the women and children. Rogers' Rangers invaded Canada and returned in rags, starving, more nearly dead than alive. There were sea fights along the coasts between traders' ships and the King's gunboats. Horses galloping in the night startled sleepers awake to hold the musket and stand by the cradle until the riders went by. In Virginia, in the Carolinas, in Massachusetts, there were uprisings against Royal Governors. British troops occupied rebellious Boston and tried to starve the city to submission, blockading it for a long year. Then the battles of Lexington, Concord, Breed's Hill; then Virginia's Declaration of Rights, and independence in Virginia; and at long last the Continental Congress made the glorious, dreadful Declaration of Independence that began six years of

invasions, battles, retreats, inflation, requisitions.

Through all this time English, French, German and Scottish women in Virginia, Swedes and Scots and Germans in the Carolinas, Delaware, and Pennsylvania, Finns in the Jerseys, Dutch on Manhattan and Long Island and in Hudson's valley, English and French women in New England, were making hooked rugs. For as we all know, women keep house and hold the world together through all the anxieties, miseries, and tragedies of all the wars.

So we have the lovely rug that Mrs. Stark planned in tones of brown and gold while the Sons of Liberty and the Green Mountain Boys were shouting "Liberty and Property!" and priming their muskets. Her husband was raising a regiment; she dyed the rags and drew the pattern. She finished the rug in 1773; he fought in the battle of Breed's Hill. And when Burgoyne's mighty army was coming down the Hudson valley triumphantly to cut the rebellious colonies in two, Captain Stark led a band of farmers against the King's troops at Bennington, with a shout: "Come on, men! We win today or Molly Stark's a widow!"

They won the battle of Bennington that saved the Revolution.

Molly Stark's is a rare survival of countless colonial rugs. All the earlier ones are gone, worn out and thrown away. We know of them only from old letters and diaries. But the skill went west with the women who followed their men over the mountain trails when the King could no longer prevent their going. They remembered it in the endless forests where sunshine never pierced the treetops, on flatboats drifting down the Ohio, trudging beside ox wagons over Cumberland

Hooked bed rug made by Molly Stark in 1773. Carnations, berries and vines are hooked onto a coarse woolen home-spun blanket and are unsheared. [MUSEUM OF THE DAUGHTERS OF THE AMERICAN REVOLUTION, WASHINGTON, D.C.]

Gap to Kentucky's bluegrass prairies, in log hovels by the malarial swamps of the Illinois country, beyond the Mississippi to the Great American Desert.

Where they stopped, again they made shelters of logs or sods, again they created farms and towns. First the men built stores and saloons and churches, then houses of sawed boards with chimneys and floors and

Antique table mat. [BROOKLYN MUSEUM, BROOKLYN, N.Y.]

Parlor rug with floral center and geometric border. Made in 1850. [CHESTER COUNTY HISTORICAL SOCIETY, WEST CHESTER, PA.]

glass windows. The women saved every emptied grain sack, washed it, ripped it, sewed the sacks together. On them they drew pictures of dog or cat, horse or cow, in a garland of flowers. Then they opened their rag bags and hooked rugs.

Few of these designs are good in proportions and flow of line; many are childishly awkward but vigorous. When you plan your own rug, look at these primitive patterns. See their candid honesty. Each one says that its maker had her own standards and did her best to live by them; she copied no one else. She used her own eyes and mind and hands; with them she did the best she could. And if in her rug the smoke blew one way and the flag blew the other way, she (as she said) "made no bones of it." She was what she was, her rug was hers, and it pleased her in her parlor.

The quiet self-reliance with which generations of forgotten men and women created our country is expressed in these rugs. It is in the art of Grandma Moses. This quality of personal moral character is the source of every lasting good in this world. These rugs are permanently valuable because they express this quality. They show us that the first essential to good work is: Trust yourself; do your own best.

A woman who copies a hooked rug is wasting an opportunity to express and truly satisfy herself. Everywhere she sees patterns of lines and masses, light and shade and color that delight her. How does she know, unless she tries, that she can't make a design to please herself? She arranges furniture in a room, flowers in a vase, and she can arrange forms and colors in a rug pattern.

Museums and libraries have inspiration to offer everyone. In hooked-rug designs you find the Persian and Indian Tree of Life, the Lotus, the Pineapple, the Horn of Plenty; the Star of David and the Star of Bethlehem; the Arabic mosaic and pointed arch; the Chinese and Japanese birds, trees and moun-

tains; the French Aubusson garlands, the English apple tree, the Scotch thistle; and the wealth of American patterns: the Pine Tree, the Liberty Tree, the Eagle of the Republic, the Clipper Ship, all the American flowers and animals, the Lemon Star, and celebrations of the wonderful machines that so swiftly abolished, here, the age-old burden of human toil: the Steamship, the Atlantic Cable, the Locomotive, the Mower and the Thresher so easily harvesting fields of grain.

For a while the machines almost abolished hooked rugs, so marvelously they were doing work that human hands had done since Adam. They made handwork old-fashioned. In the 1840's, if you could believe it, machines in factories in New England were making ingrain carpets.

Few could buy them; times were hard in the 1850's. They were much harder in the 1860's and after the war, through the 1870's. Women made hundreds of hooked rugs then, hooking many a blue or gray uniform into patterns more and more beautifully designed. These are most of the rugs that you find in museums; they are priceless now. At the time only the makers' friends noticed them, and one Yankee peddler, a down-East man of Biddeford, Maine. His name was Edward Sands Frost.

He was a veteran, home from the war, a casualty no longer able to work. So through the winters he hammered out tinwares to load a peddler's tall, gaily painted cart, and in spring, with a peddler's bell clanging in its arch above the horse's collar, he set out toward Providence, selling and trading from farm to farm.

Everywhere welcomed for the news he brought and the tales and jokes he told in the evenings after supper, he noticed and admired the housewives' rugs. I suppose he found it difficult to describe his wife's patterns; anyway, one spring he took along some drawings of them. They sold like hot cakes. Next winter he and his wife made more, still that summer he could have sold twice as many.

How to supply this demand was a problem, so he solved it. He surprised farm wives along his way by taking their leaky, worthless wash boilers in trade. That winter he beat them out flat, and with chisel and file he cut rug patterns into the tin. With these, he and Mrs. Frost stenciled each pattern on dozens of pieces of burlap. The investment was large, and risky. But in the spring he sold every pattern, for cash. His customers wanted more.

Mr. Frost set up shop in Biddeford. He hired helpers, and more helpers, to stencil hooked-rug patterns in colors on burlap. He was making money hand over fist, and hiring still more helpers, when overwork brought the old war misery on him again. He shut up shop and traveled far west for his health. In a sleepy old Spanish-mission town of Los Angeles in California, he invested his savings in real estate. Need I say that he returned to Biddeford a rich man?

For half a century the Frost stencils lay forgotten, therefore not destroyed. Today they are precious records of lost rugs, an inexhaustible source of beautiful designs for new ones. They are one of the treasures of the Henry Ford Museum in Dearborn, Michigan, proudly displayed with their stencils on burlap. You are welcome to study them to your heart's content, and may buy a stenciled pattern if you like.

Through the booming 1880's and the world-wide desperate depression of the nineties Americans kept on making the wonderful machines that lessen toil and abolish poverty. Pack trains, stagecoaches, flatboats were gone. Sitting at ease in a train, men traveled farther in an hour than ever before on foot in a day. Messages went instantly hundreds of miles on telegraph wires. Machines were now making pins, needles, nails, plowshares, shoes, stockings, table-

cloths, lace curtains—just everything. Some women had sewing machines in their own homes; others backstitched those slanting tucks in Gibson Girl shirtwaists so perfectly, by hand, that you'd think they were machine-stitched.

The 1900's were an age of affluence. We ordered ingrain carpeting from Sears, Roebuck in Chicago; we overcast the yard-wide lengths together, and after each spring and fall housecleaning we stretched the well-beaten carpet carefully over the layer of fresh straw on the parlor floor and tacked down its edges again. We thought less of a hooked rug than of a patchwork quilt or a sheet made by sewing together two lengths of muslin. (Power looms did not yet weave percale nor wide muslin.) Quilts and sheets are useful, but when you had a real machine-made carpet, what use was there for an old handmade rug? Rover could sleep on it in the barn.

In the revival of rug hooking now, we are using gifts from the makers of the machines. They have given us time; who now works from dawn to dark, six days a week, for a dollar a day? (Or for the $2.50 a week which delighted me in 1905?)

To make your own hooked rug, there is burlap machine-made more evenly than ever homespun was. There is a steel hook more perfectly machine-made and polished than any ever whittled from wood or bone. There are limitless quantities, constantly replenished, of cheap remnants of fine, machine-woven woolens; there are machines to cut them evenly into narrowest strips.

From scores of sources you can buy, cheaply, these remnants already cut, or buy them by the pound, and your own little machine to cut them. You can buy dyes to dye them (in your washing machine) or you can buy colorfast yarns in all shades and tones. You can even buy a hook which is a tiny sewing machine; you thread it with yarn and hook your rug from the wrong side with galloping stitches, if you like. True lovers of the art of hooking frown upon this swift method, and I myself prefer to enjoy watching a design grow, stitch by stitch, under my eyes; but it's fun, too, to work it sight unseen and see it all at once, suddenly, complete.

Artists are making for you now an abundance of hooked-rug designs to please whatever your taste may be: Early American, Victorian, French, Oriental, Modern American. An interest in hooked rugs opens a door to all history and the whole world of art. Whatever you find in them and choose to make your own, your hooked rug will bring into your life and your home, and keep there.

When you make it, remember that a hooked rug, cared for, lasts for centuries, and from now on Americans will care for American culture. Some day your rug will be a priceless old American.

dallion rug. [ROCHESTER MEMORIAL ART GALLERY]

*Garden bouquet in
Washington Irving's
home at Sleepy Hollow
Restorations, Tarry-
town, N.Y.*

Hearth rug, early New England. [NEW HAMPSHIRE HISTORICAL SOCIETY, CONCORD, N.H.]

Geometric hooked rug, mid-nineteenth century. [NEW HAMPSHIRE HISTORICAL SOCIETY]

How to Hook

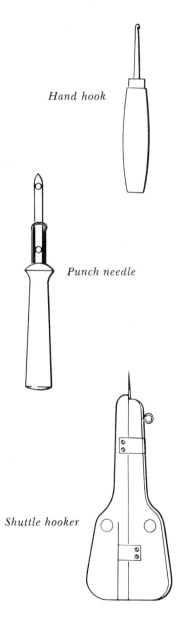

Hand hook

Punch needle

Shuttle hooker

MATERIALS

Foundation: The traditional material is burlap with a firm, even weave. Other backings are heavy, 2-thread cotton of even weave, similar to monk's cloth or linen rug base. Whatever the foundation, buy enough to allow 3″ extra on all sides of rug for hem and to allow for piecing if necessary. If you have to piece your fabric, overlap edges 2″ and stitch with strong thread before beginning to hook. Then simply hook through the overlapping thicknesses.

Filling: Wool, cotton, rayon, and other synthetic fabrics and rug yarns can be used, but woolen fabric cut in strips is the most accepted. Cut fabric strips on the straight of goods either lengthwise or crosswise. Cut materials such as wool flannel into strips ⅛″ to ⅜″ wide. Cut fabrics lighter in weight into wider strips, heavier fabrics into narrower. There are cloth-cutting machines available to cut several strips evenly at a time. Use any fabrics that are suitable in color or can be dyed for your particular rug. They may be unworn parts of discarded garments or new materials such as mill ends of cuttings. Although the amount of material varies somewhat with the individual worker, a rough estimate of about half a pound of cut wool strips to one square foot of rug is average. If materials are to be stored for any length of time, protect against moths.

HOOKS

There are two main types of rug hooks. One, called a hand hook, resembles a crochet hook set in a wooden handle. Hand hooks vary in length and size of handle, etc., so choose one that fits your hand comfortably and is easy for you to work with. The hooks are inexpensive and very popular with experienced rug hookers. You work from the front of the rug when you use a hand hook. This method allows greater versatility in design, length of loops, choice of materials and is a relaxing way to work. However, it is slower than using an automatic hook. You work from the back of a rug when you use an automatic or speed hooker. These are sold with manufacturer's directions.

PLANNING COLORS

Most designs are adaptable to varying color schemes. A few colors or a great many may be used in a rug. Choose those color combinations which you like and spread them out to plan your distribution. If there are not enough colors or shades in the materials you have, you can dye some. Dye fabrics before cutting into strips. Use any good commercial dye, following the manufacturer's directions. For five shades of one color, cut five pieces of fabric and immerse in the dye. As each desired shade is reached, remove piece from the dye. For mottled effects, which are excellent for backgrounds or large plain areas, you can spot-dye fabrics. Moisten fabric in warm water, wring it out, then spread on newspaper. Pour dissolved dye in a cup and splash spots of it over fabric with a spoon. Sprinkle salt generously over fabric and roll it loosely. Pour boiling water into a pot to height of ½″ to 1″; place fabric in it and let boil for half an hour without disturbing the fabric.

FRAME

Some people who use a hand hook work without a frame; others prefer to use one. When automatic hookers are used, a frame is necessary because the backing must be taut. Use a purchased frame or make one from strips of 1″ x 2″ lumber. Cut sidepieces about 4 feet long and crosspieces about 2 feet long. Drill ½″ holes 3″ apart down center of each strip. Lay pieces to form size of frame desired and fasten with wooden pegs through holes where strips cross. To use frame, place it across the backs of chairs so it will be at a comfortable working height when you are seated. To mount foundation on this frame, you can lace through the holes with heavy cord, or the wooden strips can be wound with cloth strips and you can sew the sides of foundation to these strips. Or the fabric can be thumbtacked to the crossbars and the tacks removed when you start hooking another section. Purchased frames come with instructions for mounting backing.

TRANSFERRING A DESIGN

If a design is graphed, enlarge it by taking a piece of wrapping paper the size of your rug and ruling the paper into the same number of equal squares, full-size. Copy the design, square by square, on the wrapping paper. To enlarge a design that isn't on a graph you can use tracing graph paper available from some art supply stores. Place this over your design and draw outline of design directly on tracing paper. Or you can mark off squares over the design to be enlarged. Use ⅛″ squares for small designs, ½″ or 1″ squares for proportionately larger designs. Cut backing to size of rug plus 3″ hem allowance on all edges. (See under Foundation, materials for piecing.) Transfer design from paper to backing as follows: Hold paper against a window, with design side against glass. Duplicate outline of design on side of paper toward you, using a heavy wax crayon or china-marking pencil. Place paper, crayon side down, on backing; iron with a hot iron. Remove paper and go over the faint impression with crayon or felt-tipped brush. If you have a knack for simple freehand drawing, you can draw the design right on your backing, using the chart as a guide. Much of the charm of old hooked rugs comes from the asymmetrical freedom of their patterns. Mark off the outside measurements of the rug, being sure to allow all around for hem. Follow the lengthwise and crosswise threads of the fabric and use a ruler to make sure you get straight edges.

HOOKING

Hooking is the process of pulling loops of yarn or thin strips of fabric, usually woolen, through a basic foundation such as burlap. If using a hand hook, hold yarn or strip of fabric in left hand under backing. Insert hook from top and draw up a loop through backing. Skip a few threads of backing and draw up another loop to same height. (*See diagram.*) Pull all ends to front and clip even with loops. Practice until you can hold strip in left hand, taut but not tight, and can manipulate hook with ease. Have loops close enough to cover the backing but not so close that rug will cup. In all hooking, first hook outline of design, then fill it in. Work background last.

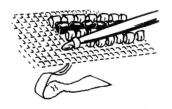

FINISHING

Some people prefer to turn under hems before starting to hook. To do this, turn under hem all around, following line drawn for edge of rug. Sew hem flat with several rows of basting. Then hook through both thicknesses out to edge. On other rugs simply turn under hem when hooking is completed and sew in place. Sew rug binding over hem if desired.

PRESSING

Dampen top of rug with cloth wrung out in warm water; place it face down on several layers of newspaper covered with brown paper and walk on it. Let dry. A special liquid may be applied to seal hooking and help hold rug in place on the floor. Sold in most needlework departments, this paintlike liquid is brushed on the back of the rug. If you prefer, you may line your rug with burlap or heavy muslin.

Directions for Hooking Bengal Tiger Rug

See general directions, pages 136-137, and graph pages 140-141.

SIZE

42″ x 67″.
Strips of both cotton and wool were cut about ½″ wide. They were hooked to a height of ½″.

COLORS

Tiger: Shades of tan and brown, outlined in reddish-brown.

Four-leaf Clovers: Pinky-tan outlined with a row of blue, then a row of white.
Background: Light olive.
Border: Inside line—brown; scallops—beige with mottled blues inside, light-olive *Background*; outer lines—olive, then a row of blue, olive at edge.

Bengal tiger hooked by "J. J." in the early 1800's. There are huge four-leaf clovers in the corners.

Hen with basket of eggs, primitive design. Note how chimney smoke blows one way and the flag the other.

Five small rugs. [SHELBURNE MUSEUM, SHELBURNE, VT.]

Mare and foal. The foal appears to be an afterthought, as mare is centered on the rug and foal breaks the border.

Aubusson-patterned floor covering, a profusion of flowers bordered with graceful scrolls. Oval, nearly 9′ x 12′, hooked about 1835. [HENRY FORD MUSEUM]

Eagle with olive branch and arrows. There are 13 stars above the wings.

Trotting pony with white socks is gay and spirited.

42" x 67"   Each square equals 2" square

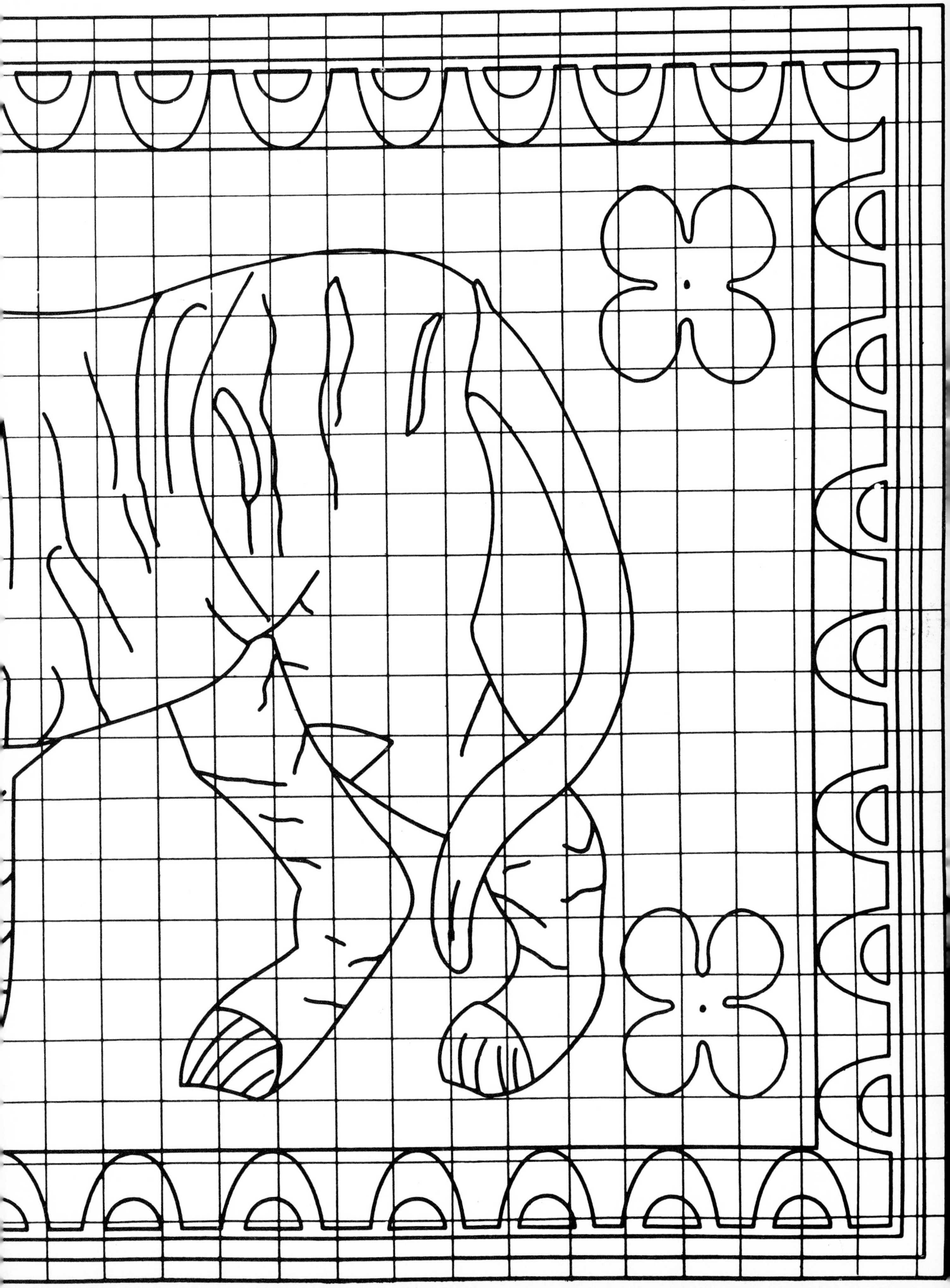

Crochet

Bedspread of white cotton yarn in popular popcorn stitch, crocheted in 12″ blocks.
[NEWARK MUSEUM, NEWARK, N.J.]

IN THE INFINITE VARIETY of these United States there are always a few women, here and there, making a few pieces of all the world's fine laces. Americans from Spain, Italy, France, Mexico, make the delicate rose prints, the traceries on net; Americans from the Near East, Austria, Germany, Belgium, make the thread laces; Americans from the Netherlands, Scandinavia, Britain, make the sturdy braid laces. Every one of us cherishes, almost reverently, a piece of any of these laces. "This is real lace," we say, though there's no need to say it. Anyone sees its handmade quality.

Yet more than a hundred years ago American women began to create American lace, and we have been making it by the mile ever since and thinking nothing of it. Ours is the only real lace without honor in its own country.

For nearly three decades I had been making it to edge handkerchiefs, petticoat flounces, sheets and pillowcases; I had made collars and cuffs of it and place mats and nightgown yokes, when one day in the National Museum of Croatia, in Zagreb, I saw ordinary crocheted lace displayed on velvet, locked under glass. Startled, I exclaimed, "What's *this?*"

My exclamation bewildered the curator. "Madame is not American?" he said. "This is our collection of the art of the American lace."

I could only gaze at it, dumb. The popcorn pattern, the filet, the spider web, the pineapple and the pinwheel, the hairpin swirls—I had made them all. Once for a petticoat I had made nine yards of a star pattern better, I thought, than the one before me. Wondering what had become of those yards distracted me while desperately I tried to think how to get out of this without lying and without admitting that an American hadn't recognized American real lace. For it struck me (like lightning) that crochet *is* real lace, and beautiful.

That was forty years ago and I haven't yet seen in an American museum such a collection of the American lace as I saw that day in the Balkans. It is a human failing to be too farsighted. We don't really see what is under our noses.

Crochet is a young lace; its inspiration came from Ireland, and it is no older than the great exodus of people from Ireland to the New World in the 1840's. Here it became wholly American, as they did. It is entirely a new lace, the only lace that a maker does not hold by threads to paper or by pins to a weighted cushion; crochet is made "in the air." Its pattern is an intangible idea in the crocheter's mind, and she realizes that idea with a free thread and a hook moving freely; the tension of the thread is hers, the hook moves to her own rhythm.

The crochet stitch itself must be nearly as old as fingers, which seem mysteriously impelled to pull a loop through a loop. I say mysteriously, remembering how this impulse baffled the American Near East Relief workers who went into Caucasian Armenia after the 1914–1918 phase of this century's World War. Russian and Turkish armies had fought back and forth across that high plateau, driving the whole population south and north and south and north again. Every hut in every village was totally destroyed. In the ruins and in the miles of wild grasses the Americans found 25,000 orphaned children hiding, lost, sick, starving and dying. They were three to ten years old and knew nothing but hunger and fear. The Americans gathered them into the murdered Czar's abandoned army barracks, cleaned, deloused, fed, healed and saved most of them alive. But it was impossible to keep bandages on their sores. Untaught, and constantly admonished not to, they could not resist pulling ravelings from the gauze and with their tiny fingers looping them into crude Armenian lace.

With the same impulse, long before recorded history, Pima Indian women in America did the first crocheting we know. They were making a kind of cloth by pounding the inner bark of trees, but some bark, pounded, crumbled to dust and fibers. Fingers pulled loops through loops of these fibers, and some woman thought of making a bowl to hold water. The loops made a sort of basket; she plastered it thickly with clay, inside and out. Sure enough, it held water. Placed too near a fire, it did not burn; when she boldly set the pot into the fire, the water boiled.

That was the beginning of crocheting, and of soups and stews and pot roasts; in the far future it led to stainless-steel double boilers and pressure cookers. Long ago those first crude pots were broken and the fibers rotted away, but their imprints remain on shards of burned clay and they are prints of single-crochet stitches. Some woman dropped a stitch at intervals and made the first crochet patterns.

The Europeans who invaded this continent centuries later had small interest in Indians, and their own forgotten ancestors had invented the potter's wheel for making pots, so colonial women knew nothing of crocheting. Martha Washington never heard of it. Dolly Madison never heard of it. Jessie Benton Frémont knew nothing of it when her husband, commanding the western army of the United States, issued the Emancipation Proclamation freeing the slaves in the West and President Lincoln annulled it and disgraced him. You and I might never have seen crocheting if Spaniards had not discovered potatoes in America or if "working classes" in Europe had had enough to eat.

Oh, by and large, in good times, usually most of them had bread and wine or ale, in summer some vegetables, but when a crop failed they died in a famine, of course, as they still do in Asia and Africa.

The discovery of tobacco, corn and potatoes in the Americas interested the upper classes. No European could think of sweet corn as food for human beings, but foppish young courtiers took to the fad of smoking, court ladies wore potato blossoms in their hair, and thinkers welcomed potatoes as food for working classes. Those classes obstinately would not eat them. Eventually, on the Continent, their betters acquired a taste for the vegetable and potatoes were reserved, by law, to the wellborn. Then the lowborn began to steal potatoes from the forbidden fields, by night, and secretly consume them.

After some two hundred years, potatoes were a staple food of the poor in Britain. To the Irish they were the staff of life. Nine months of the year they ate potatoes; they suffered from hunger only during the three "meal months," when they had eaten the last old potato, the new ones were not yet large enough to eat, and peasants survived as best they could on scanty porridge of ground grain.

During the 1840's, the years of American pioneers in California, in Ireland the potato crops failed in two successive years. A fungus infected the fields; the plants withered and died. There was famine. The whole year was "meal months."

Now the British government acted. They bought up large quantities of grain and stored it, keeping it off the market as a threat to prevent grain dealers from raising prices. Still the Irish starved; they could not buy, at any price, grain enough to keep them alive. The British government appointed experts to study the problem.

Next year again the potatoes rotted, and now the Government took measures to prevent the starving people from fatally eating them. Whoever, by any sacrifice, could get steerage passage to America, fled from Ireland to this fabulous land where work could earn food, even some shillings to send home. By tens of thousands they came, penniless, gaunt from hunger.

No statue in New York harbor was welcoming them then. But these States were truly saying to the Old World, "Keep, ancient lands, your storied pomp. Give me your tired, your poor, your huddled masses yearning to breathe free, the wretched refuse of your teeming shore." America then was truly the "Mother of exiles." And these were the starving poor, the Old World's "wretched refuse" who one day would give a charming Princess to Europe and speak to the world from the White House.

Now in Ireland came the "famine fever," the wholesale death that nobody then knew was typhus, carried by the lice that swarmed impartially on all classes from beggar to noble. The "famine fever" was usual in famines, and famines never had been unusual. The Irish were dying by hundreds, by thousands; entire villages perished; the island was being depopulated. Volunteers came from the English gentry to save the Irish peasantry, and in Cork Miss Susanna

1. *Spider web pattern as an apron trimming.* [STAMFORD HISTORICAL SOCIETY, INC., STAMFORD, CONN.]

2. *Hairpin lace.* [LAURA INGALLS WILDER HOME MUSEUM, MANSFIELD, MO.]

3. [WITTE MUSEUM, SAN ANTONIO, TEX.]
4. [WITTE MUSEUM]

5. *Spider web used as a pillow edging.* [STAMFORD HISTORICAL SOCIETY, INC.]

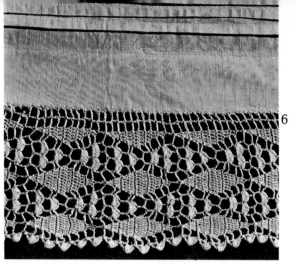

6. [FENIMORE HOUSE, COOPERSTOWN, N.Y.]

7. *One of a pair of cuffs made and worn by the writer's grandmother, Caroline Quiner Ingalls, about 1870.*

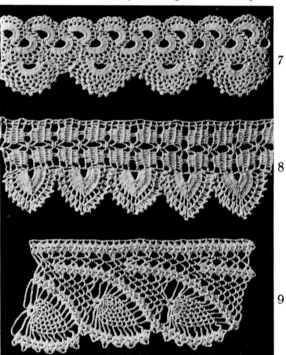

8. [WITTE MUSEUM]
9. *Pineapple.* [WITTE MUSEUM]
10. [PRIVATE COLLECTION]
11. *Popcorn stitch.* [LAURA INGALLS WILDER HOME MUSEUM]
12. [PRIVATE COLLECTION]

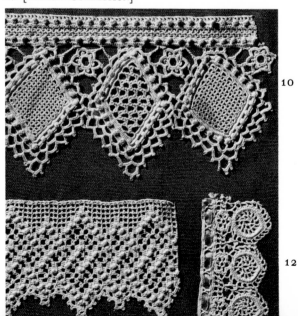

Meredith opened a school of crocheting.

The idea came from a convent in Cork, where the nuns were making crocheted lace and selling it for famine relief. In a year they had thus earned nearly $450. With tiny hooks they were making imitation Venetian rose point. Perhaps a sister from Italy or Austria had thought of this, or perhaps one from Scotland, for shepherds in the Highlands were using small wooden "shepherds' crooks" to crochet woolen *rugges* to wrap them warm in cold weather.

Whoever had thought of the idea, or of the tiny hook, the sisters were using little hooks and cotton thread to imitate old Italian laces, and these copies we now call "Irish crochet." Each rose and leaf and little motif is made separately, then with chain stitch it is crocheted to its place in the pattern.

This is the slowest method that an American crocheter knows. Few of us have patience for it, but it is much faster than lacemaking with threaded needle or bobbins. And haste was needed because lace could be sold for money and people were dying for lack of food that money would buy.

Susanna Meredith's idea spread rapidly. Many kind ladies began teaching the poor Irish women to crochet, and selling the laces in England for famine relief. Queen Victoria graciously accepted a gift of these laces, and

Filet crochet with a heart design. [PENNSYLVANIA FARM MUSEUM OF LANDIS VALLEY, LANCASTER, PA.]

instantly they were the latest vogue in highest society.

Literally for their children's lives, Irish women crocheted, while countesses, duchesses, princesses could hardly wait for new gowns trimmed with crocheted rose point. Queen Victoria herself learned to crochet, and a comfort it was to her in her later widowed years.

The new vogue spread on the Continent. Crochet was the latest thing in all the courts of Europe. Collectors bought the new laces; courtiers curried favors with gifts of them to coquettish ladies and to royalty.

Meanwhile from Boston to New Orleans housewives washed the dinner dishes and redded the kitchen, changed to their white afternoon aprons and settled down luxuriously at last to open the new *Godey's Lady's Book*, only to postpone reading the serial while they studied a crochet pattern.

Nobody ever was ahead of Mrs. Sarah Josepha Hale, the lady editor who was a lady and no shocking crusader for Woman's Rights, but who saw to it that President Lincoln established Thanksgiving as her country's unique festival. Sarah Josepha Hale herself managed *Godey's Lady's Book*, the pioneer magazine for women, first of all the American women's magazines that have followed it ever since. Sarah Josepha Hale disapproved of war; she would publish *Godey's Lady's Book* steadily month after month through the years of the War between the States without one reference to slavery, to States' rights, or to the war. But Sarah Josepha Hale was first to print, for her readers, the patterns of the very newest laces.

A year later in England Mrs. Eliza Warren, with Royal patronage, published the first book of crochet patterns: *The Court Crochet and Edging Book*, dedicated by permission to Her Majesty, Queen Victoria, of the United Kingdom of Great Britain and Ireland, and Empress of India. For this notable work Mrs. Warren had chosen Mechlin,

Crochet—a century-old adornment on household linens.

Pinwheel luncheon cloth with a pointed edging. [VALENTINE MUSEUM, RICHMOND, VA.]

Elaborate edging on a dinner cloth, on loan to the Laura Ingalls Wilder Home Museum.

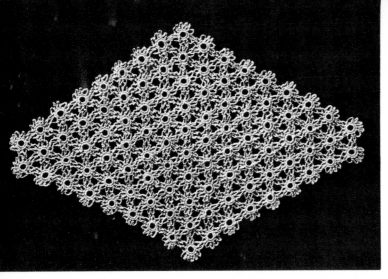

Circle motifs joined in a diamond shape. [STAMFORD HISTORICAL SOCIETY, INC.]

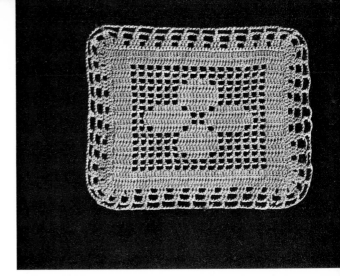

Filet crochet, made about 1840. [VALENTINE MUSEUM]

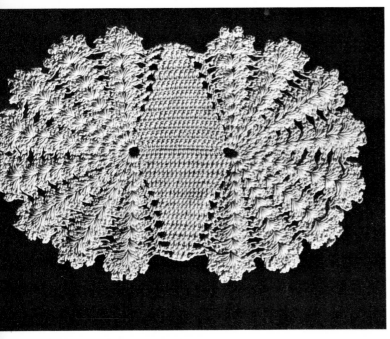

Heavy oval mat for a hot-dish pad. Crocheted about 1900. [FENIMORE HOUSE]

12" round doily, made about 1875. [WADSWORTH ATHENEUM]

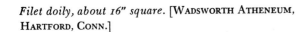

Filet doily, about 16" square. [WADSWORTH ATHENEUM, HARTFORD, CONN.]

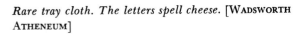

Rare tray cloth. The letters spell cheese. [WADSWORTH ATHENEUM]

Bedspread, a gift from Mrs. H. H. Thomas of Kilgore, Texas to Mr. and Mrs. Henry Ford. [NOW IN HENRY FORD MUSEUM, DEARBORN, MICH.]

Flemish, Venetian and Hungarian designs, and one made in honor of Jenny Lind, the Swedish Nightingale, whose sweet voice brought tears to listeners' eyes from New York to San Francisco and made a fortune for the shrewd Connecticut Yankee, P. T. Barnum. All these designs were in "Irish crochet," copying the old laces.

For two hundred years women in America had known the European methods of mak-ing laces and had done nothing much with them. They had been making patchwork and hooking rugs. Now they took to crocheting as ducklings take to swimming. The little hook making patterns in air was to them (and is to us) what many bobbins weaving to pattern on a weighted cushion were to lacemakers in Europe. Each method suited the worker's spirit. Europeans lived tradi-tionally in the social order of their social classes; Americans in a primeval wilderness, if they lived, had to live creatively and self-reliantly: freely. They were living in a new way, and they did not long copy old laces.

The crochet stitch is simple; the little hook is free and swift. With it in one hand and the thread running to it between fingers of the other hand, spontaneously they began to create a new lace.

Without Royal or any other patronage, unnoticed anywhere but in the backs of women's magazines, they made it. Nobody knows who they were. Who knows who we crocheters are, now? While the county fairs were small, and local, and really fairs, crocheters competed for prizes in them. When for a little while early in this century the thread manufacturers published booklets of good crochet designs, thousands of original ones were offered to them from everywhere in these states. For a century American women have been creating one of the world's beautiful laces, and still are creating it.

Out of the air they catch the thread and in the air they make a drawn-work pattern; women have gone blind working such patterns in warp threads with a needle. "In the air" crocheters fashion leaves and flowers and a web of net, airy and graceful as needlepoint laces and with a new quality. The Lemon Star, the Prince's Feathers, the Persian Pineapple old in history and young again in American patchwork are younger still in American lace; the pinwheel has countless variations in crochet, and there is no end to uses of the spider web. Every imaginable cross-stitch pattern is daintily airy in filet crochet. The popcorn stitch carves a design in three dimensions, rich and heavy; simple loops of chain stitch ruffle more lightly than Valenciennes.

All these, and more, are done easily with the little hook and nimble fingers while the lacemaker watches television. How she does this I don't know; I have no television set.

But the other day a woman told me that she does. Fingers do learn a pattern. Once I made nearly all the motifs of a bedspread while I read *Gone with the Wind*.

Of course crocheting isn't limited to lace. It repeats the patterns of weaving in coverlets and tablecloths and rugs, and the mosaics of Arabia and Persia in afghans and in place mats. With angora yarn it makes a furry bonnet for the baby; with wools it makes cosy mufflers and mittens and stocking caps; with *corde* or ribbon it makes chic hats; and if you string beads on thread, it makes a jewel of an evening purse. There's little that American women have *not* done with a crochet hook.

But the true art of crochet is the American lace. Here is a simple, primitive method. Here is the least of materials, nothing but a thread and a hook. And the whole range of human imagination, of individual creativeness, working freely in a rhythm as natural as dancing or singing, makes this new lace in the air.

Someday collectors will value American laces as now they value the laces of fifteenth-century Italy, and they will say: "The revolutionary spirit of the New World is in this lace. It follows no tradition; it is true only to eternal principles of mathematics and art. Each piece of it has its own individual character. Patterns were repeated, but the tension of the thread, the rhythm of the stitches, the effect of the whole, shows you the personality of the unknown maker."

They will say: "In that twentieth century all Americans were rich; there were no American classes. Laces were in every home; no lower classes wore their lives away making laces for superior classes. Those Americans were free people, imaginative, creative, and daring; they liked swiftness and change. American lace alone shows you that they were the people who would develop the clipper ships and the ocean steamers and the airplanes."

Popcorn bedspread inspired by the Le Moyne Star, made in blocks and crocheted together with an openwork stitch. Nineteenth century. [BROOKLYN MUSEUM, BROOKLYN, N.Y.]

How to Crochet

Crochet derives its name from the French word for little hook. Crochet hooks come in a wide range of sizes and lengths and are made of various materials. Steel crochet hooks are generally used for cotton thread and come in sizes 00, the largest, through 16, the smallest. Bone hooks are generally used for wool yarn and come in sizes 1, the smallest, through 6, the largest. Aluminum and plastic hooks, used for wool yarn and cotton thread, are sized in varying ways by different manufacturers. Some size them by letter, some by number, and others by both letter and number. Aluminum hooks usually come in sizes A through K, size A being the smallest; plastic hooks come in sizes 1 through 10½, size 1 being the smallest. Wooden rug hooks are made in large sizes only. Afghan hooks are manufactured especially for afghan stitch. They are about the length of knitting needles, either 9" or 14" long, and come in the same sizes as other crochet hooks.

CROCHET THREADS

There are many variations in weight, twist, finish, and color of crochet threads. The fine mercerized cotton threads are effective for delicate designs used in edgings, doilies, and tablecloths, while wool yarns are best for afghans, baby garments, sweaters, and other wearing apparel. The heaviest cotton, wool, and jute yarns are used for rugs. Buy all the thread or yarn you need at one time to be sure of having the same dye lot. Slight variations in weight and color can ruin the appearance of your work.

GAUGE

It is important that you crochet to the gauge specified so that your finished article will be the correct size. Gauge means number of stitches and rows to a 1" square. Make a practice piece at least 2" square, using the hook and materials specified in the directions. With a ruler, measure the number of stitches you have to 1", as in Diagram 1.

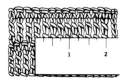

1

If your stitches do not correspond to the gauge given, experiment with a different size hook. If you have more stitches than specified to the inch, use a larger hook; if you have fewer stitches, use a smaller hook. Keep changing the size hook until your gauge is the same as that specified.

ABBREVIATIONS AND TERMS

beg	beginning
bl	block
ch	chain
dc	double crochet
dec	decrease
d tr	double treble
h dc	half double crochet
inc	increase
incl	inclusive
O	thread over
rnd	round
sc	single crochet
sk	skip
sl	slip
sl st	slip stitch
sp	space
st	stitch
sts	stitches
tr	treble
tr tr	triple treble

*—*Asterisk*—means repeat the instructions following the asterisk as many times as specified, in addition to the first time.

[ ]—*Brackets*—are used to designate changes in size when directions are given, as they often are, for more than one size. The figure preceding the brackets refers to the smallest size.

Even: When directions say "work even," this means to continue working without increasing or decreasing.

Multiple of Stitches: A pattern often requires an exact number of stitches to be worked correctly. When directions say "multiple of," it means the number of stitches must be divisible by this number. For example: (Multiple of 6) would be 12, 18, 24, etc.; (multiple of 6 plus 3) would be 15, 21, 27, etc.

( )—*Parentheses*—mean repeat instructions in parentheses as many times as specified. For example: "(Ch 5, sc in next sc) 5 times" means to make all that is in parentheses a total of 5 times.

TO BEGIN CROCHET

Make a practice piece of each new stitch and work until you are familiar with it. To practice, use medium-weight thread (a little heavier than bedspread cotton) and a No. 4 steel crochet hook.

The First Loop

1. Make a loop at the end of thread and hold loop in place with thumb and forefinger of left hand (*Diagram 2*). At left is short end of thread; at right is the long or working thread.

2

2. With right hand, grasp the crochet hook as you would a pencil and put hook through loop, catch working thread and draw it through (*Diagram 3*).

3. Pull short end and working thread in opposite directions to bring loop close around the end of hook (*Diagram 4*).

To Hold Thread

1. Measure down working thread about 4″ from loop on hook.

2. At this point, insert thread between ring finger and little finger of left hand (*Diagram 5*).

3. Weave thread toward back, under little and ring fingers, over middle finger, and under forefinger toward you (*Diagram 6*).

4. Grasp hook and loop with thumb and forefinger of left hand.

5. Gently pull working thread so that it is taut but not tight (*Diagram 7*).

To Hold Hook

Hold hook as you would a pencil but bring middle finger forward to rest near tip of hook (*Diagram 8*).

In order to begin working, adjust fingers of left hand as in *Diagram 9*.

The middle finger is bent so it can control the tension, while the ring and little fingers prevent the thread from moving too freely. As you practice, you will become familiar with the correct tension. Now you are ready to begin the chain stitch.

CHAIN STITCH (CH)

1. Pass hook under thread and catch thread with hook. This is called thread over—O (*Diagram 10*).

2. Draw thread through loop on hook. This makes one chain (*Diagram 11*).

3. Repeat steps 1 and 2 until you have as many chain stitches as you need. One loop always remains on hook. Keep thumb and forefinger of your left hand near stitch on which you are working. Practice making chains until they are uniform (*Diagram 12*).

THE BASIC STITCHES
SINGLE CROCHET (SC)

Make a foundation chain of 20 stitches for practice piece.

1. Insert hook from the front under 2 top threads of 2nd chain from hook (*Diagram 13*).

2. Thread over hook (*Diagram 14*).

3. Draw through stitch. There are now 2 loops on hook (*Diagram 15*).

4. Thread over (*Diagram 16*). Draw through 2 loops on hook. One loop remains on hook. One single crochet now is completed (*Diagram 17*).

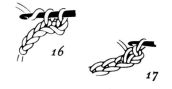

5. For next single crochet, insert hook under 2 top threads of next stitch (*Diagram 18*). Repeat steps 2, 3, and 4. Repeat until you have made a single crochet in each chain.

6. At end of row of single crochet, chain 1 (*Diagram 19*).

7. Turn work so reverse side is facing you (*Diagram 20*).

8. Insert hook under 2 top threads of first single crochet. Repeat steps 2, 3, 4, 5, 6, and 7. Continue working single crochet in this manner until work is uniform and you feel familiar with the stitch. On last row do not make a turning chain. Clip thread about 3″ from work, bring loose end through the one remaining loop on hook, and pull tight (*Diagram 21*).

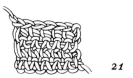

Now you have completed your practice piece of single crochet.

NOTE: In all crochet, pick up the 2 top threads of every stitch unless otherwise specified. When only one thread is picked up, a different effect is produced.

———

DOUBLE CROCHET (DC)
Make a foundation chain of 20 stitches for practice piece.
1. Thread over, insert hook under the 2 top threads of 4th chain from hook (*Diagram 22*).

2. Thread over, draw through stitch. There are now 3 loops on hook.
3. Thread over (*Diagram 23*). Draw through 2 loops. Two loops remain on hook.

4. Thread over again (*Diagram 24*).

Draw through the 2 remaining loops. One loop remains on hook. One double crochet now is completed (*Diagram 25*).

5. For next double crochet, thread over, insert hook under the 2 top threads of next stitch and repeat steps 2, 3, and 4. Repeat until you have made a double crochet in each stitch.
6. At end of row, chain 3 and turn work (*Diagram 26*).

7. On next row, thread over, skip first double crochet, insert hook under the 2 top threads of 2nd double crochet. Repeat steps 2, 3, 4, 5, 6, and 7 (*Diagram 27*).

8. Continue working double crochet in this manner until work is uniform and you feel familiar with the stitch. On last row, do not make a turning chain. Clip thread about 3″ from work, bring loose end through the one remaining loop on hook, and pull tight.

———

HALF DOUBLE CROCHET (H DC)
To make half double crochet, repeat steps 1 and 2 under Double Crochet but insert hook in 3rd chain from hook. At this point there are 3 loops on hook. Then thread over and draw through all 3 loops at once (*Diagram 28*).

Half double crochet now is completed. At end of row, chain 2 to turn.

———

TREBLE CROCHET (TR)
Make a foundation chain of 20 stitches for practice piece.
1. Thread over twice, insert hook under 2 top threads of 5th chain from hook.
2. Thread over and draw a loop through the chain. There are now 4 loops on hook.

3. Thread over again (*Diagram 29*).

Draw through 2 loops on hook (3 loops remain on hook).

29

4. Thread over again (*Diagram 30*).

Draw through 2 loops (2 loops remain on hook).

30

5. Thread over again (*Diagram 31*).

31

Draw through 2 remaining loops (one loop remains on hook). One treble crochet now is completed. At end of row, chain 4 to turn. Continue making treble crochet in this manner until you are familiar with the stitch. Finish piece same as other pieces.

———

DOUBLE TREBLE (D TR)

Thread over hook 3 times, insert hook under 2 top threads of 6th chain from hook and draw a loop through the chain (5 loops on hook). Thread over and draw through 2 loops at a time 4 times. A double treble now is completed (*Diagram 32*). At end of row, chain 5 to turn.

32

TRIPLE TREBLE (TR TR)

Thread over hook 4 times, insert hook under 2 top threads of 7th chain from hook and draw a loop through the chain (6 loops on hook). Thread over and draw through 2 loops at a time 5 times. A triple treble is now completed (*Diagram 33*). At end of row, chain 6 to turn.

33

———

BASIC TECHNIQUES
To Turn Work

You will notice that stitches vary in length. Each uses a different number of chain stitches to turn at the end of a row. Below is a table showing the number of chain stitches required to make a turn for each stitch.

Single crochet (sc) Ch 1 to turn
Half double crochet
   (h dc)   Ch 2 to turn
Double crochet (dc) Ch 3 to turn
Treble crochet (tr) Ch 4 to turn
Double treble (d tr) Ch 5 to turn
Triple treble (tr tr) Ch 6 to turn

To Decrease (DEC) Single Crochet

1. Work one single crochet to point where 2 loops are on hook. Draw up a loop in next stitch (*Diagram 34*).

34

2. Thread over, draw thread through 3 loops at one time. One decrease made (*Diagram 35*).

35

To Decrease (DEC) Double Crochet

1. Work one double crochet to point where 2 loops are on hook. Begin another double crochet in next stitch and work until 4 loops are on hook (*Diagram 36*).

36

2. Thread over, draw through 2 loops (*Diagram 37*).

37

3. Thread over, draw through 3 loops (*Diagram 38*). One decrease made.

38

———

To Increase (INC)

When directions call for an increase, work 2 stitches in one stitch. This forms one extra stitch.

———

SLIP STITCH (SL ST)

Make a foundation chain of 20 stitches for practice piece. Insert hook under top thread of 2nd chain from hook, thread over. With one motion draw through stitch and loop on hook. Insert hook under top thread of next chain, then thread over and draw through stitch and loop on hook (*Diagram 39*).

39

Repeat until you have made a slip stitch in each chain. A chain with slip stitch is often used for ties on bonnets, sacques, etc. Rows of slip stitch worked in the back loop of each stitch produce a ribbed effect.

Slip Stitch for Joining

When directions say "join," always use a slip stitch.

1. Insert hook through the 2 top threads of stitch (*Diagram 40*).

40

2. Thread over and with one motion draw through stitch and loop on hook (*Diagram 41*).

41

Working Around the Post

The "post" or "bar" is the vertical or upright section of a stitch. When directions say to make a stitch around the post or bar of a stitch in a previous row, insert the hook *around* stitch instead of in top of stitch. See *Diagram 42* for placement of hook.

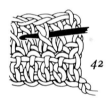

42

SPECIAL STITCHES

AFGHAN STITCH

This stitch requires a long hook in order to hold a number of stitches at one time. Though the name of the stitch implies it is used primarily for afghans, it is equally effective for crocheting sweaters, scarves, and other articles. Make a foundation chain of 20 stitches for practice piece.

1. Insert hook under 2 top threads of 2nd chain from hook; thread over and draw a loop through chain.

2. Retaining all loops on hook, draw up a loop in each remaining chain (*Diagram 43*).

43

3. When all loops are on hook, thread over, draw through one loop; thread over, draw through 2 loops.

4. Thread over, draw through next 2 loops (*Diagram 44*). Repeat this across row. The loop which remains on hook at end of row always counts as the first stitch of next row. Do not turn.

44

5. To begin 2nd and succeeding rows, insert hook in the front thread of the 2nd vertical bar (*Diagram 45*).

45

6. Draw up a loop. Retaining all loops on hook, draw up a loop in the front thread of each vertical bar across to within last vertical bar (*Diagram 46*).

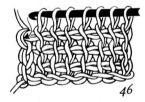

46

Insert hook in front thread of last vertical bar and the stitch directly behind it and draw up a loop. This gives a firm edge to this side.

7. Work off loops as in first row, drawing through one loop first and then through 2 loops across row. On last row of work, make a slip stitch in each vertical bar to keep edge from curling.

To Increase Afghan Stitch: To increase one stitch, draw up a loop in chain between vertical bars.

To Decrease Afghan Stitch: To decrease one stitch, insert hook under 2 vertical bars and draw up one loop.

Cross-Stitch Over Afghan Stitch: Because afghan stitch forms almost perfect squares, when an article is completed it is often embroidered with cross-stitch (*Diagram 47*).

47

BASIC SHELL STITCH

This is one of the many varieties of shell stitch. Once you have learned this basic stitch, you'll find directions for the others easy to follow. Make a foundation chain (multiple of 6 stitches plus 4) for practice piece.

1st row: Work 2 dc in 4th ch from hook (half shell), skip 2 ch, sc in next ch, * skip 2 ch, 5 dc in next ch (shell made), skip 2 ch, sc in next ch. Repeat from * across, ending with 3 dc in last ch (another half shell). Ch 1, turn.

2nd row: Sc in first dc, * skip 2 dc, shell (5 dc) in next sc, skip 2 dc, sc in center dc of next shell. Repeat from * across, ending with sc in top of half shell. Ch 3, turn.

3rd row: Work 2 dc in first sc, * sc in center dc of next shell, shell in next sc. Repeat from * across, ending with 3 dc in last sc. Ch 1, turn. Repeat 2nd and 3rd rows for desired length (*Diagram 48*).

48

KNOT STITCH

Make a foundation chain of 20 stitches (multiple of 5 sts) for practice piece.

1st row: Draw up a long loop (about ¾"), O (*Diagram 49*), draw this loop through long loop; insert hook between long loop and single strand (*Diagram 50*), O, and draw loop through, O (*Diagram 51*) and draw loop through 2 loops on hook (single knot st made). Draw up a long loop, O (*Diagram 52*), draw this loop through long loop; insert hook between long loop and single strand, O, and draw loop through, O, and draw loop through 2 loops on hook (double knot st made). Skip 4 ch, sc in next ch; * work double knot st, skip 4 ch; sc in next ch. Repeat from * across, ending sc in last ch. Make 1 double and 1 single knot st to turn.

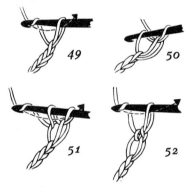

2nd row: * Sc over 2 top strands of first loop of double knot st of previous row (to right of knot), sc over next 2 top strands of 2nd loop of double knot st (to left of same knot), make a double knot st. Repeat from * across, ending sc on each side of last double knot st. Make 1 double and 1 single knot st to turn. Repeat 2nd row for desired length (*Diagram 53*).

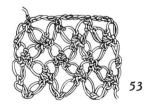

STAR STITCH

Make a foundation chain of 19 stitches (uneven number) for practice piece.

1st row: Draw up a loop in 2nd ch from hook, draw up a loop in next 3 ch (5 loops on hook), O, draw through all loops on hook (*Diagram 54*); ch 1 to form eye (one star st made), * draw up a loop in eye of star st just completed, in back of last loop of same star st and in next 2 ch (*Diagram 55*); O, draw through all 5 loops on hook, ch 1 for eye (another star st made). Repeat from * across. Turn.

2nd row: Work 2 sc in eye of each star st across to last star st, sc in eye of last star st, sc in first ch of foundation chain. Ch 3, turn.

3rd row: Draw up a loop in 2nd and 3rd ch from hook and in first and 2nd sc, O, draw through all 5 loops on hook, ch 1 for eye, * draw up a loop in eye of last st, in back loop of same st and in next 2 sc; O, draw through all 5 loops on hook, ch 1 for eye. Repeat from * across. Turn.

4th row: Work 2 sc in eye of each star st across to last star st, sc in eye of last star st, sc in first ch of turning chain. Ch 3, turn. Repeat 3rd and 4th rows for desired length.

FINISHING

Fastening Ends. After you have completed an article, thread each loose end of thread or yarn in a needle and darn it through a solid part of the crochet to fasten it securely. Cut off remaining thread close to the work. Be sure starting ends are long enough to be fastened off.

LAUNDERING

If your work has become soiled, wash it by hand before blocking. Launder cotton-thread work in thick suds of a mild soap and hot water; wash woolens in cold-water soap or mild soap and lukewarm water. Squeeze but do not wring the article. Rinse in lukewarm water several times until soap is thoroughly removed. Roll in a bath towel to absorb some of the moisture.

BLOCKING

If an article is made up of several pieces, block them before sewing together. If you have laundered your work, block it while still damp. Place article wrong side up on a flat, padded surface. Gently stretch and shape it to the desired measurements; pin to surface, using rustproof pins. Press through a dry cloth with a hot iron, being careful not to let the weight of the iron rest on the article. Let dry thoroughly before unpinning. If you have not had to launder your work, pin the dry article on a padded surface; press through a damp cloth.

SEWING

Pin together edges to be sewed, matching any pattern in rows or stitches. Thread needle with matching thread or yarn. To begin sewing, do not knot thread but take several over and over stitches, darning them, if possible, through a solid part of the crochet. Sew straight even edges with a whipped stitch, placing it at edges of the work. Sew slanting or uneven edges, caused by increasing or decreasing, with a backstitch, placing it just inside edges of work. On woolen articles leave stitches loose enough to match elasticity of garment. When sewing is completed, press seams on the wrong side and give article a light final blocking.

Directions for Five-Panel Afghan

SIZE
About 47″ x 66″.

MATERIALS
Knitting worsted, 11 ounces black (A), 3 white (B), 13 light blue (C), 2 gold (D), 10 red (E), 28 wine (F); plastic afghan hook size H or 8; steel crochet hook No. 1.

GAUGE
For striped panel, 4 sts = 1″; 4 rows = 1″. For plain panel, 5 sts = 1″; 5 rows = 1″.

STRIPED PANEL
(Make 2): Starting at narrow end with color A and afghan hook, ch 41. *1st row:* Retaining all loops on hook, O, draw up a loop in 2nd ch from hook, * O, draw up a loop in next ch. Repeat from * across. Work off loops as follows: O, draw yarn through 2 loops on hook, * O, draw yarn through 3 loops on hook. Repeat from * until 2 loops remain on hook, O, draw yarn through last 2 loops (this one loop remaining on hook is first st of next row). *2nd row:* Retaining all loops on hook, skip first vertical bar, * O, draw up a loop between next 2 vertical bars (below chain). Repeat from * across, ending with O, draw up a loop in last st. Work off loops as for first row. Repeat 2nd row for pattern and work colors as follows: Work 7 rows A, * 1 B, 1 C, 1 D, 1 E, 1 C, 1 E, 1 B (7 stripes made), 18 A, work 7 stripes as before, 18 C, work 7 stripes, 18 E. Repeat from * twice more; work 7 stripes, 18 A, work 7 stripes, 18 C, work 7 stripes, 7 A. Break off.

PLAIN PANEL
(Make 3): Starting at narrow end with color F and crochet hook No. 1, ch 43. *1st row:* Dc in 4th ch from hook and in each ch across. Ch 3, turn. *2nd row (right side):* Skip first dc, dc around post of next dc, * dc in next dc, dc around post of next dc. Repeat from * across, ending dc in ch-3. Ch 1, turn. *3rd row:* Skip first dc, sc in each dc across, sc in ch-3. Ch 3, turn. *4th row:* Skip first sc, dc in next sc, * dc around post of next dc 2 rows below, skip the sc behind the dc just made, dc in next sc. Repeat from * across, ending dc around post of last dc 2 rows below. Ch 1, turn. *5th row:* Repeat 3rd row. *6th row:* Skip first sc, dc around post of next dc 2 rows below, skip the sc behind the dc just made, * dc in next sc, dc around post of next dc 2 rows below, skip the sc behind the dc just made. Repeat from * across, ending dc in ch-1. Repeat 3rd through 6th rows for pattern. Work even in pattern until piece measures same length as striped panels. Break off.

ROPE JOINING
Hold long edge of one plain and one striped panel together, wrong sides touching. Attach 1 strand A and 1 strand D at end of strip, draw up loop through first row of each panel, using D and steel crochet hook, ch 6, remove hook, bring chain to front of work, insert hook into A loop, ch 5, skip 1 row, sc into next row, * ch 6, remove hook, bring chain to front of work, insert hook in last A ch, skip 1 row, sc into next row, ch 6, remove hook, bring chain to front, insert hook into D loop. Repeat from * to end of panels. Join all panels in this manner, alternating plain and striped panels and having end panels plain.

EDGING
Note: Draw up ¾″ loops for dc sts. *1st row:* With right side facing, attach F to any corner of afghan. Using steel crochet hook, ch 3, work 8 dc into corner st, * skip ½″ along edge, sc in edge, skip ½″ of edge, work 9 dc in edge. Repeat from * around, working 9 dc in each corner and ending with sc, skip ½″ of edge. Join with sl st to 3rd ch of ch-3. *2nd row:* Sl st in next 3 sts, * sc in next dc, ch 3, retaining the last loop of each dc on hook, dc in next 9 sts, O, draw yarn through all 10 loops on hook, ch 4. Repeat from * around. Sl st to first sc. *3rd row:* Work 6 dc in same place as sl st, * sc in first ch of ch-4, work 6 dc in next sc. Repeat from * around, ending with sc in first ch of last ch-4. Sl st to first dc of 6-dc group. *4th row:* Ch 4, * sl st in next st, ch 4. Repeat from * around, ending with sl st in first ch of ch-4. Break off.

Afghan in five panels, joined with a crocheted rope stitch. [Laura Ingalls Wilder Home Museum]

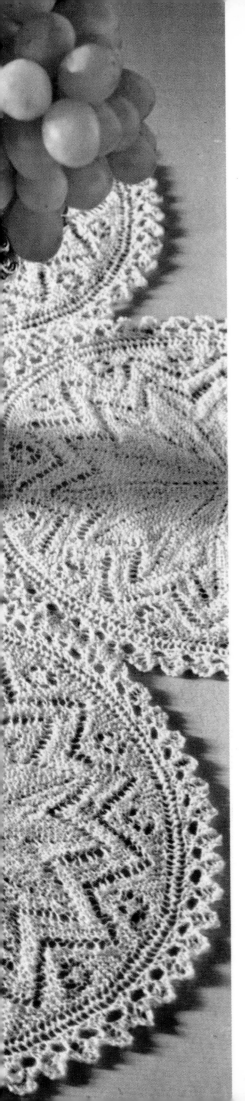

Knitting

Lace centerpiece from luncheon set knitted about 1890. [LAURA INGALLS WILDER HOME MUSEUM, MANSFIELD, MO.]

MONG AMERICAN
needle crafts, knitting is a naturalized immigrant; it came to America with the first colonists; it has been flourishing here ever since then, and Americans have changed it very little because it is both too simple and too old to change.

The knitting stitch is nothing but a loop pulled through a loop. Children's fingers do it with a bit of string; probably some idle sailor invented knitting that way. Yet this simple loop makes an endless variety of fabrics in countless textures and patterns, and everything you can think of, from bulky sweaters to babies' caps, from cozy afghans to filmy laces.

Thousands of knitters had made them all, long before the lookout on Columbus's flagship sighted land in the Western Ocean. If you have a piece of plain knitting on your needles today you are copying a piece that Egyptians laid in a tomb six thousand years ago, when they packed it with things that a soul would need on its journey to judgment and beyond.

Nobody knows how that Egyptian knitter held the wool, but if your right forefinger loops the yarn over the needle's point, you are using the English method. On the Continent, knitters hold the yarn over the left forefinger, as crocheters do; then the needle in the right hand picks up the yarn through the loop. Or they let the yarn run from a ball in the apron's pocket through a safety pin on the apron bib and hold only the needles in their hands. In the Balkans the yarn runs up from the pocket, around the knitter's neck, and down to the grabbing needles. From the English Channel to the Black Sea women are knitting at this minute, swiftly, beautifully, in a way that (to me) is upside down.

Americans are knitting in all these ways. The method makes no difference; the result is always the same simple loop through loop. In thousands of years ingenuity has done almost everything that can be done with this stitch; many expert knitters don't know the half of it. It would take a book to describe the twists and crossings, combinations and skippings of this one stitch and its reverse, the purled stitch; indeed, many books. Fortunately they have been written. They are waiting for you in your public library, and if you don't yet know them, they will surprise you.

Let me warn you that a genuine interest in knitting can keep you fascinated, eagerly pursuing it and never satisfied, through a lifetime. If a woman knew all there is to know about knitting there would be little under the sun that she didn't know.

My grandmother taught me to knit when I was five years old and I have been knitting, off and on, for more than seventy years. I thought I knew something about knitting.

Do you know that it is Arabic? I didn't. Ancient Arab traders, knitting as they sat on the little donkeys leading the long, slow, bell-chiming caravans of loaded camels, took the craft east across India and far west to Egypt, where one may have taught it to the knitter of that piece found in the tomb.

From then until little longer than a century ago, knitting was man's work. Of course! you say. But I had never thought of that. Of course, knitting was a skilled trade. Since Adam left Eden, knitting and weaving were the only ways of making cloth and the two crafts were equally efficient until power looms began to weave, in the nineteenth century.

The fact lends plausibility to the legend that the Roman soldiers cast lots for Christ's seamless garment because it was knitted. They could not divide it without raveling and destroying it.

From an enthralling little book picturing every way of knitting every combination of stitches, *Mary Thomas's Knitting Book*, I learn that while the Pilgrim Fathers were in Holland, apprentices were serving six years to learn knitting. The ambitious boy spent three years serving and learning in his master's shop, then three years traveling to study methods in foreign shops and to see the latest styles in design. Then (as a scholar today earns his Ph.D. degree) in thirteen weeks he must make his Master pieces.

Typically, these were:

1. A carpet about five feet square, of his own design, composed of flowers, foliage, birds and animals, all in their natural colors.
2. A beret.
3. A woolen shirt.
4. A pair of hose with Spanish clocks (or, sometimes, "in the English style").

To do all that knitting in thirteen weeks, or in even less time when he was required also to felt his work, I think would daunt the swiftest knitter of Argyle socks. (Argyle socks doubtless come from Scotland, as afghans come from Afghanistan.) But when the young man had done all this knitting, and when the Masters of his master's Knitting Guild had examined it, and had approved it, then he was one of them: a Master Knitter.

For centuries in their craft monopolies chartered and enforced by their Kings or Princes the diligent European knitters made those carpets, large and small, as intricately patterned and colored as Oriental rugs. They stranded the colored yarns along the back of the work, and they must have enjoyed it. As every woman who has done it knows, knitting colors into your own design, watching it grow, is a pleasure more than worth the bother of keeping all those yarns from tangling as badly as they try to.

Then silk returned to Europe, a marvel rarely seen there for a thousand years, a sensation in the workshops. Traders were bringing it again from the legendary East in years-long voyages over perilous seas, far around Africa. This was a cargo to make men's fortunes; it was a precious rarity not to be touched by an apprentice. The Master Knitters used it reverently. Clinging to the skillful fingers, its stranded threads knitted into richly patterned, richly colored, shimmering stuffs glinting with spun gold. This was a fabric fit for the kings who wore it.

So in a winter morning of 1649—January 30, it was—axes rang frostily in the woods along Charles River, and Puritans muffled in dark homespun trudged through the snow in Charles' Town, the settlement at Boston Harbor in Massachusetts Bay Colony. In London the time was two hours after noon, and splendid in silk knitted by a Master, King Charles stood on a scaffold.

Within a broad wall of guards his enemies courteously attended him; beyond the guards, too far to hear him speak, a close-packed crowd of thousands stood silent, gazing. To those around him the doomed Monarch spoke his last words.

No man desired the liberty and freedom of his people more truly than he, he said. "But I must tell you that their liberty consists in having government. It is not their having a share in government; that is nothing appertaining unto them. A subject and his sovereign are clean different things."

He knelt and laid his neck on the block. The ax fell. "At the instant whereof . . . ," said a witness later, "there was such a groan from the thousands then present as I never heard before and desire . . . never to hear again."

Ships sailing down the Thames took many weeks to bring to the settlers in New England the incredible news that their fellow subjects in England had killed their King. Fly overnight to England now for a holiday, and you can see in London Museum the marvelously knitted silken shirt that he wore that day.

These intricately colored patterns must be done in plain knitting—knit across and purl back—to give each colored stitch its due value. So this use of colors is the easiest way to knit your own original designs. You can knit any colored pattern you please, if you dot its colors into the squares of graph paper. You can adapt any cross-stitch or needlepoint pattern. All knitters enjoy knitting, but one who hasn't watched her own colored design growing from her needles hasn't had all the joy of the craft.

Of course the effect depends on the yarn you use and the size of the needles. Carpet yarns and wooden needles made a handsome rug, silk threads and fine needles an entrancing stole. Once I reveled in knitting a bed jacket of white angora straight across (except for widening and narrowing) from snug cuff through flowered full sleeve to flowered sleeve and snug cuff, a slit in the middle for the neck. (Must bed jackets waste their warmth on a pillow and keep trying to leave our chests bare?) I dreamed up the flowers as I went; colors were luscious under the misty rabbit-fur yarn.

Naturally mere women (though some were Queens) could never be admitted to the craftsmen's guilds, but I suspect that privately we always have knitted. It's a matter of record that Mistress Lee, who lived in Calverton, England, four hundred years ago,

Knitted Laces. [BELOW: WITTE MUSEUM, SAN ANTONIO, TEX. RIGHT: STAMFORD HISTORICAL SOCIETY, INC., STAMFORD, CONN.]

Bedspread in shell design with fringed edging (tester is netted). [NEWARK MUSEUM, NEWARK, N.J.]

kept her needles flying to help support her family. She knitted goodness knows how many pairs of stockings; and it is believed that her husband William helpfully invented the first knitting machine so that she could make more, faster.

Certainly he invented it, in 1589; I'm not saying why. The rumor that Scots invented one earlier is only a rumor, though Scots have always been renowned for their beautiful knitted laces.

Perhaps from them came that wondrous

gift to Queen Elizabeth, which no other Queen (nor King) had ever dreamed of: a pair of *silk* stockings. Only genius could have thought of such a gift. When Her Majesty superbly trod on silk, hidden of course by yards and yards of royal robes, but well known for all of that, her bowing courtiers must have felt unusual awe, and their ladies a pang of envy. In no time they were buying silk stockings, extravagantly.

It would be nearly four hundred years before knitting machines made silk stockings

so cheap that, in these states, working girls wore them. I remember my first pair of silk stockings as vividly as my first nervously brave use of a telephone. But when my mother was a girl, American women were wearing something that few of us could afford today: hand-knitted lace stockings.

They were beautiful things, sheer lace knitted of finest white thread (sometimes silk) on the tiniest steel needles, with snug garter tops and finely knitted plain soles. Knitted round and round, they were seamless and their elasticity fitted a leg as perfectly as its skin. Though of course they never were seen in public, often their lace pattern matched that of the knitted lace mitts (without fingertips) which were.

Whether of silk or the more usual cotton, these lace stockings and mitts were "for best" —for Sundays and parties and brides. Everyday stockings were plain knitted, and fingers made them without thought; a woman glanced from her book only to change needles. Plain knitting was a woman's second nature because all little girls learned it, often before they learned to read.

In our country knitting always has been women's work. The Guilds could not thrive here; they were communes and the early Americans were too poor to survive in them. They brought communes with them from feudal Europe, but both in Virginia and in Plymouth Colony they died until they abolished them.

In those days a man used all his energy in fighting the sea or the forest for his family's food, while his wife spent hers in cooking and preserving it, and in making soap, thread, yarn, cloth; she rested while she knitted and rocked the cradle with her foot. Safe on a low stool beside her, the small daughter "knitted" with bare wooden needles until Mother trusted her with a length of thread and showed her how to "cast on."

She was a plain knitter before (when her father could spare a shilling) she went to Dame School to learn her letters, Bible lessons, deportment, and a lady's "plain sewing and fancywork." There she did the knitting patterns, raveling out every mistake and doing the work again until it was perfect. Finally, with fresh thread, she knitted the patterns one after another in a long sampler. This proof of the Dame School's excellence was also her graduation certificate and a pattern book for her future use.

So if you have the good fortune to find in some old trunk a strip of knitting about six inches wide and a yard or so long, done in a succession of patterns not repeated, a thing without any conceivable use today, do not wonder about it. It was a knitting sampler; now it is an heirloom. Unless you are sure that your grandchildren will treasure it, do give it to a museum with a record of names, dates, and anything else you can learn about it. Every decade will add to its value. An eighteenth-century American knitting sampler would be priceless now.

Perhaps all of the early samplers are lost. We can only show you one that a little girl knitted ninety years ago. Her name was Bernadin Loeffler. She had three younger sisters and a little brother, and after her

Sampler of knitting patterns mastered by Bernadin Loeffler, aged ten, in 1870. [LAURA INGALLS WILDER HOME MUSEUM]

father died she and her mother were responsible for them all. The family had come across the ocean to Brooklyn, where there were aunts and cousins and Bernadin went to a public school. Late in the nineteenth century the public school teachers did not teach knitting, but Bernadin learned the new language and new ways, and she already knew how to knit, anyway. She did her sampler at home when she was ten years old.

She grew up to be a governess. During the Armistice in the World War she was able to see Germany again, with her charges, two little boys. But she married in Brooklyn and went with her husband to live in Nebraska. She lived to be ninety years old, coming back to Brooklyn after her husband died. She had always kept the sampler. The patterns that she knitted into it are older than anyone knows.

The knitted leaf pattern is very old, too. It is the hardiest of perennials; knitters are knitting it into bedspreads all over this country this minute, while goodness knows how many are cherishing it in counterpanes that grandmother's grandmothers knitted. In Damariscotta, Maine, there is one that is linked with the whole unwritten history of these United States.

A remarkable woman knitted it—but how countless many remarkable American women there have been, and are. She was Lovey West Mero; did you ever hear of her?

She was a granddaughter of Josiah Robbins, who "took up land" on the Fox Islands

in Maine when Maine was part of Massachusetts Bay Colony. She married Herman Mero, a grandson of the fighting Irishman, Hezekiah Mero, whose intimate friend was a Boston silversmith named Paul Revere. Herman Mero's other grandfather was Lovey's grandfather's brother Phillip, who took his family and all their earthly goods to the farthest settlement on Georges River and farther into the wilderness to hew out a cabin where Union, Maine, now is. You know about them if you have read Ben Ames Williams' *Come Spring*; their lives inspired that book and are told in it.

In 1860, Lovey West Mero's son Charles was fifteen years old. He ran away to join the 20th Maine Regiment, and gaily playing the fife he marched with the troops in many a parade and into more than one battle. Waiting for news of him, his mother knitted. At Gettysburg he was distinguished for heroism on the battlefield. The news could not have lessened his mother's fears. She endured them three years longer. Then he came home, alive, uninjured, safe. Later the veterans elected him Commander of the Grand Army of the Republic.

As soon as the war was over, Lovey Mero moved the family to Waldoboro, Maine. Energetic, resourceful, a magnetic person, she was a driving force at home and in the little German settlement; warm and generous, she was true to her given name. The neighbors mourned when she decided to go west. They made a Friendship Quilt, each writing

her name in ink on her patchwork block and all working together to quilt and bind it, and together they presented it to her as Waldoboro's farewell gift. She packed it carefully with her leaf-pattern counterpane and its matching pillow shams.

In covered wagons and on horseback the Robbins and Mero families, with dogs and cows, got over the mountain ranges, plodded along the woods' wagon trails, forded rivers, detoured around swamps, all the way to fertile empty land by the falls of the upper Mississippi. There they settled. Diligently and thriftily, they farmed the land, profiting from the growing market of the Twin Cities, Minneapolis and St. Paul. When Lovey West Mero was an old woman, her family was wealthy.

Then she could well afford an occasional trip to visit old friends in Waldoboro. She traveled by stagecoach, of course, and her daughter always remembered how merry and witty she was on the long and tiring journey. In her nineties she continued to travel all the way from Minnesota to Maine and back. She always carried a lunch basket with a teapot dangling beside it, and every time the driver stopped the jolting coach to rest the horses, she hopped out and built a little fire to make a pot of tea for the travelers' refreshment.

On one of these journeys she brought back the leaf-pattern counterpane with its matching pillow shams and gave them to her grand-niece Laura Castner. In time they came back to her own line and her daughter Sarah's grandson, Harold W. Castner, has them now in Damariscotta, Maine. Lovey West Mero lived a hundred years, but the longest lives are short; our work lasts longer.

Knitted laces. [*1, 3 and 5:* WITTE MUSEUM; *2, 4 and 6:* STAMFORD HISTORICAL SOCIETY, INC.]

Rug knitted in 1850 from scraps of wool yarn.
[HENRY FORD MUSEUM, DEARBORN, MICH.]

How to Knit

KNITTING NEEDLES

Knitting needles come in a wide range of sizes, types, and lengths and are made of various materials. Straight needles with single points are used when you work back and forth in rows. Circular needles are usually used for knitting skirts or other tubular garments, when you work in rounds. They are also used when a straight needle is not long enough to hold a large number of stitches. Double-pointed needles come in sets of four. They are used for socks, mittens, or other tubular garments, when you work in rounds. There are also steel double-pointed needles that come in sets of five, called knitting pins, that are very fine for making lace doilies. Large needles are used for heavy yarn and smaller needles for thinner yarn.

YARNS AND THREADS

There are many types of yarn and thread used for knitting. They differ as to twist, size, texture, and weight. The material specified in directions has always been chosen to suit the article which is being made. Only an expert knitter should attempt substituting materials. Buy all the thread or yarn you need at one time to be sure of having the same dye lot. Slight variations in weight and color can ruin the appearance of your work.

ABBREVIATIONS AND TERMS

Here are the common abbreviations and an explanation of the terms and symbols most frequently used in knitting.

beg	beginning
dec	decrease
dp	double pointed
inc	increase
k	knit
O	yarn over*
p	purl
psso	pass slipped stitch over
rnd	round
sl	slip
sl st	slip stitch
st	stitch
sts	stitches
tog	together

* Occasionally shown as YO

*—Asterisk—means repeat the instructions following the asterisk as many times as specified, in addition to the first time.

[]—Brackets—are used to designate change in size when directions are given, as they often are, for more than one size. The figure preceding the brackets refers to the smallest size.

Even: When directions say "work even," this means to continue working without increasing or decreasing, always keeping pattern as established.

Multiple of Stitches: A pattern often requires an exact number of stitches to be worked correctly. When directions say "multiple of," it means the number of stitches must be divisible by this number. For example: (Multiple of 6) would be 12, 18, 24, etc.; (multiple of 6 plus 3) would be 15, 21, 27, etc.

()—*Parentheses*—mean repeat instructions in parentheses as many times as specified. For example: "(K 3, p 2) 5 times" means to make all that is in parentheses 5 times in all.

Place a Marker in Work: This term means to mark with a safety pin a certain point in the work itself to use as a guide in taking future measurements.

Place a Marker on Needle: This term means to place a safety pin, paper clip, or bought plastic stitch marker on the needle between the stitches. It is slipped from one needle to the other to serve as a mark on following rows.

Slip a Stitch: When directions say "slip a stitch" or "sl 1," insert right needle in stitch to be slipped as if to purl and simply pass from left to right needle without working it.

GAUGE

It is most important that you knit to the gauge specified so that your finished article will be the correct size. Gauge means the number of stitches to 1″ and the number of rows to 1″. Make a practice piece at least 4″ square, using the needles and yarn specified in the directions. With a ruler, measure the number of stitches you have to 1″. If your stitches do not correspond to the gauge given, experiment with needles of different size. If you have more stitches than specified to the inch, you should use larger needles. If you have fewer stitches to the inch, use smaller needles. Keep changing the size needles until your gauge is exactly the same as that specified.

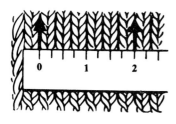

TO BEGIN KNITTING

For a practice piece, use knitting worsted and No. 6 needles.

How to Cast on

Make a slip loop and insert point of needle through it (*Diagram 1*). Tighten loop. Hold in

left hand. Hold second needle in right hand, with yarn in working position as shown in *Diagram 2*.

Insert point of right needle in loop on left needle from left to right. With index finger bring the yarn over the point of right needle (*Diagram 3a*).

Draw the yarn through the loop (*Diagram 3b*).

Insert left needle through new loop (*Diagram 3c*) and remove

right needle. You now have 2 stitches cast on. You can make the 3rd and all succeeding stitches the same way, or, for a stronger edge, you can insert right needle between stitches just below left needle instead of through loops (*Diagram 4*).

Cast on 15 stitches for a practice swatch. You are now ready to begin knitting.

THE KNIT STITCH

Hold needle with cast-on stitches in left hand. Insert right needle in front of first stitch on left needle from left to right. With right hand bring yarn under and over the point of right needle and draw the yarn through the stitch; slip the old stitch off the left needle. This completes first stitch of row. Repeat in each stitch (*Diagram 5*) until the stitches have been knitted off left needle. Always push work along left needle so that stitch to be worked is near tip. When row is completed, you should have 15 stitches on right needle as you had on left originally. Count stitches occasionally to make sure that you keep the same number. At the end of row, turn work so needle with stitches is in your left hand. Continue working rows

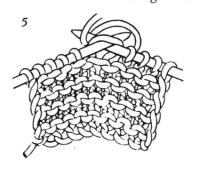

in this manner until work is uniform and you feel familiar with the stitch. When you knit each stitch in each row, it's called garter stitch.

To Bind Off

You are now ready to finish off your practice piece. This process is called binding off. Loosely knit 2 stitches. With point of left needle pick up first stitch and slide it over second; slip it off needle. * Knit next stitch and slip preceding one over it. Repeat from * across (*Diagram 6*).

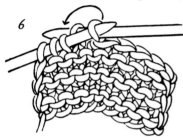

When you come to your last stitch, cut yarn about 3″ from the needle. Bring loose end through last stitch and pull tightly. Darn in end with tapestry needle so that it will not show.

The Purl Stitch

To make this stitch the yarn is in front of work instead of back and needle is inserted in stitch from the right instead of left. The wrong side of a purl stitch is a knit stitch. The purl stitch is rarely used alone, so to practice the stitch proceed with stockinette stitch.

Stockinette Stitch

Cast on 15 stitches for practice swatch. Knit first row. Turn work. Insert right needle in front of first stitch on left needle from right to left. With right hand bring yarn over the point of right needle and draw yarn through the stitch; slip old stitch off left needle. This completes first purl stitch. Keeping yarn in front of work, repeat in each stitch across (*Diagram 7*).

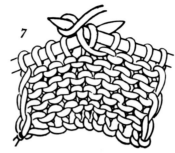

Knit next row, purl next row. Repeat these 2 rows until your work is uniform and you feel familiar with the purl stitch. Bind off. If you bind off on a purl row, purl the stitches instead of knitting them.

Note: The bumpy surface of stockinette stitch is the purl side, the smooth surface (this is usually the right side of work) is the knit side (*Diagram 8*).

You have now learned the two simple and basic stitches from which all knitting is derived.

Ribbing

Ribbing is a combination of purling and knitting in which you alternate a specified number of stitches of each. The most common form is knit 2, purl 2. It is always worked so stitches fall in columns. Because of its elasticity, it is generally used for waistbands and neckbands. It is easier to rib if you identify the stitch for what it is when it's facing you and purl the purl stitches, knit the knit stitches.

How to Increase

Increases are generally used to shape garments. First work knit (or purl) stitch as usual into front of stitch but leave stitch on left needle. Then knit (or purl)

in back of this same stitch (*Diagram 9*).

How to Decrease

There are two ways of decreasing and directions always tell you which one to use. The first, and most often used, direction will say "dec 1" and will specify where to do it. To do this simply knit or purl 2 stitches together (*Diagram 10*).

The second way is used only on knit rows. Directions will say "sl 1, k 1, psso." To do this, slip 1 stitch (simply pass the stitch from left needle to right without working it), knit the next stitch, then pass the slipped stitch over the knit stitch (*Diagram 11*).

To Make a Yarn Over

Yarn over automatically increases a stitch and is used mostly in lace patterns since it produces a hole in the work. On a knit row, bring yarn under tip of right needle, up and over needle, then work next stitch (*Diagram 12*).

On a purl row, bring yarn over right needle, around and to

front again, then work next stitch (*Diagram 13*).

A yarn over forms an extra loop on right needle. On next row work as other stitches.

How to Attach a New Yarn. Plan to attach a new yarn at beginning of a row. Tie in a single knot around old yarn, then knit several stitches with new yarn. Pull up old yarn so first stitch is same length as other stitches and knot again. When work is completed, weave both ends into back of knitting.

How to Pick Up Dropped Stitches. Beginners and even advanced knitters often drop a stitch or stitches. They must be picked up or they will "run" just like a stocking. Use a crochet hook. Catch the loose stitch and draw the horizontal thread of the row above through it (*Diagram 14*).

Repeat until you reach the row on which you are working. Then place on needle. *Diagram 14* shows picking up a knit stitch. *Diagram 15* shows a purl stitch.

How to Pick Up Stitches. This is usually done along an edge

of a piece already knitted. With right side of work facing you, tie yarn to spot where picking up is to start. Work with yarn and only one needle. Insert point of needle through knitting a short distance from the edge, wrap yarn around needle as if to knit and draw loop through piece. Continue in this manner across edge, spacing stitches evenly (*Diagram 16*).

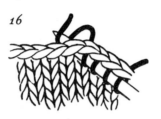

WEAVING OR KITCHENER STITCH

This is a method of joining two pieces of knitting together such as the toe of a sock. The effect is a continuous piece of knitting. There must be an equal number of stitches on each of two needles. Break off yarn, leaving about a 15″ end. Thread into tapestry needle and work as follows: Hold 2 needles even and parallel, having the yarn come from the right end of back needle, draw tapestry needle through first stitch of front needle as if to purl (*Diagram 17*),

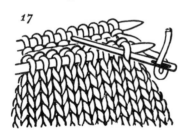

draw yarn through but leave stitch on needle; draw tapestry needle through first stitch of back needle as if to knit but leave stitch on needle; *draw tapestry needle through first stitch of front needle as if to knit and slip stitch off needle; draw tapestry needle through next stitch on front needle as if to purl but leave stitch on needle; draw tapestry needle through first

stitch of back needle as if to purl and slip stitch off needle; draw tapestry needle through next stitch on back needle as if to knit but leave stitch on needle. Repeat from * until all stitches are worked off. Draw end through one remaining loop and fasten.

How to Block. To insure a smooth professional look, block, then sew pieces together. Blocking is the process of steaming and shaping a garment. If it has been made in several pieces, block two similar pieces at the same time. With right sides together, pin to padded board with rustproof pins or thumbtacks. Pin to desired measurements. Place a damp cloth over knitting and press with hot iron. Keep iron moving lightly over work and don't press down hard on knitting.

How to Sew Edges Together. Seams should be as invisible as possible. Thread a tapestry needle with same yarn as garment. There are two methods of sewing. The first is used on straight edges. Place two pieces to be joined side by side, flat on surface and with right sides up. Draw sewing yarn through first stitch at bottom edge of one piece, then draw through corresponding stitch of other piece. Continue in this manner, just picking up edge stitch of each piece until seam is complete. The second method is used on shaped edges such as sewing in a sleeve. With right sides facing, sew just inside edge, using a backstitch. Leave stitches loose enough to provide elasticity.

DUPLICATE STITCH

This is used to work a design on top of knitting. Thread a tapestry needle with contrasting color yarn and work as follows: Draw yarn from wrong to right side through center of lower point of stitch. Insert needle at

Bedspread knitted in raised-leaf pattern, a favorite for four generations. [Brooklyn Museum, Brooklyn, N.Y.]

top right-hand side of same stitch. Then holding needle in horizontal position, draw through to top left side of stitch.

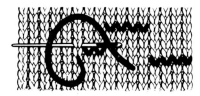

Insert again into base of same stitch. Keep work loose enough so it completely covers stitch being worked over. Almost any design that appears on a chart or graph can be used to work this stitch.

WORKING WITH TWO OR MORE COLORS

Fair Isle Knitting. This term is used for a pattern where two colors are involved and the color changes every few stitches. The yarn not being used is carried on wrong side of work throughout the whole pattern.

To work it, the color yarn used most is held in right hand as usual, the second color is held in the left hand. If yarn is carried more than 3 stitches, catch carried yarn in order to avoid having a long loop at back of work. Work as follows: * Insert right needle in regular manner, but before picking up yarn to work this stitch, slip right-hand needle under the carried yarn, work stitch in usual manner, slipping off carried yarn as stitch is completed. Work next stitch in regular manner. Repeat from * across. Be careful not to draw yarn too tightly as work will pucker or to work too loosely as loops will hang at back of work.

Bobbin Knitting. This term is used for a pattern where color appears in a definite block or line and you attach a color as it appears in the pattern. A small amount of yarn may be wound on a bobbin for easier working. When changing colors, simply twist yarn by bringing new color under yarn you are working with to avoid holes in work. Break off colors where not needed in design, leaving 5" ends to weave in.

HOW TO READ CHARTS

When working duplicate stitch, Fair Isle or bobbin knitting, a chart is given with directions. It is easier to knit a design or motif by following charts than by working from written directions. Simply think of each little square on the chart as one stitch in your work.

Directions for Raised-Leaf Bedspread

(See color photograph on preceding page.)

SIZES
Small (76½" x 90") or large (90" x 103½").

MATERIALS
Bucilla Blue Label Crochet and Knitting Cotton, 24 (500-yard) skeins for small size, 29 for large; knitting needles, 1 pair No. 1 (English needles No. 12).

GAUGE
Average 6 sts = 1". Each block measures 13½" square and consists of 4 triangles sewn together. Width of edging 4½".

TRIANGLE
(Make 120 for small size to make 30 squares; make 168 triangles for large size to make 42 squares): Cast on 3 sts. *1st row (right side):* (O, k 1) 3 times. *2nd row:* O, p 6. *3rd row:* O, p 1, k 2, O, k 1, O, k 2, p 1. *4th row:* O, k 1, p 7, k 2. *5th row:* O, p 2, k 3, O, k 1, O, k 3, p 2. *6th row:* O, k 2, p 9, k 3. *7th row:* O, p 3, k 4, O k 1, O, k 4, p 3. *8th row:* O, k 3, p 11, k 4. *9th row:* O, p 4, k 5, O, k 1, O, k 5, p 4. *10th row:* O, k 4, p 13, k 5. *11th row:* O, p 5, k 6, O, k 1, O, k 6, p 5. *12th row:* O, k 5, p 15, k 6. *13th row:* O, p 6, sl 1, k 1, psso, k 11, k 2 tog, p 6. *14th row:* O, k 6, p 13, k 7. *15th row:* O, p 7, sl 1, k 1, psso, k 9, k 2 tog, p 7. *16th row:* O, k 7, p 11, k 8. *17th row:* O, p 8, sl 1, k 1, psso, k 7, k 2 tog, p 8. *18th row:* O, k 8, p 9, k 9. *19th row:* O, p 9, sl 1, k 1, psso, k 5, k 2 tog, p 9. *20th row:* O, k 9, p 7, k 10. *21st row:* O, p 10, sl 1, k 1, psso, k 3, k 2 tog, p 10. *22nd row:* O, k 10, p 5, k 11. *23rd row:* O, p 11, sl 1, k 1, psso, k 1, k 2 tog, p 11. *24th row:* O, k 11, p 3, k 12. *25th row:* O, p 12, sl 1, k 2 tog, psso, p 12. *26th row:* O, k 26. *27th row:* O, k 27. *28th row:* O, p 28. *29th row:* O, k 29. *30th row:* O, p 30. *31st row:* O, p 31. *32nd row:* O, k 32. *33rd row:* O, p 33. *34th row:* O, k 34. *35th row:* O, k 35. *36th row:* O, p 36. *37th row:* O, k 37. *38th row:* O, p 38. *39th row:* O, k 2, (O, sl 1, k 1, psso) 18 times; k 1. *40th row:* O, p 40. *41st row:* O, k 2, (O, sl 1, k 1, psso) 19 times; k 1. *42nd row:* O, p 42. *43rd row:* O, k 2, (O, sl 1, k 1, psso) 20 times; k 1. *44th row:* O, p 44. *45th*

row: O, k 45. *46th row:* O, p 46. *47th row:* O, k 47. *48th row:* O, k 48. *49th row:* O, p 49. *50th row:* O, k 50. *51st row:* O, p 51. *52nd row:* O, k 52. *53rd row:* O, k 53. *54th row:* O, p 54. *55th row:* O, k 55. *56th row:* O, p 56. *57th row:* O, (p 2, k 1, O, k 1, O, k 1, p 5) 5 times; p 2, k 1, O, k 1, O, k 1, p 2. *58th row:* O, (k 2, p 5, k 5) 5 times; k 2, p 5, k 3. *59th row:* O, (p 3, k 2, O, k 1, O, k 2, p 4) 5 times; p 3, k 2, O, k 1, O, k 2, p 3. *60th row:* O, (k 3, p 7, k 4) 6 times. *61st row:* O, (p 4, k 3, O, k 1, O, k 3, p 3) 6 times; p 1. *62nd row:* O, (k 4, p 9, k 3) 6 times; k 2. *63rd row:* O, (p 5, k 4, O, k 1, O, k 4, p 2) 6 times; p 3. *64th row:* O, (k 5, p 11, k 2) 6 times; k 4. *65th row:* O, (p 6, k 5, O, k 1, O, k 5, p 1) 6 times; p 5. *66th row:* O, (k 6, p 13, k 1) 6 times; k 6. *67th row:* O, (p 7, k 6, O, k 1, O, k 6) 6 times; p 7. *68th row:* O, k 7, (p 15, k 7) 6 times; k 1. *69th row:* O, p 8, (sl 1, k 1, psso, k 11, k 2 tog, p 7) 6 times; p 1. *70th row:* O, k 8, (p 13, k 7) 6 times; k 2. *71st row:* O, p 9, (sl 1, k 1, psso, k 9, k 2 tog, p 7) 6 times; p 2. *72nd row:* O, k 9, (p 11, k 7) 6 times; k 3. *73rd row:* O, p 10, (sl 1, k 1, psso, k 7, k 2 tog, p 7) 6 times; p 3. *74th row:* O, k 10, (p 9, k 7) 6 times; k 4. *75th row:* O, p 11, (sl 1, k 1, psso, k 5, k 2 tog, p 7) 6 times; p 4. *76th row:* O, k 11, (p 7, k 7) 6 times; k 5. *77th row:* O, p 12, (sl 1, k 1, psso, k 3, k 2 tog, p 7) 6 times; p 5. *78th row:* O, k 12, (p 5, k 7) 6 times; k 6. *79th row:* O, p 13, (sl 1, k 1, psso, k 1, k 2 tog, p 7) 6 times; p 6. *80th row:* O, k 13, (p 3, k 7) 6 times; k 7. *81st row:* O, p 14, (sl 1, k 2 tog, psso, p 7) 6 times; p 7. *82nd row:* O, p 70. *83rd row:* O, k 2, (O, sl 1, k 1, psso) 34 times; k 1. *84th row:* O, p 72. *85th row:* O, k 2, (O, sl 1, k 1, psso) 35 times; k 1. *86th row:* O, p 74. *87th row:* O, k 2, (O, sl 1, k 1, psso) 36 times; k 1. *88th row:* O, p 76. *89th row:* K 77. Bind off. After you have made four triangles, sew them with their points together to make one block. Sew by picking up the O at edge of triangles.

ASSEMBLY

Sew blocks together arranging them 5 across and 6 in length for small spread; 6 across and 7 in length for large.

BORDER

Cast on 33 sts. *1st row:* K 2, (k 1, O, k 2 tog) 3 times; p 2, O twice, k 2 tog, k 18 (34 sts). *2nd row:* K 20, p 1, k 3, (k 1, O, k 2 tog) 3 times; k 1 (34 sts). *3rd row:* K 2, (k 1, O, k 2 tog) 3 times; p 2, k 21 (34 sts). *4th row:* K 8, O, k 1, O, k 15, (k 1, O, k 2 tog) 3 times; k 1 (36 sts). *5th row:* K 2, (k 1, O, k 2 tog) 3 times; p 2, (O twice, k 2 tog) twice; k 8, p 3, k 8 (38 sts). *6th row:* K 9, O, k 1, O, k 11, (p 1, k 2) twice; k 1, (k 1, O, k 2 tog) 3 times; k 1 (40 sts). *7th row:* K 2, (k 1, O, k 2 tog) 3 times; p 2, k 14, p 5, k 8 (40 sts). *8th row:* K 10, O, k 1, O, k 19, (k 1, O, k 2 tog) 3 times; k 1 (42 sts). *9th row:* K 2, (k 1, O, k 2 tog) 3 times; p 2, (O twice, k 2 tog) 3 times; k 8, p 7, k 8 (45 sts). *10th row:* K 11, O, k 1, O, k 13, (p 1, k 2) 3 times; k 1, (k 1, O, k 2 tog) 3 times; k 1 (47 sts). *11th row:* K 2, (k 1, O, k 2 tog) 3 times; p 2, k 17, p 9, k 8 (47 sts). *12th row:* K 12, O, k 1, O, k 24, (k 1, O, k 2 tog) 3 times; k 1 (49 sts). *13th row:* K 2, (k 1, O, k 2 tog) 3 times; p 2, (O twice, k 2 tog) twice; O twice, sl 1, k 2 tog, psso, O twice, k 2 tog, k 8, p 11, k 8 (52 sts). *14th row:* K 13, O, k 1, O, k 15, (p 1, k 2) 4 times; k 1, (k 1, O, k 2 tog) 3 times; k 1 (54 sts). *15th row:* K 2, (k 1, O, k 2 tog) 3 times; p 2, k 20, p 13, k 8 (54 sts). *16th row:* K 8, sl 1, k 1, psso, k 9, k 2 tog, k 23, (k 1, O, k 2 tog) 3 times; k 1 (52 sts). *17th row:* K 2, (k 1, O, k 2 tog) 3 times; p 2, (O twice, k 2 tog) twice; (O twice, sl 1, k 2 tog, psso) twice; O twice, k 2 tog, k 8, p 11, k 8 (55 sts). *18th row:* K 8, sl 1, k 1, psso, k 7, k 2 tog, k 10, (p 1, k 2) 5 times; k 1, (k 1, O, k 2 tog) 3 times; k 1 (53 sts). *19th row:* K 2, (k 1, O, k 2 tog) 3 times; p 2, k 23, p 9, k 8 (53 sts). *20th row:* K 8, sl 1, k 1, psso, k 5, k 2 tog, k 26, (k 1, O, k 2 tog) 3 times; k 1 (51sts). *21st row:* K 2, (k 1, O, k 2 tog) 3 times; p 2, (O twice, k 2 tog) twice; (O twice, sl 1, k 2 tog, psso) 3 times; O twice, k 2 tog, k 8, p 7, k 8 (54 sts). *22nd row:* K 8, sl 1, k 1, psso, k 3, k 2 tog, k 10, (p 1, k 2) 6 times; k 1, (k 1, O, k 2 tog) 3 times; k 1 (52 sts). *23rd row:* K 2, (k 1, O, k 2 tog) 3 times; p 2, k 26, p 5, k 8 (52 sts). *24th row:* K 8, sl 1, k 1, psso, k 1, k 2 tog, k 29, (k 1, O, k 2 tog) 3 times; k 1 (50 sts). *25th row:* K 2, (k 1, O, k 2 tog) 3 times; p 2, (O twice, k 2 tog) twice; (O twice, sl 1, k 2 tog, psso) 4 times; O twice, k 2 tog, k 8, p 3, k 8 (53 sts). *26th row:* K 8, sl 1, k 2 tog, psso, k 10, (p 1, k 2) 7 times; k 1, (k 1, O, k 2 tog) 3 times; k 1 (51 sts). *27th row:* K 2, (k 1, O, k 2 tog) 3 times; p 2, k 38 (51 sts). *28th row:* Bind off 18 sts, k until there are 23 sts on right-hand needle, (k 1, O, k 2 tog) 3 times; k 1 (33 sts). Repeat first through 28th rows for pattern.

Work in pattern until border is large enough to fit all around spread, allowing for gathering at corners and ending with a 28th row. Bind off remaining sts. Sew border to edge of spread.

Weaving

Plaid linen woven in New York, early nineteenth century. The same pattern is often used in iron-rust, yellow and white, or in a combination of the three colors. [NEW YORK STATE HISTORICAL ASSOCIATION, COOPERSTOWN, N.Y.]

VERYONE KNOWS that weaving is crisscrossing strands together to make a fabric, but only weavers think about it. If you're simply taking it for granted, as so many of us do nowadays, just try to imagine what would happen if everything woven suddenly vanished.

We would be naked; there would be no clothes, no bedding, no carpets, curtains, not so much as a towel; mills, factories, cars would stop running; in warehouses and cargo ships everything sacked or baled would flow into heaps; clothbound books would be loose pages, typewriters would have no ribbons. And that's hardly the beginning of it.

Weaving is a primary essential to civilization. It was one of our savage ancestors' first efforts to climb out of savagery; its history is inseparable from the history of the ageslong struggle toward a truly civilized human world. So in that continuing effort it has a special meaning now; for it was women in America, quietly weaving, who began the world revolution for individual freedom.

King George III was a good ruler, sincere and conscientious. He worked hard and unselfishly to do his duty of managing his subjects for the common good. When he decided to permit them to weave in England and forbid them to weave in America, he was acting as good rulers always had acted. When King Louis XIV decided to protect his vintners in France, and ordered his subjects in America to stop making wines, they stopped. But French kings had selected their American colonists carefully, had given them food and seeds and tools—a hoe to every child more than six years old—and had set over them commanders who always told them what to do and took care of them.

Refugees had made the English colonies, with no help nor government from England. They starved until in utmost desperation they learned that God gives every person, with life, the responsibility for it.

With this knowledge they had lived, they had prospered for nearly two centuries. Now their King asserted his own control of their lives, his responsibility for them. He would permit them to raise flax and wool to ship to his weavers in England, but it was not his plan to have weavers in his colonies.

An American housewife had made the flaxen thread, from seed to hank. She had made the woolen yarn in a year of tending sheep, washing and carding and spinning the oily fleeces. Her fingernails were blue from the indigo vat, and she may even have raised the indigo. Her husband had made for her the spinning wheel and the loom, hewed and whittled and smoothed and pegged together of wood from the living tree. These things are *mine*, she said.

The King said that she must not use them? When the children needed clothing, the new bed lacked bedding?

She warped the thread and beamed the warp and threaded it through the heddles and the reed; she wound the weft on the shuttle. She sat down, her feet on the treadles. Then in the village street and by the cabin in the clearing men heard the thump-thud of the busy looms, drum-beating the battle cry that they would shout from Bunker Hill to Yorktown: "Liberty and Property!"

Already these women were weaving the American patterns that we cherish now. In Europe's chartered guild monopolies the workers and their masters were weaving the patterns prescribed, large patterns of blended colors, tapestries and brocades, so many threads of warp and so many threads of woof to the inch, by order of the King. Once the orders did not come, and for a whole year not a shuttle moved in France, where the barefooted peasants and serfs wore only a single garment. In America the independent women each wove her own pattern. She set the small motifs on creamy white, on indigo blue, on brown from the walnut husk or yellow from the peach leaf. Each motif stood alone, clear and firm, and together the colors sang from the cloth.

There was nothing new in the loom. Thousands of years of trying, failing, thinking, trying again, had made that eighteenth-century loom. One of its predecessors was the "wrap-around" loom, that we are still using. It's the little Weave-It which you can buy. Or a child can make a version of one by driving a row of brads into the top and bottom of an old wooden picture frame. You

Plaid in twill or diagonal weave.
[FARMERS' MUSEUM, COOPERSTOWN, N.Y.]

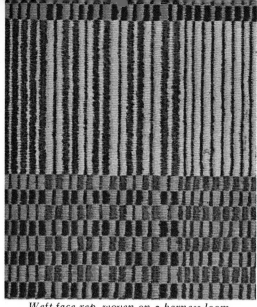

Weft-face rep, woven on 2-harness loom.
[NATIONAL GALLERY OF ART, WASHINGTON, D.C.]

Log-cabin design for 2-harness loom.
[FARMERS' MUSEUM]

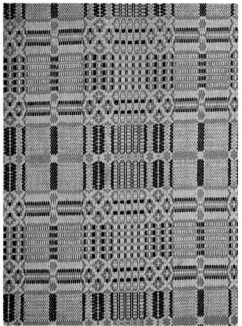

Five-star and Table pattern.
[SHELBURNE MUSEUM, SHELBURNE, VT.]

Double Chariot Wheels for 4-harness loom.
[SHELBURNE MUSEUM]

Double-star and Table pattern (opposit
[FARMERS' MUSEUM]

Nine-block and Table design.
[SHELBURNE MUSEUM]

Both sides of reversible piece in summer and winter weave.
[FARMERS' MUSEUM]

Coverlet from the Knapp family of Morris, N.Y. Technique is overshot weaving, the weft skipping over a number of threads (see detail, above). [FARMERS' MUSEUM]

wind the warp back and forth on the brads and darn across it with a long needle.

It's fun to make small things on this primitive loom. Scraps of colored wools or floss make bookmarks, ties, belts, scarves, or dozens of squares or strips which, sewed together, may be a baby bonnet or sweater or afghan. Worn-out stockings, slashed round and round diagonally into strips, have made many a mat and cushion top and stair tread on a wrap-around loom.

This archaic way of weaving, though, makes you want to do what countless weavers must have wanted to do for ages before they could think how to do it; that is, to get the weft under all the "every other" threads of warp at once, instead of one by one.

The ancient Romans did it. Americans did it, too, probably at about the same time, for Navaho women still are weaving their colorful serapes on something like the old Roman loom.

They ran a wide, thin strip of wood under every second thread of the warp; then they turned it on edge, raising all those threads. This made an opening, called a "shed," through which the shuttle went (and goes) under all those alternate threads in one swift flight. Now the problem is: how to get it back as quickly, under all the other threads?

In time they solved that. They looped a string around each one of those other threads and tied each string, in its order, to a stick. Eureka! How easy to weave now! Turn the strip of wood on edge, pass the shuttle through the shed, lay the strip flat again. Now lift up the stick; it pulls up all the threads on the dangling strings; hold them up with one hand and with the other hand throw the shuttle back through this shed. Lay the stick down on the warp; turn the flat one on edge again, and repeat.

Almost any day in Arizona you can watch weavers doing this, though the Indian loom hangs perpendicular; the weaver does not lift and drop the warp threads, but pulls and pushes them.

You can buy a small loom which lies on a table and works on the same principle. On it, all the threads of warp run through loops tied to sticks named "harnesses," and we call the loops "heddles" because the early Saxons did. To them the word meant "heavers," and the loops heave up the threads.

There's no tabby weaving that you can't do on this simple table loom, much more easily and quickly than you may think. Tabby is plain weaving, smooth, as taffeta is. (Both words are Arabic, from '*Attabi*, the name of the weavers' quarter in old Baghdad.) The many qualities and sizes of warp and woof threads give a great variety of textures in tabby weaving and there's an endless range of possible color combinations.

At such looms in ancient Rome thousands of slaves wore out their wretched lives weaving *sarge*. A *sarge* was a strip of woolen cloth. With a hole in the middle for a head to go through, and a belt, it was an ordinary Roman's only garment. It was the common soldier's tunic, blanket, umbrella, knapsack, anything it could be used for. Through the centuries of ceaseless war the government's demand was insatiable, and *sarge* contractors became millionaires in the grandeur that was Rome, gone now. Only our word "serge" remains.

The loom had been invented then. During two thousand years Europeans improved it. They added more harnesses and a swinging "comb" with teeth (faster than fingers) to drive each strand of weft firmly against the previous one. They wound the warp and the woven fabric on beams that could be revolved, and so made long lengths of cloth.

When someone thought of attaching treadles to the harnesses, he set the loom on legs; then a weaver could sit down to work, his feet walking on the treadles, closing and opening the sheds, his arms throwing the shuttle left and right. This was the loom that began the drumbeat of the world revolution, not two centuries ago.

In the little while that free men have been beginning to make a wholly new world, they have transformed that ax-hewn loom into the vast, air-conditioned, steel-shining, humming factory pouring out endless streams of such fabrics as Aladdin could not dream. The ranks of dancing heddles are steel needles with eyes in their middles through which warp flows faster than eye can see, and the flying shuttles jeer at Aristotle, the great Greek thinker who said that men must be slaves because work must be done, so society will have slavery "as long as a shuttle will not fly by itself."

Free men make shuttles fly by themselves. Before the revolutionary little Republic was half a century old, men from the whole Old World were beginning to abolish age-old poverty and toil here. In the 1840's New England's mill girls were proud, happy, prosperous, admired, and envied. Highly skilled, stylishly dressed, properly chaperoned, they tended the swift machines and competed for the fame of their mills. In each mill they organized a literary club; they gave concerts and wrote stories, essays, and poems to read to audiences at "literary evenings"; they published little magazines. There never had been such workers on earth before; there were no others like them then. The shuttles did the work for them, and required from them diligence, prudence, intelligence, honesty.

In England the weavers were smashing the machines that did in factories the work that families had been doing from dawn to dark in crowded, damp, working-class hovels. In America, home weaving was already becoming what it is now, an art. Thrifty women told themselves that it was economical, but also it was (as it is) a pleasure not easily given up.

A century ago on a farm in New York State my father's mother could well afford to buy whatever she wanted, and she and her daughters did wear French calicoes on summer Sundays, silks and velvets to church in winter. Still she continued for twenty years to clothe her family well besides, in linen and linsey-woolsey and good woolen broadcloth from the flax field and the Merinos. As long as she lived her sheets and tablecloths were hand-woven linen, and into this century, though her parlor carpets were Aubusson, her own richly colored, woven rag carpets were beautiful on the floors of sitting room, dining room, and bedrooms.

Nothing wears like good homespun, she used to say, fingering the soft, smooth cloth that she didn't weave any more. Even then I knew that she was mourning a lost pleasure. Indeed there is no other like weaving. It is the only artcraft that engages and delights all one's mind and muscles together. There is never a trace of tedium in it.

The loom is set before you begin. You have wound and chained-off and beamed the warp; you have threaded it according to pattern through the heddles and the reed, stretching it evenly. This takes time and patience and precision but there's pleasure in the skill itself and anticipation increases that. You have wound the shuttle. Now you sit at the loom, feet on the treadles, shuttle in hand and pure joy begins.

Every muscle, *every* one, moves in rhythm with the rising and falling harnesses, the crisscrossing maze of warp, the shuttle's flight to and fro. Slowly under your eyes the pattern unfolds and grows as if alive. It holds you fascinated, watching it grow. The rhythm is in your blood; a warmth spreads to the very tips of fingers and toes. A radiance, a harmony, seems to encompass everything. The harnesses rise and fall; the mazy warp engages and disengages; the pattern grows, and all's well with the world.

Doctors should prescribe weaving for most of our ills and all our woes.

On Weaving

This is the one needlecraft in the book where we cannot present general directions. Today, people are usually taught weaving in classes. Specific directions are needed for each pattern, each loom and each type of weaving.

During the two centuries in this country when almost all of the textiles worn and used in the home were produced by the family, the women of America wove great quantities of plain material. The simple 2-harness loom could produce not only plain linens and woolens but also rep materials, plaids and patterned carpeting.

The most usual looms had 4 harnesses and on those could be woven most of the coverlets in overshot weave, patterned linens, and clothing woolens and blankets in twill weave. Coverlets in summer and winter weave were also a possibility if the less common 6-harness loom was available. Usually only a professional weaver had the 16-harness loom which was necessary for producing fancier linens like the diaper damask tablecloths or the double-woven coverlets.

The patterns used in weaving were written down as drafts or threading plans on strips of paper for convenience in use. These were handed down in families and copied by friends and neighbors just as were the recipes for cooking and baking. The notation looked very much like music as it was written on four or more bars which represented the frames or harnesses of the loom. Marks or numbers indicated the position of each warp thread in its heddle on its respective harness. One kept one's place in the pattern while threading the loom by sticking a pin into the strip of paper, and much-used drafts are full of pinholes. A modern graphic system of notation is used here as it is more easily understood by the weavers of today. Any size yarn needed could be produced when yarns were spun at home, and even when the cotton yarns were spun in the factory and purchased for home use, there was a good choice of yarn sizes. Now, when we wish to duplicate the results which they obtained, we find ourselves handicapped by the limited range of yarn sizes available to the hand-weaver. We have to adapt their patterns and particularly the sett of warp to our available yarns.

Bed blanket, woven in plaid sometime in the first quarter of the nineteenth century. [SHELBURNE MUSEUM, SHELBURNE, VT.]

Overshot woven coverlet, nine-wheel patterns, made as the early ones were, in two strips. [SHELBURNE MUSEUM]

Crib coverlet woven near Ephrata, Pa. in a design of a 16-pointed star, enclosing an 8-pointed star, enclosing a rectangle and diamond. [SHELBURNE MUSEUM]

Rag carpet fragment, woven in western New York (about 1850) of narrow strips of cotton rags on a cotton warp and used for hall runners. [FARMERS' MUSEUM, NEW YORK STATE HISTORICAL ASSOCIATION, COOPERSTOWN, N.Y.]

Striped carpeting, woven about the year 1830, of cotton weft and homespun woolen yarn dyed with natural dyes. [FARMERS' MUSEUM]

Directions for M's and O's Pattern Tablecloth

Tablecloth made in the nineteenth century in the popular M's and O's pattern draft, a favorite for woven linen. [FARMERS' MUSEUM]

Worked on a 4-Harness Loom

WARP: Single-ply cotton, bleached
SETT: 36 to the inch
WEFT: Single-ply linen, bleached

WOVEN: In checks, alternating pattern shots to square the blocks

SUGGESTIONS:
WARP: Linen 40/2 or 20/1 or cotton 20/2, sett 30 to 36
WEFT: Linen 20/1

 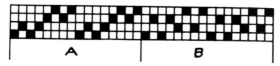

Tie-up for Sinking Shed
Tie-up to Blank Spaces for Rising Shed

Repeat—32 ends
Treadling
A Block—3, 4 x 7
B Block—1, 2 x 7

Candlewicking

Center motif of a hand-woven linen spread, embroidered with candlewicking in French knots, about 1825. Made by Laura Collins, descendant of three early settlers of Guilford, Connecticut and of the Reverend Timothy Collins of Litchfield, Connecticut. [SHELBURNE MUSEUM, SHELBURNE, VT.]

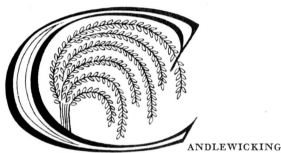ANDLEWICKING
is as American as lemon meringue pie, fun
to make, a delight to have. And not easy to
define more precisely without fear of successful contradiction.

Say that it is a traditional American needle art; true, but it's hardly older than the
Republic, which isn't two centuries old yet.
Say that candlewicking is embroidery; yes,
but it is weaving too. Show its prim, geometrical, almost flat designs, or its boldly firm
curves raised in almost sculptured bas-relief;
neither is at all like the airy softness of the
candlewick coverlet on your bed. No needlework is more popular; everyone admires it;
even its machine-made imitation called
"chenille" is everywhere. Yet how popular
is it? Are you making a piece?

Today tufted candlewicking is a lazy
woman's artcraft, just suited to me. It's done
swiftly with galloping stitches; it is finished,
clipped, tufted in almost no time at all. It is
as thrifty of cash as of time. You can hardly
believe how much you get for so little.

First, you want cloth that will wash and
shrink in washing. The shrinking is important, and shrinkable cloth is cheapest. Then
you must have a huge darning needle and
candlewicking thread. You may have in-
herited a candlewicking needle with two big
eyes in it, at right angles to each other, one
below the other.

Now, the pattern. There isn't a design that
you can't do in candlewicking. In slim lines
or solid masses you can copy or adapt any
pattern of any other needlework. Truly, all
the patterns of embroidery, patchwork,
crewel, cross-stitch, hooking, crochet, weaving, are yours to choose, and all the forms of
flowers and fruits, insects, birds, animals,
buildings. This is the time to have a simple
mind; it is easier to make up.

So transfer a pattern or sketch one, or do
this: Take a square of paper, fold it into a
small square or oblong or triangle; with scissors carve its edges, then unfold it and surprise yourself. You have a geometrical pattern. If you like it, you have an original
candlewicking pattern; use it repeatedly for
an allover design or in a row for a border. If
you don't like it, throw it away; there's always the fun of making another.

When your pattern is lightly chalked on
the cloth, there's no more to do but baste
swiftly along its lines. With the threaded
needle you take small stitches, evenly one or
two or three inches apart, letting the candlewicking lie lazily on the cloth between
them. You need not bother with embroidery
frames; simply baste *loosely*, not puckering
the cloth. And with careful eye, keep equal
distances between stitches.

The basting done, take the scissors and cut
the candlewicking in the middle of the
spaces between stitches, and that is all. The
cluster of cut threads stands up in a tuft over
each stitch. If the stitches are close together,
the tufts will be a solid line or a mass. If the

stitches are farther apart, the tufts will be a dotted line.

Now all goes into the washing machine where hot water shrinks the cloth, tightening its warp and woof to grip every tuft firmly. In the drier or on a clothesline the tufts become fluffier. They will shake out fluffier still, and shaking is all you do to candlewicking; you never iron it.

This tufted work is the latest form of candlewicking and the easiest and quickest to do. The technique is nothing but basting; the beauty is in material and design. The effect is velvety soft. In white on white it can be as subtle as quilting. In white on clear light blue or green, pink or yellow, it is dainty and gay.

In this artcraft you can make curtains, cushions, bedspreads, even little soft rugs. I can think of a breath-taking, wholly unique bedroom and bath . . . but so can you.

It's a far cry from the first American candlewicking to this latest form of it. The very name, candlewicking, makes you think of those pioneer women, working year long to make the candlewicking, and of the frugal poverty saving and using every inch of it left over when the last drop of bayberry wax was cooling in the candle molds.

In fact, it wasn't that way at all. Our candlewicking comes from wealth well earned and royally spent. This needle art represents America's aristocracy of mind and manners, talents and culture. An earliest example of

Unsheared candlewicking on a hand-woven spread made by Martha Freeman in 1823. It is believed to be part of her trousseau. Note the bows in the shapes of hearts. [NEWARK MUSEUM, NEWARK, N.J.]

it was created in Gunston Hall.

If you have not yet seen Gunston Hall in its formal gardens, beyond its *allées* of venerable boxwood, see it before you fly to Europe or the Orient. George Mason planned this noble home and watched its building for three years while his friend George Washington was planning the remodeling of the farmhouse at Mount Vernon, some five miles farther up the Potomac. Finer by far than finished Mount Vernon, to some of us Gunston Hall is the most beautiful mansion ever built in England's American colonies.

The men who planned these beautiful houses and gardens were the men who invented the first political organization ever designed to prevent a Government from suppressing individual liberty. George Mason lived twenty years in Gunston Hall, a country squire responsible for hundreds of lives, a businessman managing a large, productive property profitably, a scholar reading and thinking in his library, and a gentleman serving in the colony's House of Burgesses.

Then he wrote the Virginia Declaration of Human Rights, and saw its adoption with Virginia's Declaration of Independence, weeks before Thomas Jefferson repeated it in the Continental Congress's Declaration of Independence, and thirteen years before nine free and sovereign States joined the federation based on it. Gunston Hall represents the Revolution as truly as a cabin in a clearing did.

George Mason's oldest son, George, built another house for his bride, Elizabeth Mary Ann Barnes Hooe. They named their new home for a then recent battle in Massachusetts, and young George Mason became George Mason of Lexington. Mrs. Mason of Lexington had a handsome candlewick bedspread. You can see it now in Gunston Hall.

Possibly she made it there; she and her husband were his father's guests while workmen were finishing Lexington Hall. Probably she didn't. She was no older than sixteen; her second child was born when she was eighteen. Certainly one of her accomplishments was fine needlework. No doubt she sat decorously in these beautiful, wax-polished, satin-damask-lined rooms, her little slippers hidden under flowing skirts and a ringlet brushing her cheek as her head bent over crewel work or needlepoint. But her candlewick bedspread was made on a huge loom; it is ninety-two inches wide and seamless.

It was "made by her or for her," the document says. And at Gunston Hall, as at all such manorial estates, the looms were in workrooms which were as much a part of the household as kitchens, pantries, smokehouses, and stables. Workrooms were the province of the most skillful and honored slaves; there they carded, spun, dyed, wove the wool from the sheep and the cotton from the fields into all the fabrics needed for the household. This way of living was many thousands of years old.

When Gunston Hall was built, slavery was everywhere taken for granted, as we ourselves take old customs for granted without thinking about them. Of the few who did think at all about slavery, nearly all decided that it was natural, necessary, and good.

When George Washington was ending his second term, and refusing a third, as President of the United States, the wise old librarian of Count Waldstein at Dux was writing that there would always be galley slaves in Italy because of the narrowness of those eastern Mediterranean waters.

This was Europe when the nineteenth century began. We forget how recently a few men in America declared to a world of slaves, that "all men are created equal . . . endowed by their Creator with . . . unalienable . . . Liberty," and risked—and most of them lost—their lives and fortunes to defend that truth and establish it on earth.

They thought it would be a long time before the whole earth's population knew it, and how right they were. They expected slavery to be ended in their own little federation of States before their slaves' children grew up. Nobody dreamed that Eli Whitney would invent a cotton gin and that states from the Atlantic to the Rio Grande would be dependent on slave labor.

So I think that among the chattering women in Gunston Hall's weaving room a proudly skillful and respected slave wove young Mrs. Mason's candlewick bedspread. The great loom was threaded with fine white cotton, the shuttle wound with "roving," as the soft-spun wicking was called. She made the pattern by picking up certain loops of roving from the web, onto a long, slender reed. The reed held up the loops while she stepped on the treadle; the harnesses rose and fell, the crisscrossing warp encircled the strand of wicking and held the loops firmly. She pulled the reed out of them, passed the shuttle again through the "shed" and deftly picked up the next row of loops.

These patterns made on looms are the earliest American candlewicking. They come from the great houses of late colonial days and like the architecture, the furniture, the pictures, and books, they show novel patterns in an old way of weaving.

How ancient that is, I don't know; nobody knew in the Near East, where Moslem grandmothers strictly ruling their busy harems smiled to see me learning it on the hand-worn old looms under the fig trees.

In the early American candlewicking, the reed picks up only certain loops, making geometrical patterns on a surface of tabby weaving. Their squares, stars, triangles and pine trees come mostly from patchwork, and usually the pattern's surface is flat, raised evenly from the cloth. Sometimes a weaver used two reeds of different diameters, making longer and shorter loops to give more height and emphasis to parts of her design, and in her work you see the individualism continually changing old ways into new.

The first free people began immediately the changes that transformed everything in these multiplying States with faster and faster speed. The greater the individual freedom, the faster is human progress, for free minds think of even more new things to be done than men can do in the limits of space and time. So Americans hurry; we are more aware of Time and we chafe against it more vigorously than people living anywhere else. Candlewicking shows this, as everything in our lives does.

Weaving was too rigid and too slow. The Republic was no sooner safely established in the nineteenth century's teens than American women were making candlewicking in a wholly new way. They wound the soft, fat clusters of threads into huge French knots on their sewing needles and stitched the knots to the cloth in lines and masses of firm bas-relief; their patterns were no longer geometrical, held to the square meshes of weaving. The free needle followed the mind's fancies of curving stems and petals, of eagles and peacocks and crescent moons. The early nineteenth-century candlewicking puts borders of swags and tassels around such patterns and once, for a bride, tied up the tassels with heartshaped bows.

Today our candlewicking is freer still and even faster. We do it with the darning needle and the automatic washing machine. This basted, clipped, tufted work is late nineteenth century at earliest; most of it is no older than our own century. Through the mountains from the Carolinas to Oklahoma you may see, on any summer day, multitudes of candlewick bedspreads in many colors, displayed for sale. These are products of cottage industries supplying a wholesale market for "chenille" bedspeads; they are made with small machines even swifter than basting needles and the wholesale buyers prescribe patterns and colors.

Pretty as some of them are, there is all the difference imaginable between these chenille bedspreads, in the mountains or in shops, and the candlewicking that you do so easily in your own unique pattern, pleasing your own taste, belonging in your own home.

No needlework is more suited to our times, which seem to have so few hours in a day. Nothing is more traditionally American, for our tradition is progress, constant change. Today we are making mid-twentieth-century candlewicking. Only remember that there will be a twenty-first American century, and a twenty-second, and then some. So have a heart; be kind to curators unborn and work your name *and the date* into your design, won't you? Or, if you must be so shy, embroider them small, underneath.

Sunflower, pineapple and leaves on a hand-woven spread of about 1820. [Henry Ford Museum, Dearborn, Mich.]

Eagle, the traditional American emblem, embroidered in candlewicking on a woven cotton counterpane. [Mount Vernon Ladies' Association, Mount Vernon, Va.]

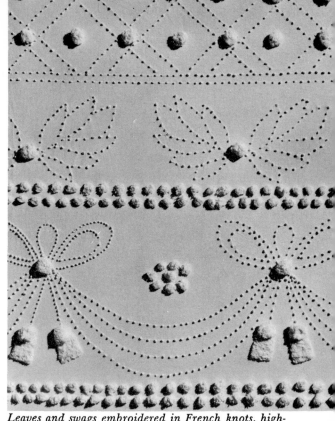

Leaves and swags embroidered in French knots, highlighted with appliquéd clipped tufts of candlewicking. [Henry Ford Museum]

Robbing Peter to Pay Paul, pieced quilt pattern in candlewick embroidery on a nineteenth-century spread. [Henry Ford Museum]

Medallion worked with French knots and satin-stitch candlewicking. [Farmers' Museum, New York State Historical Association, Cooperstown, N.Y.]

How to Do Candlewicking

BACKGROUND FABRICS

Use fabrics that have not been preshrunk and need no ironing, fabrics like bark cloth, homespun, or 2 x 2 basket-weave monk's cloth. After embroidery is completed, the spread is washed so that fabric shrinks and the candlewicking threads are held in place more firmly. Be sure to start out with a piece large enough to allow for shrinking. Candlewicking is traditionally worked on off-white fabric.

THREAD

For early American candlewicking, 4-, 6-, and 8-ply thread was used. Today the only candlewicking thread readily available is an 8-ply thread which can be separated to get the desired number of strands. The thread can be obtained by mail from mail-order houses sold in units of two-pound cones. For most spreads one two-pound cone is sufficient; more thread can be reordered if necessary. This thread comes only in off-white. When candlewicking is completed, your spread can be bleached to whiten both threads and fabric. Or, if you want to make a tinted spread, use a commercial dye, following manufacturer's directions to obtain the desired shade.

NEEDLES

Use couching or darning needles with an eye large enough for the number of strands you are working with. For working traditional tufts (*see Method 1*) you can use a darning needle or a candlewick needle. A candlewick needle is long with a large eye and has a wide shaft. Old candlewick needles used to be made with single or double eyes with a special widened point.

HOOPS

You may use an embroidery hoop if you wish. However, if you find it more comfortable to work without one, be sure to sew loosely enough to keep fabric from puckering.

TRANSFERRING DESIGNS

Trace outline of your design on tracing paper, pin in place on fabric over a piece of dressmaker's carbon. Carefully and firmly go over design or dots with a pencil or pointed object such as a knitting needle. Check to see if design is visible on fabric; you may have to bear down harder.

FINISHING

After candlewicking is completed, wash the spread to shrink the fabric. Dry spread in drier or hang it over a clothesline, changing its position several times to prevent fold lines. If not using a drier on a spread with tufts, shake vigorously to make threads separate and fluff when it is almost dry. Do not iron.

Bedcover, quilted and embroidered in French knots with candlewicking thread. Cover has an inner lining. [BROOKLYN MUSEUM, BROOKLYN, N.Y.]

STITCHES

Embroidery stitches most frequently used in candlewicking are backstitch, French knot, and satin stitch.

TUFTS

Note: The thread will fluff into tufts when spread is washed and dried.

Method 1: The traditional method of making tufts is to work a row of evenly spaced running stitches as shown in diagram, threading needle with several strands, depending on the desired fullness of the tufts. For example, 15 strands of 8-ply thread make a tuft ¾″ in diameter. Then with sharp-pointed scissors cut halfway between stitches. If tufts are far apart, cut away part of the connecting threads.

Method 2: On some pieces the tufts are made by laying strands in position on top of fabric. With sewing thread, the strands are tacked down before cutting between stitches.

Single Tuft: Single tufts can be made with a single stitch through the fabric, or by tacking the strands in position on top of fabric. Then cut threads to length desired.

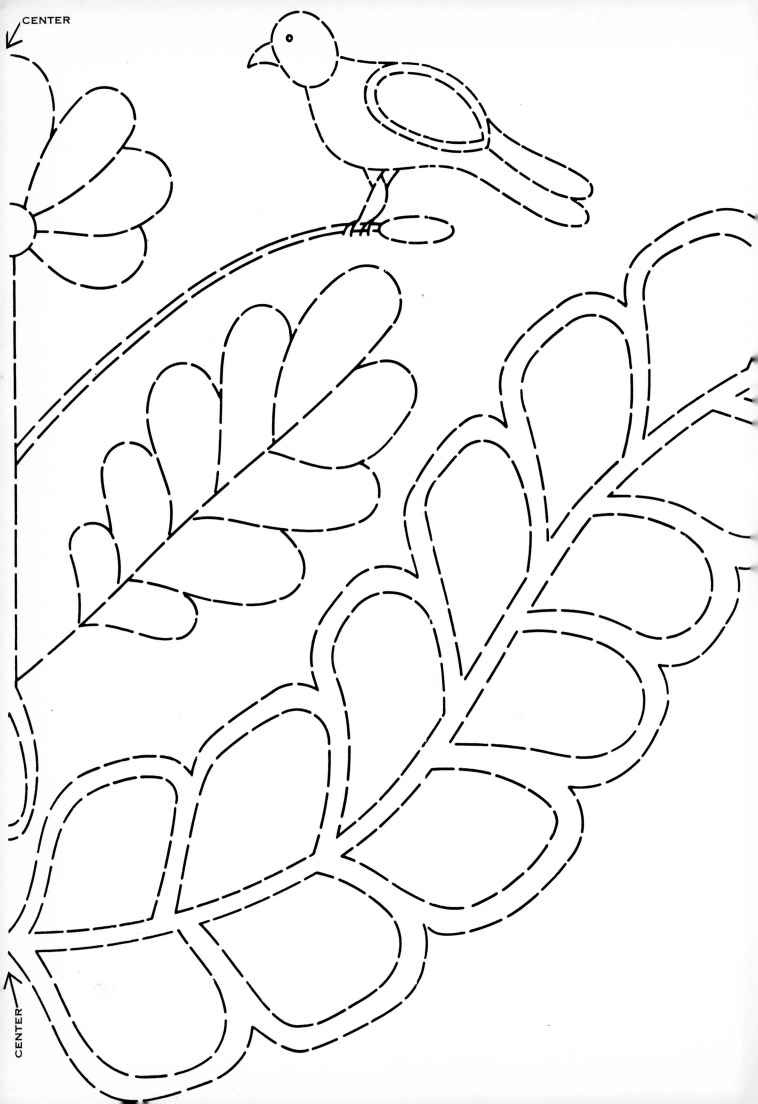

CENTER

CENTER

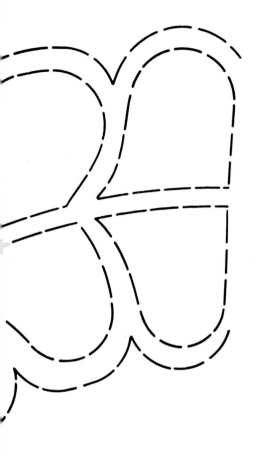

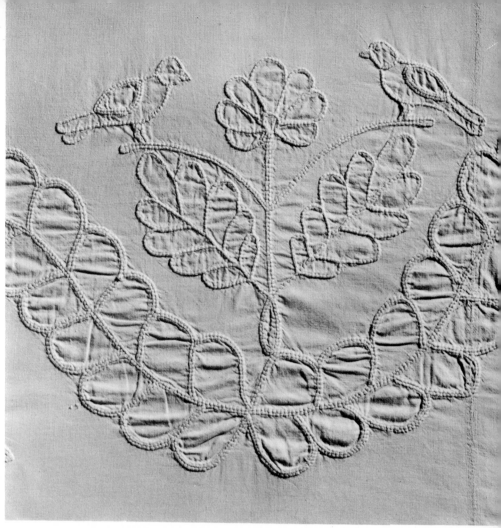

Prince's Feather quilt design: birds, flowers and leaves chain-stitched on reverse side with candlewicking. [HENRY FORD MUSEUM]

Directions for Prince's Feather

SIZE
Design area is 11½″ x 23″.

MATERIALS
Fabric; candlewicking thread.

TRANSFERRING DESIGN
Right half of complete design is shown. Trace off on transparent paper. After transferring first half (see transferring instructions, page 195) reverse paper and transfer left half, matching centers.

CANDLEWICKING
Work with 6-ply strand of thread. Broken lines indicate backstitch.

The original design was on a bedspread and was repeated all around the border, center was plain. You can plan the pattern to fit a bedspread or coverlet of your dimensions, or use the design as a border on plain curtains.

Reminder: In laying out design, work from the centers to the corners.

Rug Making

Yarn-sewn rug, worked over a slender gauge.
[New York State Historical Association, Cooperstown, N.Y.]

two things that are humdrum commonplace to us; the chair, which was a throne, and the carpet or rug, which not long ago was royal.

When the Kings of Spain and France and England were giving this unexplored continent to their favorites, they lived in castles where cellars were open cesspools and floors were covered with layers of dirty rushes. Their serfs, peasants, and workers lived crowded in damp, floorless hovels.

For centuries the nabobs of the distant Orient had enjoyed marvelous rugs made in the imperial factories. The Persian Emperors had one Winter Rug, for their pleasure in the gloomy seasons, which measured 150 by 75 feet. Woven of silk, it pictured a garden in spring where a path wandered by a brook, trees and shrubs were blossoming and flower beds filled a wide border with masses of blooms. The brook was crystals, the earth was gold; the boles and branches were silver and gold; leaves were emeralds and flowers were pearls, rubies and sapphires.

The Orient's working classes lived in floorless hovels, of course, as many of them still do. The nomad tribes wove coarse cloth on primitive looms, as American Indians were doing. The priceless rugs were made in the emperor's factories, for royalty and royalty's favorites.

When Moslems conquered Persia in the seventh century, they cut up that famous Winter Carpet and divided it; each soldier got a bit worth about $2,000. Two centuries later they conquered Spain, and there for six hundred years free weavers produced multiplying quantities of Oriental rugs for the free market that flourished in Islam from Spain to Samarkand to Burma. But that prospering brilliant civilization did not cross the Pyrenees and slowly the Europeans backed it out of Spain.

Late in the fifteenth century a Genoese sea captain, Christopher Columbus, rode into the army camp of King Ferdinand and Queen Isabella outside the walls of Granada. They were besieging the Moslems' last Spanish stronghold. He made his deal with them there. They dubbed him Lord High Admiral of the Western Seas and gave him and his heirs forever 10 per cent of all revenues from the lands he might reach; and while he was sailing westward, their troops stormed Granada. Rugmaking ceased in Europe when the last vestige of Moslem learning and trade and industry was driven out.

In India the Emperor Akbar's servants piled rug on silken rug from his factory while in England Queen Elizabeth walked majestically on layers of dirty rushes in her great halls. Her servants sprinkled herbs over the rushes and her courtiers held perfumed handkerchiefs to their noses to endure the stench in which they lived.

When Cardinal Wolsey ordered clean rushes spread daily in Hampton Court Palace, he was charged with foolish extravagance. The powerful Cardinal demanded one hundred rugs from Venetians permitted to trade in London. It was a monstrous demand. Ransacking the world's markets and offering exorbitant prices, the Venetians could get no more than sixty. There was a sensation at court; the Queen had a rug. It was laid over three layers of "sweet" rushes.

In Virginia and Massachusetts the first refugees from the terror and tortures of Europe were living in floorless hovels as the poor always had lived. But here nothing kept them from climbing out of that age-old depth of poverty. Here, a peasant was not permitted to have only the dead wood that fell from trees in his lord's hunting forests. Here, a poor man was not punished for cutting down a tree.

The men first made crude bedsteads and did not sleep on mud. Then they hewed logs roughly flat on one side and laid puncheon floors. Damp came up through the cracks. To stop that, women spread sand inches thick on the puncheons and we all know why they drew patterns on the sand with the bundles of twigs that were their brooms. Footprints spoiled the pattern but next morning they made their floors pretty again.

Slowly, year by year, they improved their way of living, and they made a great discovery, unknown till then: that progress on this earth is possible.

They learned that living in freedom is not easy because a free person must rely on himself, but free men make living easier, cleaner, better for everyone. Some of them lived to enjoy smooth, clean floors of boards sawed at the water mill. And during that seventeenth century some began to make American rugs.

We can guess that women began it in the eastern colonies where winter's cold blowing under doors made floor coverings more useful than in the warmer South. We can imagine a woman having—and instantly rejecting—an impulse to stop that icy draft by putting against it, on the floor, the treasured yarn-sewn coverlet from her bed.

In the Brooklyn Museum there is a beautiful yarn-sewn coverlet surviving from the seventeenth century. It is worked in wool of many strands (like candlewicking) dyed in shades of blue from lighter to darker, solidly covering the cloth with long stitches. The shading of color makes it beautiful; the depth of wool makes it cuddly warm. Nobody would put it on a floor; every toe would catch in those long stitches. But we can surmise that some such coverlet, a variation of the Scandinavian *rugge*, was an ancestor of American rugs.

Their material was rags, so dire poverty inspired their invention. Yet today, when free persons in this classless society have abolished that ancient wretchedness and every worker here is richer than King George was, our rugmaking is flourishing as never before.

There is no longer a need for handmade rugs. Making them now is an art, and everywhere in these states more and more homekeeping women are making them, using all the needlework arts: hooking, knitting, patchwork, embroidery, tufting, and weaving, and braiding. And the end is not yet, for in mid-twentieth century the renaissance of our artcrafts is part of the American Renaissance now only beginning.

Braided Rugs. Braiding is a major American artcraft, probably older than hooking and certainly as thriving today. Decorators value our braided rugs as highly as hooked rugs and both more highly than most of the contemporary Oriental rugs. True aristocrat that it is, a braided rug is at ease and gracious in any company, with Swedish Modern, French Provincial, English Adam or Jacobean, as with Early or Modern American.

The technique is basically simple, merely braiding rags together, right over left, left over right, as every woman has braided hair. American women may have braided corn-shuck mats before they could spare rags to braid. Many a corn-shuck mat lay on porches outside farmhouse doors when I was a girl, and my father's little-girl sisters braided shining wheat straws to make their summer hats.

Anyone can braid; almost everyone does. But the art of braiding rugs is not so simple. The size, the shape, the texture, the choice and blending and shading of colors, their harmonies and contrasts, are as important to a braided rug as to a picture. Their possibilities are endless and as endlessly alluring to a rugmaker as to any other artist.

The technique, too, requires the most skillful precision. The rug's texture derives from the folding of the rags, their tension in the hands, the accuracy of braiding, the care in lacing the braids together.

Each rag's edges must be folded in, and the rag then folded lengthwise to make a firm tube that will not wrinkle in braiding, for the surface of the rug must be smoothly molded. Originally, of course, the only tools were hands and a precious sewing needle. But profit seekers in a free market abolish drudgery as well as poverty. No sooner are increasing numbers of us braiding rugs again, than we are offered newly invented tools and quantities of new, cheap materials.

You can buy cheaply clever little steel "braiders" which magically do all the folding of the rags while you braid them; and a clamp to hold the braid's tension; and a little machine with a gauge, which cuts the cloth the width you want; and even pins made especially to mark and hold a braid's end while you taper it or butt two ends together. And you can buy mill ends of new woolen cloth by the pound, in fadeless colors, plain and plaid and checked and figured. There is stout linen thread for lacing the braids together; there are bodkin-needle lacers.

Our grandmothers didn't dream of such pampering, but they would approve our practicality, for nothing is more practical than a braided rug. It is (practically) inde-

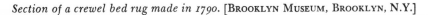

Section of a crewel bed rug made in 1790. [BROOKLYN MUSEUM, BROOKLYN, N.Y.]

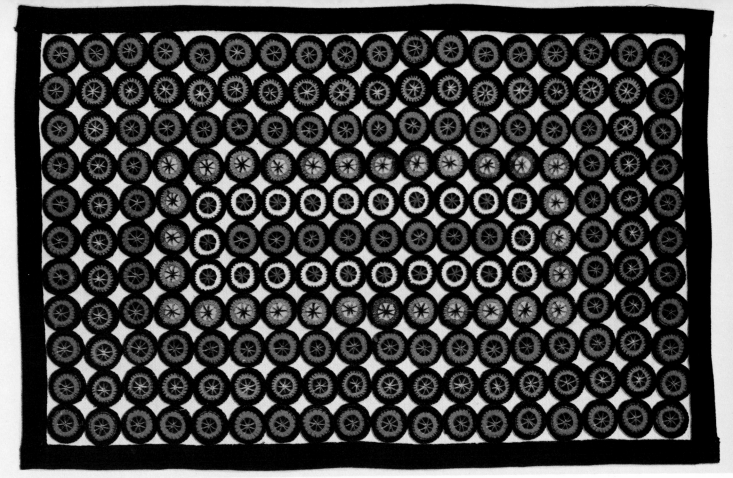

Button rug: circles of felt and wool, three deep, appliquéd and embroidered with buttonhole and star stitches on a flannel background. [WENHAM HISTORICAL ASSOCIATION AND MUSEUM, WENHAM, MASS.]

structible. It is reversible. Butt the ends of braid together to make each round complete and lace it separately to the other rounds, and no stain or burn is fatal; you simply snip out the injured round and lace in a new one. If you move, or want to move the rug, easily you make it larger or smaller.

You can even spend years in making a braided rug and use it all the time. My busy next-door neighbor, Ruth McKee, made a charming little braided rug to lie under a coffee table. In odd moments while a cake was baking, and such, she braided. From time to time she added a few rounds to her rug and now, large and handsome, it "makes" her whole admirable living room.

There is a rapidly growing literature of the newest techniques and the timeless art of braiding rugs. It will tell you useful facts, such as exactly how to begin a round rug, or that the center braid of an oval rug is precisely as long as the difference between the rug's width and its length, or that you lace the braids together on a flat surface (with pictures showing how) and from time to

time lift the rug and drop it, to make sure that it always will lie flat.

You will find colored pictures of beautiful rugs, with their color charts given, round by round, so that you can duplicate one if you like. But color is a subtle thing, and so personal. When once you see how colors blend and change their qualities in braiding, you will be enthralled as all artists are, happily fascinated and using color in your own way in your own rug.

Woven Rugs. Though hooked and braided rugs are made of rags, only these are called "rag rugs." I'd guess that they were the very first American rugs; they are simply tabby weaving, using rags for weft with carpet warp. But everywhere in these States some woman is still weaving them. I wouldn't think of keeping house without them.

My grandmother always dyed her rags (though at last guiltily she bought bolts of machine-woven cloth to dye and tear up) and she planned richly colored, room-size patterns. Often shading colors by twisting together two rags, she wove in narrow strips and sewed them together invisibly to make the pattern whole.

My own rag rugs are short hit-and-miss ones with only a band of solid color, or colors, across the warp-fringed ends. One color of warp blends all colors and kinds of cloth (though don't mix wool with silk or cotton or nylon). Or the warp can be stripes of different colors, of course. All worn-out clothes from overcoats to stockings, and sheets and blankets and curtains, will make these little beauties.

They are perfect with Early American maple or pine. The washing machine is their beauty parlor. They'll always go into it and come out looking younger. I wish I had a loom and time to make them. If you haven't, either, get one; you'll be glad you did.

Appliqué Rugs. These little button and petal rugs, with the knitted and crocheted ones, are the nineteenth century's American scatter rugs, quaint now and amusing. Few survive and few are being made.

In the dire depression of the 1870's women made many a blue and gray uniform into button and petal rugs. In the tragic depression of the 1890's my mother made a petal rug from totally worn-out overalls. Any stout cloth will line a petal rug, but you must have the right color for a button rug's lining because it will show.

For a button rug, cut three rounds of cloth; one 2½ inches in diameter; the second, 2 inches; the third, 1½ inches. Buttonhole their edges (we can afford embroidery floss) and stack them, largest on bottom, smallest on top. Arrange these stacks to your taste, touching each other on the lining, and fasten each stack down with a cross-stitch or French knots in its center.

The petal rug thriftily uses fewer scraps and they hide the lining. Cut oblongs to petal points at one end, buttonhole their sides and the point, lay a row of them side by side with points extending beyond the edges of the lining. Sew the wide ends to the lining. Lay another row overlapping the first row and sew down the wide ends. Continue, of course using fewer petals in each successive row, until the wide ends meet in the rug's middle. Cover them in the center with a piece of cloth buttonholed down. The rug may be any shape you want.

The patterns of these rugs are the arrangements of colors. Harmonies and contrasts, shadings and tones, are innumerable and you can make them delightful.

Knitted Rugs. The character of knitted or crocheted rugs depends on the material. Sturdy ones were knitted of rags on big wooden needles. Knit squares or strips, arrange them to please you and sew them together with stout thread. Knitted strips will make a round or oval rug; if you'd rather knit than braid, it can have the rippling shading of a braided rug.

"Waste not, want not," we used to say, and all the ends of yarns left over from other knitting made knitted rugs. Plain knit-and-purl-back to make strips three inches wide. Cut and hem a lining of narrow-striped ticking and firmly sew *both* edges of a knitted strip along every stripe of the ticking. You will have something indeed rare today, a corded rug. (There's no law against sewing the knitted strips round and round, should you want a round corded rug.)

If you'd rather have a fluffy rug, simply with scissors cut every cord open straight along its middle, and shake. Again, it is the arrangement of colors that makes these little rugs pleasing. Or not.

Crocheted Rugs. These are mid-nineteenth century at earliest. Usually round, they were crocheted in single stitch, of rags, using a wooden crochet hook of giant size. Ch 3, sl st in 1st ch; ch 1, 2 sl st in each ch st—every crocheter knows the routine, and the problem of widening just enough to keep the work flat. If we failed, we patted the rug flat on a flat surface, dampened it with starch and let it dry. Then it behaved until it was washed. And flattened again.

Candlewicking, or stockings cut diagonally round and round in wide strips, will crochet more easily into softer rugs. But crochet these over a firm cord; we used the farmers' binding twine. It gives the rug body and holds its shape. A final round of slip stitches over the cord is advisable, too.

Embroidered Rugs. For durability, these should be done in needlepoint or cross-stitch on canvas. A famous one, now in the Metropolitan Museum of Art in New York City, is known as the Judge Pliny Moore rug, though it was his convent-taught daughters who spent four years (1808–1812) making it for their drawing room in Champlain, New York. It is twenty feet square. They washed, carded, spun and dyed the yarn of wool sheared from their father's sheep but they had canvas imported from Montreal. They stretched it on a frame larger than a quilting frame and made the rug with some 1,500,-000 needlepoint stitches. For many years it was the pride and beauty of Judge Moore's drawing room.

Rugs always had been handmade, of course. An Oriental rug, tufted by hand on each strand of weft in the ancient loom, was then rare indeed in the seventeen states. A woman who wanted a rug made it by hand. But Judge Pliny Moore's rug had been on the floor only two years when a boy was born in West Boylston, Massachusetts, who would change that. He was named Erastus Brigham Bigelow.

His parents were poor. In the Old World they would have been serfs or peasants, so he could have been only a serf or peasant. Had he been born half a century earlier in the colonies, he would have earned his living from the age of seven, but already it was easier to be poor here; Erastus was not doing a hired farmhand's work until he was ten years old. He never was able to go to school but he learned reading, writing, arithmetic, and got a clerk's job.

When he was twenty-three he invented a loom that wove lace. He developed this into a power loom weaving patterned fabrics, and ended the four-thousand-year-old labor of hand weaving. He and his brother Horatio built a mill and hired helpers; they made ingrain carpets and a town, Clinton, Massachusetts, grew around the mill. In the 1850's, little more than a century ago, Erastus Bigelow invented the first power loom weaving Brussels and Wilton carpets.

English manufacturers adopted this magical loom and prospered for decades from the advantage it gave them over Continental weavers. The Bigelow Carpet Mills, expanding to supply an increasing demand, employed more and more workers. Erastus Bigelow became a renowned economist and one of the founders of the Massachusetts Institute of Technology. He died in 1879, seven years before I was born; our lifetimes almost overlapped. So quickly, in freedom, men took the ancient drudgery out of human lives.

You do not need at all to make your wall-to-wall carpeting or your beautiful rugs. You have them, of course. Nine-tenths of the energy that makes the stupendous quantities of luxurious carpeting on millions of floors in these states is the tireless energy of machines, very costly machines which millions of us own. The little human energy spent in tending the swift machines in clean, air-conditioned factories is more the energy of minds than of hands.

A handmade rug, now, is a work of art. Making it engages hands and minds, and more. You put into it your own personality, your knowledge, your taste, your character, yourself. You make it with love, love of your home, your family, your American culture and way of life, love of the intangible quality that, to you, is beauty.

These rugs that thousands upon thousands of homekeeping women are making now with their hands, in moments of happy leisure taken from busy days, truly express the spirit of our revolutionary country, the spirit of individual human beings in freedom.

On Rugmaking

Many of the crafts covered in other chapters can be utilized to make American rugs: embroidery, cross-stitch, needlepoint, appliqué, hooking, knitting, crochet, weaving, and tufting. One more method is braiding, which is worked with strips of fabric.

FIVE-STRAND BRAIDING

MATERIALS

Cut fabric in strips about 2″ wide, depending on weight of fabric. The strips should be of the same weight so that braiding is even and of a uniform width. To join strips, cut ends diagonally and sew together on bias. Roll strips into balls until you are ready to use them.

METHOD

Pin ends of 5 strips together. Starting with strip at extreme right side, weave this strip over next strip, then under, over, and under remaining strips. Repeat, always weaving with strand that is then at extreme right side. Turn under raw edges of strip and fold in half lengthwise as you braid, and pull fabric taut

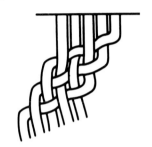

so that braid is firm. For a smoother braid, try to stagger joinings of strips so that no two joinings fall at exactly the same spot in the braid.

ASSEMBLING RUG

Work on a flat surface to keep rug from curling. Start at center with a 6″-long braid of the black and white braid. Wrap braid around until it measures about 15″ long. Then continue with white and print braid to complete rug. Sew as you wrap. Use carpet thread, and sew through outside strand on coiled braid, then through outside strand on braid being added. Sew braids together firmly but not so tightly that rug curls.

Directions for a Five-Strand Braided Rug

SIZE

About 22″ x 30″; 5-strand braid, about ⅞″ wide.

MATERIALS

The original rug was braided of cotton fabric.

COLORS

On the original rug, center braid was worked with 4 strips of black and 1 strip of white. Remainder of rug was worked with 3 strips of white, 1 strip of purple print, and 1 strip of red and white print. When braiding is complete, assemble as above.

Braided five-strand rug, made by the author's mother, late nineteenth century. [LAURA INGALLS WILDER HOME MUSEUM, MANSFIELD, MO.]

Index

All page numbers printed in italic type denote illustrations.